Palgrave Studies in Economic History

Palgrave Studies in Economic History is designed to illuminate and enrich our understanding of economies and economic phenomena of the past. The series covers a vast range of topics including financial history, labour history, development economics, commercialisation, urbanisation, industrialisation, modernisation, globalisation, and changes in world economic orders.

More information about this series at
http://www.palgrave.com/gp/series/14632

Silvia A. Conca Messina · Stéphane Le Bras ·
Paolo Tedeschi · Manuel Vaquero Piñeiro
Editors

A History of Wine in Europe, 19th to 20th Centuries, Volume I

Winegrowing and Regional Features

palgrave
macmillan

Editors
Silvia A. Conca Messina
Department of Historical Studies
University of Milan 'La Statale'
Milan, Italy

Paolo Tedeschi
Department of Economics, Management
and Statistics (DEMS)
University of Milano-Bicocca
Milan, Italy

Stéphane Le Bras
University of Clermont Auvergne
Clermont-Ferrand, France

Manuel Vaquero Piñeiro
University of Perugia
Perugia, Italy

Palgrave Studies in Economic History
ISBN 978-3-030-27771-0   ISBN 978-3-030-27772-7 (eBook)
https://doi.org/10.1007/978-3-030-27772-7

Cover illustration: © Winery Scacciadiavoli of Pambuffetti, Montefalco (Umbria, Italy)

This Palgrave Macmillan imprint is published by the registered company Springer Nature Switzerland AG
The registered company address is: Gewerbestrasse 11, 6330 Cham, Switzerland

Contents

List of Figures

Viticulture and Winemaking in Abruzzo from the Unification of Italy to the Development of the Cooperation System

List of Tables

The "Grapes Country": Portuguese Viticulture from the Early Nineteenth Century Until the New Millennium

History of a Vineyard in Champagne: From Eighteenth to Twenty-First Century

The Development of Winegrowing, Winemaking and Distribution of Wine in the Lower Moselle (Eighteenth–Twentieth Centuries)

The Mountain Wine, 1800–1900: Case Studies from the Provinces of Sondrio and Trento

The Development of Winegrowing and Oenology in Southern Piedmont and Oltrepò Pavese

The Improvement of the Production and Quality: The Case of Wine Production in the Eastern Lombardy During the Nineteenth and Twentieth Centuries (Provinces of Bergamo and Brescia)

Viniculture in the Italy of the Mezzadria (Tuscany, Umbria and Marche)

Viticulture and Winemaking in Abruzzo from the Unification of Italy to the Development of the Cooperation System

Winegrowing in Slovenia in the Twentieth Century

Terroir, Institutions and Improvements in European Wine History: An Introduction

Silvia A. Conca Messina, Stéphane Le Bras, Paolo Tedeschi and Manuel Vaquero Piñeiro

The Research Project and the Relevance of the Topic

The project of a book collecting papers about different European wine regions was developed during Spring 2017 by Paolo Tedeschi and Manuel Vaquero Piñeiro, scholars in economic history and members of the informal group of research about the Italian Oeno-History.

Considering that, from food and agricultural history points of view, the wine sector is at the core of the present scientific debate and the social, economic and legislative relevance of the products of the terroir

S. A. Conca Messina (✉)
Department of Historical Studies, University of Milan 'La Statale', Milan, Italy
e-mail: silvia.conca@unimi.it

S. Le Bras
CHEC, University of Clermont Auvergne, Clermont-Ferrand, France
e-mail: stephane.lebras@uca.fr

S. A. Conca Messina et al. (eds.), *A History of Wine in Europe, 19th to 20th Centuries, Volume I*, Palgrave Studies in Economic History,
https://doi.org/10.1007/978-3-030-27772-7_1

are receiving ever more attention in the field of scientific literature,[1] this research project and the consequent two volumes which were realized aim to show that the wine history has to start by the analysis of the evolution of the single wine regions. This evidently does not imply that the State was not important for the improvement of the quality and quantity of the European wine production: the mainstream idea is that local winegrowers and winemakers' choices were fundamental to develop a successful wine conquering the world wine market or, in the opposite, to explain the decadence or the limited diffusion of a wine. The State and, more in general, public institutions (local or European) guaranteed a support (minimum or relevant) and established rules to follow during the winemaking, but they were not able to create homogeneous wines. Face the changes of laws and other relevant exogenous factors (as the arrival of diseases and new technological innovations) each wine region gave a different answer and so chose a different way of development allowing (or not) the winemakers to improve the quality of their production and to extent their market. So, only for the mass media and the statistics, it exists a French (or an Italian or a Spanish,

[1]For the increasing interest and relevance of the "wine history and wine economics" and the rapid rise of its social and economic relevance throughout the world, it is important to remember the launch in 2006 of the "Journal of Wine Economics" (Cambridge UP) edited by the American Association of Wine Economists: it joined the "International Journal of Wine Business Research", the official outlet of the Academy of Wine Business Research, which was launched in 1989 (under the name of "International Journal of Wine Business Marketing"). Concerning in particular the wine history see, among others, the following publications which also include relevant studies on legislation in the wine sector: Unwin (1996, 236–321), Bisson et al. (2002, 696–699), Campbell and Guibert (2007), Simpson (2011), Lukacs (2012), Harvey et al. (2014), Harvey and Waye (2014), Tattersall and De Salle (2015), Meloni and Swinnen (2016), Anderson et al. (2017), Anderson and Pinilla (2018), and Alonso et al. (2019).

P. Tedeschi
DEMS, University of Milano-Bicocca, Milan, Italy
e-mail: paolo.tedeschi@unimib.it

M. Vaquero Piñeiro
Department of Political Science, University of Perugia, Perugia, Italy
e-mail: manuel.vaqueropineiro@unipg.it

etc.) wine: in the real oenologic world there only exist the wine regions of Barolo, Bordeaux, Champagne, Chianti, La Rioja, Tokaj etc.

As the proposal was considered original and interesting and met the favourable answer of lots of colleagues working in European universities, it was possible, thanks to the precious collaboration of Silvia A. Conca Messina and Stéphane Le Bras, to produce two volumes analysing the wine history of lots of different European wine regions and, at the same time, illustrate the role of national and European institutions in the development of the wine sector.

The two volumes show how the wine market was made and shaped by three actors, that is producers, sellers and public authorities (municipalities, countries and European Union) and that there existed (and continue to exist) different wine markets depending on price and quality of the product (the wine for old taverns and modern supermarkets is very different from the wine for three stars restaurants or niche luxury market) and consumers' regional customs and tastes (German wines always have a few market in France and Italy, rose wines are only for young people and they were often created by producers who want to diversify their products and create a new wine market, etc.). It is important to note that all wine producers had to constantly achieve compromises with their consumers, including those making high-quality wines: the example of the best production in the Champagne region is evident (Perron 2010). Besides it was important, in particular from the last decades of the twentieth century, the historical relevance of the concept of terroir, the wine producers' appropriation and invention of the tradition and the related marketing based of the (clearly false) concept that in the past the wine was more organic and good (Marache and Meyzie 2015; Reckinger 2012; Demoissier 2010; Charters 2006). Again the French market (or the Italian and Spanish ones) and the related average prices exist only in the statistics: they did not really explain what has happened in the wine history (and also in the present wine world) with the important, but rare, exception represented by local analyses which are able to use long term prices concerning one defined product (Chevet et al. 2011). Furthermore, these volumes aim at underlining that the history of wine should be based on data and information from both archives and official statistics. The combination would make it possible to better highlight the actual decisions taken by winemakers about wine production production in a defined wine area (Le Bras 2019).

In these two volumes most of the contributions concern Italian and French wine regions: this is obviously linked to the origin of the project and the editors, but it is also related to the evolution of the European wine history. The modern viticulture was born in France and the first producers in the world are (and had been for the last two centuries) France and Italy. The others European countries simply copied the innovations coming from France thanks to the network of the agrarian reviews and congresses which started in Europe during the first half of the nineteenth century (Locatelli and Tedeschi 2015): this network allowed the international diffusion of the know-how concerning winegrowing and winemaking. This transfer of knowledge was implemented by migrants coming from Italy, France and Spain who progressively developed a local viticulture in Chile, Argentina, USA, New Zealand, Australia etc.: new wines progressively entered in the world wine market and this last became more competitive (Anderson 2004; Lukacs 2005; Anderson and Pinilla 2018). The French wine sector (the most modern in the world) obviously represented the most important reference for all people who wanted to invest in the wine industry, but the diffusion of the ampelographic know-how allowed to better imitate the French productive system and so some wine producers started to make products whose quality was not so inferior to the French wines. In particular, during the second half of the twentieth century, the Italian wine production progressively increased in quality and quantity: in the new Millennium the Italian wine sector became the first in the world for the total production (about the primacy concerning quality authors of these volumes obviously do not enter in the debate). All this clearly explain why the studies about the history of the French and Italian vines, wines and winemakers are so numerous and it is very difficult to indicate all of them.[2]

These volumes also include some contributions that allows readers to discover the evolution of the viticulture and winemaking in

---

[2]It is impossible to quote every recent article and book about French and Italian wines in the nineteenth and twentieth centuries. Only considering the volume and papers published by academic historians and agronomies in the new Millennium it is possible to see, among others: for France see Lachiver (1988), Sagnes (1993), Paul (1996), Stengel (2013), Bodinier et al.

other European regions (or small countries) as the Mosel (Germany), the Slovenia, the Catalonia, the Luxembourg and Porto (Portugal). There are unfortunately some relevant absences, e.g. some Spanish or German regions (as La Rioja, Castilla-La Mancha, Franconia, Palatinate, Rheinland, etc.) or the Hungarian Tokay[3]: this simply depends on the fact that no other colleagues accepted to write because they had no time.

Even these lacks, these volumes allow scholars the opportunity to make interesting comparisons between different European winemaking regions. They, in particular, put in evidence that the "road to success" followed by lots of European wines can share the same characteristics, in particular when terroirs are located under the same public authority and legislation, but it is also possible that there exist very different trajectories depending on the different wine producers' decisions and their ability in lobbying with the public authorities. For example the choice to create cooperatives was very important to overcome the negative effects of the crises linked to the fungal and insect attacks and to improve the ratio quality/price of the wine production and moreover the distribution of the wine, before in the local market and then in the national and international ones.[4]

The European wine regions had in fact to face the following events arriving from the last decades of the nineteenth century and the end

(2014), Le Bras (2017, 2019). For Italy, Pedrocco (2000), Failla and Scienza (2001), Agnoletti (2002), Gangemi and Ritrovato (2002), Tedeschi (2003, 2017), Zoia (2004), Leonardi (2006), Ciuffoletti (2009), Dandolo (2010), Maffi (2010, 2012), Ottolino (2011), Mainardi and Berta (2013), Mocarelli (2013), Gasparini (2014), Carassale (2014), and Zanotti (2015). In Italy the substantial interest in this topic is also demonstrated in particular by the eight volume collection concerning the regional history of vines and wine (*Storia regionale della vite e del vino in Italia*) and by the other numerous books edited by important experts in oenology as well as professional *sommelliers*.

[3]Among the major limits of this collection, the lack of contributions on Castilla-La Mancha, the Spanish region that currently covers 46% of the Spanish vineyard area and 13.6% of that of the EU, and on other relevant French and Italian wine regions. However, it is evident that it was not possible to consider all European wine regions. About the Spanish wine sector see Muñoz Moreno (2009). Besides about the German wine sector, other the contribution of Thomas Schuetz in these volumes, see Bird (2005) and Brook (2006). Finally, about the Hungarian wine sector see Rohály et al. (2003).

[4]The relevance of the cooperative wineries for the European wine sector is put in evidence in lots of contributions of these volumes. See also, among others, Planas (2016) and Simpson (2000).

of the twentieth one: the reduction of the land set aside for vineyards, a careful selection of vine varieties, the growth in investments for the improvement of manufacturing techniques and of the quality of the cellars, a progressive differentiation of wines according to the geographical origin of vines and an increased attention towards the retailing sector and to consumer tastes. Even if some events were similar, e.g. the strong increase of the productive costs following the arrival of the fungal diseases (*oidium* and *peronospora*) and insect (*phylloxera*) attacking the European vineyards, it is possible to note different evolution in France, the country where lots of wines showed a high-quality level during the nineteenth century, when in other European areas the high-quality wines represented some exceptions in a context presenting a low quality for most of the production arriving from the terroirs. In this case it became very relevant the considerable differences in the social and economic position of viticulturists and winemakers: French winemakers, for example, were able to organize mass protests against the government policy on wine (in particular in the early twentieth century) and set up a number of powerful regional associations (like the *Confédération générale des vignerons du Midi* or the *Fédération des Syndicats de la Champagne*). They were able to influence the legislation: they laid down a set of guidelines for winegrowers during the 1930s and the related birth of the Controlled Designation of Origin (in French language Appellation d'Origine Controlée, AOC) (Wolikow and Humbert 2015). They acted on behalf of their members and, in an attempt to reduce distribution costs, they held negotiations with wine retailers and bottle maker's associations (particularly in the case of *Champagne*).[5] In other European countries this did not happen or it arrived later or it had small dimensions, that is it was limited to a discrete lobbying action to obtain some tariff protection or subsides and, moreover, the discussions about the CDO finished without guidelines and some winemakers who underlining that CDO protected the worst producers and that the

[5]On French viticulturists and winemakers and their relations with the State and with wine retailers see, among others, Sagnes (2008), Bagnol (2010), Lucand (2011), Palaude (2012), Le Bras (2013), and Planas (2015).

best wineries had in their name and history all the necessary to conquest the wine market.[6]

It is evident that where the legislation regulated the winegrowing and winemaking it was very important the ability of local producers to obtain rules which were favourable to the characteristics of their wines. Where the public authorities were absent, the winegrowers and winemakers associations assumed the role of the main player and, by the definition of the guidelines and orienting the investments to modernize the productive system, decided the future of the local viticulture. The role of investments was fundamental because, although viticulture naturally remained a rural activity, it gradually became industrialized. In particular during the last few decades of the twentieth century, winemakers who wished to remain competitive in the new worldwide wine market had to modernize their interactions with consumers and retailers and become fully integrated into the industrial sector: this arrived both in the European terroirs and in non-European wine regions (Doloreux and Lord-Tarte 2013). This has been accompanied over the last 25 years by the rapid rise of wine tourism, which has had the effect of increasing the social and economic impact of the wine sector (and justifying new academic studies).[7]

Notes About the Terroir, Technology, Public Institutions and Related Improvements in European Wine History

Over the past 150 years, the total world volume of wine production has grown from 10 to 27 billion litres per year (Anderson et al. 2017). In the 1860s, almost all of it was produced in Europe; after a century and

[6]About the relevance of rules established by the European institutions for the European wine secter see, other the contributes in these volumes, Gaeta and Corsinovi (2014).

[7]For recent studies on the wine industry see also *The Journal of Wine Economics*, *The International Journal of Wine Business Research*, as well as the *Conference proceedings of the Academy of Wine Business Research* from 2003 to 2014 (http://academyofwinebusiness.com). For wine tourism see, among others, Hall et al. (2000), Carlsen and Charters (2006), Asero and Patti (2009), Boatto and Gennari (2011), Cavicchi and Santini (2014), and Vaquero Piñeiro (2015b).

a half—despite the emergence of new competitors and the globalization process—the volume of wines produced in European countries is still around six-tenths globally, while exports exceed two-thirds of the wine traded throughout the world. In the last two decades of the twentieth century, exports from the old continent represented, in monetary value, more than 90% at the global level; while they fell to slightly above 70% in the first 16 years of the twenty-first century alone. In 2016, out of the $32 billion of wine exported throughout the world, France held the record with $9.13 billion, Italy (which had reached first place in volume of production) followed it with $6.22 billion, ahead of Spain ($2.96 billion).

Therefore, Europe has been able to maintain clear leadership both in the volume of production and in monetary value, despite the process of globalization. This process of "slowed down" and "delayed" globalization in the wine sector has undergone a change in very recent times, beginning in the last three decades, with the strengthening of important competitors (e.g. Australia, New Zealand, Argentina and the United States) and, in last few years, with the development of new markets such as China, which in turn is fostering the growth of the sector. Nevertheless, outcomes are not easily predictable, mainly because wine is not like other "agro-industrial" products. Producing good wine requires certain skills and factors which are not so easy to relocate: they are complex, variable, difficult to reproduce. Probably, the main feature of wine is the variety of its products and the complexity of all the factors that make it possible to achieve a certain quality and a diversified, typical and unique offer.

The history of wine is inextricably linked with the history of Europe, its agrarian systems, its territories, its institutions and its local traditions. Its success in the world in the last two centuries should not be taken for granted. The essays collected in this volume try to offer a picture of the wine industry's production and retailing systems in various European regions over the last two centuries. In order to better understand its economic significance, the authors have tried to set the production and sale of wine in their historical context, namely the European rural society and its institutions as well as the wine merchants. Thus, the essays allow us to trace the transformation of production, marketing and distribution, the evolution of trading and consumption markets.

They also highlight the advancements in science and techniques, the issues of cultural representations, the role of agricultural and educational institutions, the influence of economic policies, as well as the emergence on the scene of economic actors and entrepreneurial initiatives of various dimensions and social origins: from the small–medium enterprise to the large multinational, from the family business to the consortium, from producers belonging to the aristocratic classes to merchants or peasants.

As it emerges from this collection of contributions, Europe now reaps the benefits of a slow and contrasting evolution that began in the first half of the nineteenth century, when France started to establish the modern global wine industry. The search for wine quality—the key element of its economic success—required a series of cultural, institutional, political and entrepreneurial components strongly linked to the wine producers and terroirs. During the nineteenth century, some radical changes were introduced regarding the two main production systems into which the sector was divided: on the one hand, the production for self-consumption or local sales; on the other hand, specialized production aimed at satisfying external, interregional or international demand. Although in several European regions—including Italy and France—the mixed system remained largely predominant for a long time, from then onwards, the growth of markets, the refinement of production methods, cultural values, scientific knowledge applied to cultivation and winemaking processes underwent sweeping changes. In terms of quantity, the volume of wines destined for sale during the year continued to be prevalent for a long time as this kind of production was within the reach of small winemakers. However, at the same time, the experimentation and refinement of vintage wines increased and required much greater investments (e.g. in cellars, barrels for preservation) in view of a considerably higher profit.

The aristocratic and bourgeois classes that emerged from the Napoleonic wars were the first to embrace this tendency towards the qualitative improvement of wines, often emphasized in this volume. They considered the production of wine and the consolidation of oenological science as an effective factor for social identity and investment. In the beginning, these improvements were undertaken with the liqueur wines (Porto, Marsala, sherry) launched by the British on the national and international colonial market. Then—also in the wake of the reputation and appeal created by Champagne—came the turn of the most widely consumed table wines, which also became the subject of vigorous modernization. While liqueur wines were intended to satisfy the narrow demand of the élites, in the case of the much more widespread red and white wines, it was a matter of introducing changes into a fully consolidated sector, rather behind in its ways but based on centuries-old knowledge handed down from generation to generation. Therefore, the innovations did not always find a fertile ground on which to develop. There was much resistance and the wine had to be suitable for certain tastes: changing it also meant bringing changes to everyday life and, in the long run, social practices. Moreover, for many farmers and owners it was a question of continuing to have wine for domestic consumption, completely leaving aside the unknown world of the market and commercial trade.

Nevertheless, as several of these essays highlight, a common trend was underway throughout Europe: the transition from an oenology aimed at the production of large quantities of wine for local or national consumption to one which was more attentive to quality, safety and the promotion of a precise image. The research and development of bouquet and taste, which are typical of good wine, involved a growing number of operators throughout Europe. They accumulated more precise knowledge about vines, the condition of grapes at harvest time and winemaking methods. All of the most intricate aspects of wine handling (types of barrels, periodic decanting, contact with oxygen, control of temperatures and environmental conditions) were investigated and studied by local institutions and the most advanced operators (generally those in contact with international markets).

Vine diseases, which affected crops all through the nineteenth century (*oidium*, *phylloxera*, *peronospora* or downy mildew, black rot), led to a dramatic reduction in harvests in France, the major European producer, but represented an opportunity for viticulture expansion in Italy and Spain, which were hit only later. Each country reacted with its own systems, but generally, the diseases increased the attention that was paid to the vineyards and stimulated the qualitative improvement of production. Although only a few producers decided to specialize in high-quality production, the characteristics of European wines improved everywhere, at least regarding the way wines were produced and sold. In southern Spain and Italy, the great variety of traditional vines required extensive experimentation in order to identify the most suitable rootstocks, while other areas focused on growing better quality grapes and abandoned marginal vineyards. In Slovenia, after the outbreak of *phylloxera*, viticulture and winemaking were re-established in line with the rules and methods applied in the Habsburg monarchy.

The variable influence of the diseases from region to region and the temporal differentiation of their effects are recurrent themes in the essays of this volume, which capture the turning points and the transformation from a variety of local oenological traditions to a larger agronomical and technical landscape on a continental scale. Around 1850, the birth of European oenology was underway, later to spread worldwide. The fight against these plagues had long-term effects on European viniculture and was the driving force in bringing producers and scientists together and creating local institutions, schools and producers' associations. Some general consequences of *phylloxera* and *peronospora* are easily recognizable: a decrease in the number of small producers due to the growing costs of new grafts and of monitoring and looking after the crops; the increase of the capital required both to combat the diseases of the vine and to expand the production of vintage wines; the growing recourse to science; the development—or at least the planning—of legislation aimed at guaranteeing the origin of wines, both to fight against the increasing chemical sophistication of wine as well as to support exports; the growing urban demand for popular wines improved transport systems, the increasing power of commercial houses; beginning in the nineteenth century, the expansion of viticulture in the colonies by Europeans.

The recurrent crises of overproduction (and therefore of prices) were among the most difficult economic problems for European winemakers. The crises depended on variable productivity from year to year and on the fact that investments encountered difficulties in following such unpredictable market trends (also considering that newly planted vines required a certain number of years before they started to produce grapes). Fraud was as well an important issue and a market-confusing variable, leading to regional uprising in France and legislative response. Many of the changes in the wine industry introduced during the twentieth century were aimed precisely at reducing this variability as much as possible, e.g. the vertical integration of production, technical progress aimed at creating wines with the most constant characteristics, the growing importance of, first, major producers and then large multinationals which were able to provide the vast capital necessary to invest in new technologies and marketing.

Everywhere in Europe, regardless of the agricultural structure and the characteristics of wines, public institutions played a decisive role, with the creation of schools, cooperation systems, industrial exhibitions, experimentation centres and the application of scientific knowledge. Beginning in the nineteenth century, the creation of new agricultural schools and public institutions for the improvement of rural activities helped winemakers in various ways: lectures, conferences, bulletins, newspapers, the dissemination of news concerning innovations in viticulture (wine production and preservation, the prevention of and cures for diseases, etc.). Various competitions and exhibitions for scholars and producers were organized with the specific aim of increasing the productivity of the vines, while for others it was to improve the resilience of the wine during transport. Moreover, other means such as agricultural almanacs and calendars contributed to the dissemination of knowledge concerning ampelography and oenological practices. The regional studies collected here help to better define the tangible systems of transferring know-how and its impact on production practices. France was—and has remained—the country of reference for wine producers and consumers, a leadership based on an enduring institutional tradition in supporting French products and on maintaining the quality of a product whose roots lie in the early-modern age. The creation of institutions to support the sector was decisive even in areas such as Bordeaux, which had long enjoyed international prestige. In this area too, it was the institutions which led initiatives in promoting local wines, marketing and various other actions aimed at improving every aspect of production and trade: vineyards, commercial networks and logistics facilities, brokerage houses, brand promotion and enhancement and state-endorsed ranking (1855). Besides, the economy—and the reputation—of the area included not only the most prestigious brands and names, but also small producers, winegrowers and wines of average quality. At every stage of this story, cohesion—which does not necessarily mean solidarity—was at stake, to preserve or rebuild the brands and the overall reputation of the region.

A further important aspect which emerges from reading the essays is the close relationship between the wine and its terroir—i.e. the land, the region where the vineyard is cultivated. Even if "terroir" is a highly debated concept—especially because it fosters a strong geological determinism that excludes or underestimate the role of other factors (e.g. human interventions)—it is a practical one, allowing territorial and cultural comparisons. Wine is a typical product of European civilization and culture, has shaped the agricultural landscape and, more recently, has assumed increasing importance in the tourism industry. It is no coincidence that wine is one of the main strengths for territorial brands and for the creation of tourist destinations whose appeal lies in "authentic" food or wine and short supply chains.

Last but not least, the volume also tries to consider the differentiated impact of legislation concerning indications of the product's origin. Although several price-dependent markets persisted, the average quality of European wines progressively improved after the establishment of the Common Agricultural Policy. In Italy, the new CAP rules made an important contribution to the improvement and qualitative diversification of wine, a differentiation which involved both the production processes as well as the logistics and supply chains. In France, campaigns of uprooting from the 1970s to the 1990s changed the face of mass-production vineyards: thanks to the bonuses granted by the CAP, new qualitative vine stocks were planted, improving the general level of the French wine sector, especially the ordinary wines.

As a whole, the process of transformation of the European oenological industry appears as variegated as its wines. It has been a journey of modernization that every country, every region and every territory has interpreted in an original way and at its own pace. Nevertheless, its common ground lies in its transition from an oenology aimed at producing large quantities of wine, to one which places greater value on the product's quality, safety, promotion and reputation.

The editors thank a lot the anonymous referees (all papers were in fact subject to double-blind refereeing) for their precious suggestions and advice which contributed to further improve the quality and historical interest of the contributions included in these two volumes.

References

Agnoletti M. (2002), *Bois et vigne dans une ferme toscane (XVIIIe-XIXe siècle)*, in A. Corvol (ed.), *Foret et vigne, bois et vin, XVIe-XXe siecle*, Paris, L'Harmattan, pp. 49–66.

Alonso Ugaglia A., Cardebat J.M., Corsi A. (eds.). (2019), *The Palgrave Handbook of Wine Industry Economics*, London, Palgrave Mcmillan.

Anderson K. (2004), *The World's Wine Markets: Globalization at Work*, Cheltenham (UK), Edward Elgar Publishing.

Anderson K., Nelgen S., Pinilla V. (2017), *Global Wine Markets, 1860 to 2016: A Statistical Compendium*, Adelaide, University of Adelaide Press.

Anderson K., Pinilla V. (2018), *Wine Globalization: A New Comparative History*, Cambridge University Press.

Asero V., Patti S. (2009), *From Wine Production to Wine Tourism Experience: The Case of Italy*, AAWE Working Paper, 52.

Bagnol J.M. (2010), *Le Midi viticole au Parlement. Édouard Barthe et les députés du vin de l'Hérault (années 1920–1930)*, Montpellier, Presses Universitaires de la Mediterranee.

Bird O. (2005), *Rheingold—The German Wine Renaissance*, Bury St Edmunds, Suffolk, Arima publishing.

Bisson L.F., Waterhouse A.L., Ebeler S.E., Walker M.A., Lapsley J.T. (2002), "The Present and Future of the International Wine Industry", *Nature*, 418: 696–699.

Boatto V., Gennari A.J. (eds.). (2011), *La roadmap del turismo enologico*, Milan, FrancoAngeli.

Bodinier B., Lachaud S., Marache C. (eds.). (2014), *L'Univers du vin. Hommes, paysages et territoires*, Caen/Rennes, PUR.

Brook S. (2006), *The Wines of Germany*, London, Mitchell Beazley.

Campbell G., Guibert N. (eds.). (2007), *Wine, Society, and Globalization: Multidisciplinary Perspectives on the Wine Industry*, London, Palgrave Macmillan.

Carassale A. (2014), *Problemi e prospettive della vitivinicoltura nella provincia di Porto Maurizio (1960–1923)*, in A. Carassale, L. Lo Basso (eds.), *In terra vineata. La vite e il vino in Liguria e nelle Alpi Marittime dal Medioevo ai nostri giorni. Studi in memoria di Giovanni Rebora*, Ventimiglia, Philobiblon, pp. 109–131.

Carlsen J., Charters S. (eds.). (2006), *Global Wine Tourism: Research, Management and Marketing*, Cambridge, MA, CAB International.

Cavicchi A., Santini C. (eds.). (2014), *Food and Wine Events in Europe: A Stakeholder Approach*, London/New York, Routledge.

Charters, S. (2006), *Wine and Society. The Social and Cultural Context of a Drink*, Amsterdam, Elsevier.

Chevet J.M., Lecocq S., Visser M. (2011), "Climate, Grapevine Phenology, Wine Production, and Prices: Pauillac (1800–2009)", *American Economic Review: Papers & Proceedings*, 101(3): 142–146.

Ciuffoletti Z. (2009), *Alla ricerca del "vino perfetto". Il chianti del Barone di Brolio. Ricasoli e il Risorgimento vitivinicolo italiano*, Florence, Olschki.

Dandolo F. (2010), *Vigneti fragili: espansione e crisi della viticoltura nel Mezzogiorno in età liberale*, Neaples, Guida.

Demossier M. (2010), *Wine Drinking Culture in France: A National Myth or Modern Passion?* Cardiff, University of Wales Press.

Doloreux D., Lord-Tarte E. (2013), "The Organisation of Innovation in the Wine Industry: Open Innovation, External Sources of Knowledge and Proximity", *European Journal of Innovation Management*, 16(2): 171–189.

Failla O., Scienza A. (2001), *Vitigni e viticoltura lombarda alle soglie del '900*, in O. Failla, G. Forni (eds.), *Le piante coltivate e la loro storia. Dalle origini al transgenico in Lombardia nel centenario della riscoperta genetica di Mendel*, Milan, FrancoAngeli, pp. 299–327.

Gaeta D., Corsinovi P. (2014), *Economics, Governance, and Policy in the Wine Market: European Union Developments*, New York, Palgrave Mcmillan.

Gangemi M., Ritrovato E. (2002), *Vigne, vin et bois en Terra di Bari (1875–1914)*, in A. Corvol (ed.), *Foret et vigne, bois et vin, XVIe-XXe siecle*, Paris, L'Harmattan, pp. 67–88.

Gasparini G.P. (2014), *Il vino delle Cinque Terre e le sue trasformazioni otto-centesche*, in A. Carassale, L. Lo Basso (eds.), *In terra vineata. La vite e il vino in Liguria e nelle Alpi Marittime dal Medioevo ai nostri giorni. Studi in memoria di Giovanni Rebora*, Ventimiglia, Philobiblon, pp. 88–108.

Hall C.M., Sharples E., Cambourne B., Macionis N. (eds.). (2000), *Wine Tourism Around the World: Development, Management and Markets*, Oxford, Butterworth-Heinemann.

Harvey M., Waye V. (eds.). (2014), *Global Wine Regulation*, Pyrmont, ThomsonReuters.
Harvey M., White L., Frost W. (eds.). (2014), *Wine and Identity: Branding, Heritage, Terroir*, London/New York, Routledge.
Lachiver M. (1988), *Vins, vignes et vignerons. Histoire du vignoble français*, Paris, Fayard.
Le Bras S. (2013), *De l'emprise locale à l'influence nationale: formes d'actions, impacts et dynamiques du Syndicat régional des vins du Midi (1920–1965)*, in D. Fraboulet, C. Druelle-Korn, P. Vernus (eds.), *Les organisations patronales et la sphère publique. Europe XIXe et XXe siècles*, Rennes, PUR, pp. 243–255.
Le Bras S. (ed.). (2017), *Les Petits vignobles. Des territoires en questions*, Rennes/Tours, PUFR/PUR.
Le Bras S. (2019), *Le négoce des vins en Languedoc. L'emprise du marché (1900–1970)*, Tours, PUFR.
Leonardi A. (2006), *Collaborare per competere: il percorso imprenditoriale delle Cantine Mezzacorona*, Bologna, Il Mulino.
Locatelli A.M., Tedeschi P. (2015), *A New Common Knowledge in Agronomics: The Network of the Agrarian Reviews and Congresses in Europe During the First Half of the 19th Century*, in S. Aprile, C. Cassina, P. Darriulat, R. Leboutte (dir.), *Une Europe de papier. Projets européens au XIXe siècle*, Villeneuve d'Ascq, Presses Universitaires du Septentrion, pp. 187–203.
Lucand C. (2011), *Les négociants en vins de Bourgogne. De la fin du XIXe siècle à nos jours*, Bordeaux, Féret.
Lukacs P. (2005), *American Vintage: The Rise of American Wine*, New York/London, W.W. Norton.
Lukacs P. (2012), *Inventing Wine: A New History of One of the World's Most Ancient Pleasures*, New York/London, W.W. Norton.
Maffi L. (2010), *Storia di un territorio rurale. Vigne e vini nell'Oltrepò Pavese. Ambiente, società, economia*, Milan, FrancoAngeli.
Maffi L. (2012), *Natura docens. Vignaioli e sviluppo economico dell'Oltrepò Pavese nel XIX secolo*, Milan, FrancoAngeli.
Mainardi G., Berta P. (eds.). (2013), *Ampelografia italiana del 1800. Atti del convegno di storia della vite e del vino in Italia: Canelli, 26 novembre 2010*, Canelli, OICCE.
Marache C., Meyzie P. (eds.). (2015), *Les produits de terroir. L'empreinte de la ville*, Rennes/Tours, PUFR/PUR.
Meloni G., Swinnen J. (2016), "The Political and Economic History of Vineyard Planting Rights in Europe: From Montesquieu to the European Union", *Journal of Wine Economics*, 11(3): 379–413.

Mocarelli L. (2013), *The Long Struggle for the Chianti Denomination: Quality Versus Quantity*, in G. Ceccarelli, A. Grandi, S. Magagnoli (eds.), *Typicality in History: Tradition, Innovation, and Terroir / La typicité dans l'histoire. Tradition, innovation et terroir*, Bruxelles, Peter Lang, pp. 323–340.
Muñoz Moreno A. (2009), *Geología y vinos de España*, Madrid, Ilustre colegio oficial de Geólogos.
Ottolino M. (2011), *Produzione e commercio di vino e dei suoi derivati in Terra di Bari tra XIX e XX secolo. Le iniziative societarie*, in G. Gullino, P. Pecorari, G.M. Varanini (eds.), *Studi di storia economica e sociale in onore di Giovanni Zalin*, Sommacampagna, Cierre, pp. 313–337.
Palaude S. (2012), *Le Groupe des Verreries champenoises, syndicat méconnu des fabricants de bouteilles à vins de Champagne (1899–1939)*, in D. Fraboulet, P. Vernus (eds.), *Genèse et morphologies originelles des organisations patronales en Europe (XIXe–XXe siècles)*, Rennes, PUR, pp. 259–267.
Paul H.W. (1996), *Science, Vine and Wine in Modern France*, Cambridge, CUP.
Pedrocco G. (2000), *Viticoltura ed enologia in Italia nel XIX secolo*, in M. Da Passano et al. (eds.), *La vite e il vino: storia e diritto (secoli XI–XIX)*, 2 v., Rome, Carocci, I, pp. 613–627.
Perron F. (2010), "Quel goût pour le "vin des rois et roi des vins"? Une mediation complexe entre les preferences du consommateur et l'offre des producteurs au tournant du XVIIIe et XIXe siècles", *Food and History*, VIII(2): 135–154.
Planas J. (2015), *State Intervention in Wine Markets and Collective Action in France and Spain during the Early 20th Century*, Documentos de Trabajo, Asociación Española de Historia Económica.
Planas J. (2016), "The Emergence of Winemaking Cooperative in Catalonia", *Business History*, (2): 264–282.
Reckinger R. (2012), *Parler Vin. Entre norms et appropriations*, Rennes, PUR.
Rohály G., Mészáros G., Nagymarosy A. (2003), *Terra Benedicta: The Land of Hungarian Wine - Tokaj and Beyond*, Budapest, AKO' Publisher.
Sagnes J. (ed.). (1993), *La viticulture française aux XIXe et XXe siècles*, Béziers, Presses du Languedoc.
Sagnes J. (ed.). (2008), *La révolte du Midi viticole cent ans après, 1907–2007*, Perpignan, Presses Universitaires de Perpignan.
Simpson J. (2000), "Cooperation and Cooperatives in Southern European Wine Production", *Advances in Agricultural Economic History*, 1: 95–126.
Simpson J. (2011), *Creating Wine: The Emergence of a World Industry 1840–1914*. Princeton/Oxford, Princeton University Press.

Stengel K. (2013), *Traité du vin en France: Traditions et Terroir*, Paris, Sang de la terre.

Tattersall I., De Salle R. (2015), *A Natural History of Wine*, New Heaven/London, Yale University Press.

Tedeschi P. (2003), *Il rinnovamento colturale. Aspetti della viticoltura bresciana fra Ottocento e Novecento*, in G. Archetti (ed.), *La civiltà del vino: fonti, temi e produzioni vitivinicole dal Medioevo al Novecento*, Brescia, Centro culturale artistico di Franciacorta e del Sebino, pp. 789–816.

Tedeschi P. (2017), "Note di eno-storia economica: viticoltura e produzione di vino nei terroirs italiani (secoli XVIII-XX)", *Proposte e Ricerche*, (79): 101–111.

Unwin T. (1996), *Wine and the Vine: An Historical Geography of Viticulture and the Wine Trade*, London, Routledge.

Vaquero Piñeiro M. (2015a), "El turismo enológico en Italia: origen y desarrollo", *RIVAR*, II(5): 117–137.

Vaquero Piñeiro M. (2015b), *L'enoturismo in Italia. Paesaggi e imprenditoria*, in P. Avallone, D. Strangio (eds.), *Turismi e turisti. Politica, innovazione, economia in Italia in età contemporanea*, Milan, FrancoAngeli, pp. 285–305.

Wolikow S., Humbert F. (eds.). (2015), *Une histoire des vins et des produits d'AOC. L'INAO*, de 1935 à nos jours, Dijon, EUD, 2015.

Zanotti E. (2015), *I Folonari: un'antica storia di vini e banche*, Milan, Mursia.

Zoia D. (2004), *Vite e vino in Valtellina e Valchiavenna: la risorsa di una valle alpina*, Sondrio, L'Officina del Libro.

The "Grapes Country": Portuguese Viticulture from the Early Nineteenth Century Until the New Millennium

Conceição Andrade Martins
and Ana Cardoso de Matos

Introduction

Historically, vines have been cultivated all over the country and wine is an important production and a key article of our balance of trade.[1] From the fifteenth century, the Portuguese expansion process increased

[1]At least since the fourteenth century, Portuguese wines were shipped, mainly through the ports of Lisbon, Oporto' and Viana, to the northern Europe markets. It was estimated that, by the middle of the fourteenth century, would be exported, annually, between 12,000 and 30,000 barrels (pipas) of wine, the majority of which the "well-known" Lisbon wines. In value, wine exports would amount to about one million pounds, what was, "by far", the main source of revenue of Portuguese foreign trade. See, Castro, 1971, pp. 274–276; Brito, 1889, pp. 450–469.

C. Andrade Martins (✉)
Institute of Social Sciences, University of Lisbon, Lisbon, Portugal

A. Cardoso de Matos
University of Évora-CIDEHUS, Évora, Portugal
e-mail: amatos@uevora.pt

S. A. Conca Messina et al. (eds.), *A History of Wine in Europe, 19th to 20th Centuries, Volume I*, Palgrave Studies in Economic History,
https://doi.org/10.1007/978-3-030-27772-7_2

the demand for wines by the vessels that annually left the Tagus River in the search of lightening the unknown and discovers "new worlds". Not just because wine was an essential product for the survival of the crews of the sea fleets that crossed the South Atlantic and the Indian Ocean, but also because it was an important commodity of the world's maritime trade.[2] Despite this, Portuguese wines trade overseas was quite irregular until the beginning of the eighteenth century. Its take off dates back to the last quarter of the seventeenth and is directly connected, firstly with the international political-diplomatic and military context of the second half of that century and the rivalry between the British and the French.[3] Secondly, with the development of the Portuguese–British trade encouraged, largely, by the 1654 treaty (Westminster Treaty) which awarded "huge" privileges to English merchants trading in the Portuguese "*economic space*", above all in Brazil, including entitlement to lower duties.[4] And thirdly, with the maritime and commercial competition between the British and the Dutch's which, "crossing" the Portuguese sea ports, increased the demand of national products, among which wine proved to be a good "*return merchandise*". By the end of the eighteenth, wine products—wine, spirit, and vinegar—already accounted for about half of mainland's articles exports, but for the United Kingdom, Portugal's major trade partner, their weight was much higher: 84%.[5]

[2]There is evidence that during the *Quattrocento* many fields had been cleared to plant vineyards and wine supply was quite abundant. See Lobo, 1903, secção I, p. 15.

[3]Devolution war (1667), Augsburg Alliance war (1688/1697) and Spain Succession war (1701/1713). Increase of English royalties on French wines in 1660, 1689 and 1697. Barriers or even ban on French wines importations into the UK between 1667–1670 and 1679–1685. Throughout these years the exports of Portuguese wines to England rose from less than 200 barrels (pipas) to over 12,000. See Martins, 1990, pp. 77–79 and 217–218.

[4]About this treaty considered the "*Magna Carta*" of the British dominance in Portugal, see Shillington, V. M., and Chapman, A. B. Wallis., *The Commercial Relations of England and Portugal*, London, s/d, p. 204.

[5]Since the beginning of eighteenth, Portuguese wines were at the top of British wine imports. Their share climbed from 41% in 1695/1704 (50% the Spanish wines and 3% the French) to 75% in 1740/1804 (20% the Spanish and 5% the French). See, Public Record Office, *Accounts and Papers*, XXXIV.

It is, therefore, not surprising that viticulture has become such an important branch of the national economy that, from the mid eighteenth on, imposed itself as a national "question" and compelled the state to interfere and regulate it. Especially the Port wine sector where, from 1756 onwards "*the state was always present* (… and even) *in the periods of economic liberalism and free trade, its presence was stronger than in the rest of the economy and society*" (Barreto 1988, p. 374). It was, in fact, in that year (1756) that Prime Minister Pombal demarcated the first wine district in the world—the Alto Douro's vineyards demarcated region—regulated all the winegrowing process inside Douro's wine district and established a company with royal privileges to supervise the wine production, manufacture, transport and trade inside and outside this region, namely in the warehouses of Gaia and Oporto.[6] Thus, Port is the oldest controlled denomination of origin.

A century and a half later (1907/1908) six new wine regions would be demarcated: Two in the north and central north of the country (Vinho Verde and Dão); three in the south, nearby Lisbon (Carcavelos, Colares and Moscatel de Setúbal), and one in the islands (Madeira). At present, there are much more oenological *terroirs* protected spread out all over the mainland and islands (See Map 1), and, as a major old world wine country, Portugal boasts two wine producing regions UNESCO world heritage sites: the Douro valley wine district and the Pico island wine region in the Azores.

At the turn of the millennium the importance of wine sector in Portugal can be measured by the following indicators: (i) the cultivated area under vines was around 250,000 hectares (the 8th at world level), which corresponds to 6.8% of the Portuguese agricultural surface, the higher vineyard's density in EU and in the main world wine countries[7];

---

[6]About this company (the General Company of Agriculture of Alto Douro Vineyards), the demarcation of the Douro wine growing district and the regulation of its production and manufacture process, see, Pereira, 1990; Martins, 1998; Sousa, 2006.

[7]The second is Moldavia (6% of agricultural surface), the third Italy (5%), and the fourth Spain (4%). For vineyard acreage by country see, European Commission, DG Agriculture and Rural Development, elaboration based on notifications from EU Member States under Reg. (EU) 555/2008, Annex XIII, Table XIV; and for agricultural areas, *FAO Statistical Yearbook* 2013, Table 4, pp. 34–37.

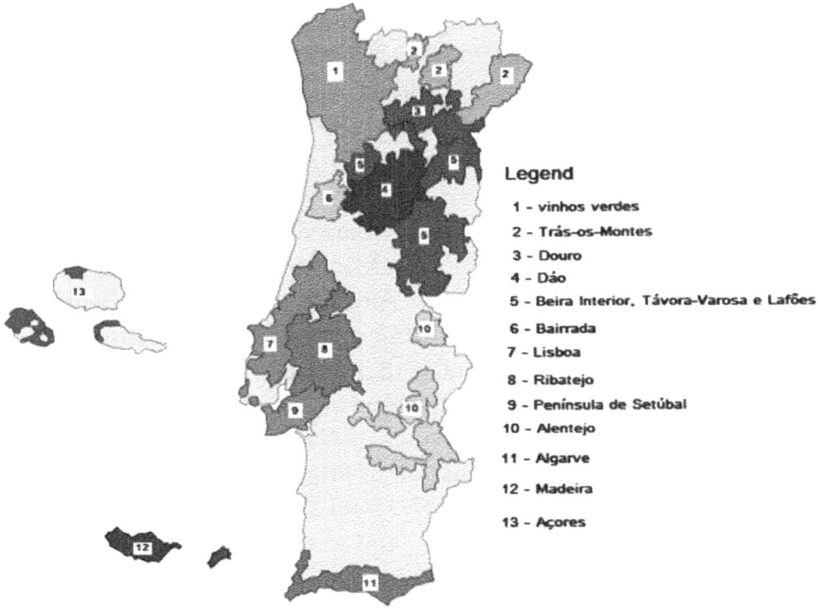

Map 1 Portuguese wine-growing districts (*Source* Authors eleboration of Infovini's Regiões Vitivinícolas Map)

(ii) almost 40% of this acreage is dedicated to quality wines (VQPRD), rising this proportion to higher values in the north-west and north-east of the country (See Table 1); (iii) at the same period (1995/2005), the wine production exceeds 7 million of hectolitres (10° world wine producer and 5° EU), corresponding to 4% of EU production and 2.6% of the whole world production; (iv) the value of this production in the agriculture branch is over 8%, less than the French (around 10%), close to the Italian (9%) and higher than the Spanish (3%); (v) exports amount to about 2.5 million hectolitres (3.5% of the world market) and its value rounds 530 million Euros; and (vi) this branch involves almost 250,000 wine farming companies, the majority of small and very small scale, and more than 100 cooperative wineries accounting for half of the wine production.

The aim of this chapter is to highlight the relevance of *vitivinicul-ture* and wine trade to Portuguese economy and society, and to put in

Table 1 Portuguese viticultural land (2010)

Wine regions	Land in wine (hect)	% total land in wine	Land in VQPRD[c] (hect)	% VQPRD[c] regional land in wine
Northwest (Minho)	31,010	13.0	29,388	94.8
Northeast (T Montes[a])	68,765	28.9	41,358	60.1
Center (Beiras)	56,663	23.8	12,555	22.2
South Center (Estremadura, Lx e Vale Tejo[b])	52,752	22.2	5058	9.6
South (Alentejo and Algarve)	25,473	10.7	9125	35.8
Mainland Portugal	234,663	98.7	97,484	41.5
Azores	1700	0.7	228	13.4
Madeira	1423	0.6	497	34.9
Total Portugal	237,786	100.0	98,209	41.3

Notes
[a]Includes Douro's wine district where the proportion of VQPRD wines is much higher (around 85%)
[b]Includes Setúbal Peninsula
[c]VQPRD are Quality Wines Produced in a Specified Region
Source IVV, *Yearbook* 2011 as at 31 July 2010–

evidence the main changes and progresses of this branch since the turn of the nineteenth century.

Wine Tradition in Portugal

The suitability of Portugal for wine was highlighted by many renowned experts, namely the MP and head of the central Agriculture department, Moraes Soares (1811/1881), who assured, in the prologue of his studies on Portuguese vine-growing to the London International Exhibition of 1874 and the Paris Universal Exhibition of 1878, that "*If Portugal is not the 'native' country of the vine is, at least, its homeland 'of adoption*'" (Soares 1874, p. 3, 1878). A similar opinion expressed Villa Maior (1809/1884) in his Report to the 1867 International Exhibition.

There he stated that Portugal had, not only all the conditions to be a first-rate wine country but, more than any other, the ability to export wines of all categories. For them to be excellent, winegrowers only needed to improve their manufacture and treatment, since even when the vines were treated with little care and the wines made "*by chance*" we manage to make good wines.[8] For his part, the scholar and politic Elvino de Brito (1851–1902) argued that, if it were not for the high taxes imposed on wines by the majority of the importing countries, the cultivation of vines could have expanded in such a way across the country, that all the other, including that of cereals, would be subsidiary (Brito 1889, p. 459). Finally, Lopes de Carvalho argued that "*Viticulture has been at every age the alma mater of Portuguese agriculture*" (Carvalho 1890–1891, p. 229).

Plant rather widespread in Portugal, like in the majority of the Mediterranean countries, grape growing had been strongly encouraged and supported either by the crown, the church or the monastic orders since the beginning of "*nationality*" (twelfth century). On one hand, exempting from the payment of rents, for a few years, the tenants who planted vineyards at their domains or at the fields surrounding the villages and cities (Porto, for instance), and on the other, charging lower rents to vines than to cereals.[9] The main reasons for such a "*protection*" are known and connected with the growth of the religious and laic wine demand, the good adaptability of vineyards to thinner, poor and arid soils and its capacity to fix populations. Besides, for those who farmed the land, vines had the advantage of being subjected to fewer constraints than cereals and provide surpluses for the market. The expansion of the country's winegrowing area did not change, however, the "*original characteristics*" of this culture. In fact, wine remained a mixed and

[8] Villa Maior, 1868. About Portuguese participation in nineteenth century international exhibitions see, Matos and Martins, 2003.

[9] Vines paid census between 1/5 and 1/10 and grains usually around ¼. On this subject and the one of the wine-growing expansion in Portugal throughout the twelfth and sixteenth centuries. See, Alves, 1943; Barros, 2003, vol. 16, pp. 217–308; Coelho, 1977, 1983; Gonçalves, 1987, pp. 73–97; Lencastre, 1953; Rodriguez, 1997, vol. 3, pp. 17–28; Santana, 2003, vol. 15, pp. 11–24; Trincade, 1974.

supplementary production, even in districts relatively well integrated into the mercantile economy and with better connections with the marketplaces (local, national or international).[10]

So, although, historically, vines have been enough disseminated throughout Portugal, it has been just around the middle of the seventeenth century that its culture started to become predominant and almost exclusive in some regions, especially around the Douro river's valley. Encouraged by the domestic and external demand (mainly British, Dutch, German and Northern Europe), the viticulture specialization of this region began taking shape during the second half of the seventeenth century and has speeded up throughout the eighteenth and nineteenth centuries.[11] This process was led by the monks and the rural aristocracy, but seldom or never within the framework of the large farming. In fact, it has been, above all, the small and middle landowners and farmers who ensured and guided the Herculean labour of transforming the flaky schistose soils of the Douro valley into vineyards.[12] By doing so, they gave up audaciously the traditional self-consumption productions on behalf of the most commercial one, wine, and went ahead with the winegrowing specialization on the Douro valley, although the natural resources of this region were, at first sight, unfavourable compared with other places where viticulture was either in dissemination or was already intensively cultivated, like, for example, near the main cities and maritime ports (Lisbon, Porto, Viana do Castelo, Aveiro, Setúbal,

---

[10]The dispersion of cultures around Aveiro was characterized by Silva as a "selective mixed-farming", due the "predisposition" for concentrating cereals cultivation at certain places and vine's rather at the vicinity of the cities and the slopes of Este where, moreover, new vines had been planted. Silva 1994, pp. 90–91. On the "logic" of wine expansion in "low" Mondego, see Durand, 1972; Gonçalves, 1987.

[11]In the seventeenth and eighteenth centuries those were important overseas markets for both Port and Madeira wines, but also for other Portuguese wines, namely the well-known Lisbon wine, that used to be sent to northern Europe and América through the Lisbon, Faro, Figueira, Setúbal and Viana harbours in vessels carrying other commodities, such as salt, fruits and colonial products. Further more, the British demand for wines strongly grew after the Restoration (1660) and the development of the maritime trade with its colonies, which Francis regarded as the "turning point" of its wine trade. See, Francis, 1972.

[12]This process involved the building of walled terraces in the steep slopes of the Douro valley.

etc.).[13] In reality, due to the rocky soil and the hot dry climate of that part of the country, the yields are very low (around half a litre per vine in top estates, nowadays), but the juice is very rich and concentrated.

Given that until the 1850s (appearance of powdery mildew in Portuguese vines) there are no evidences of the use of chemical fertilizers on most productive grape varieties, and, therefore, no significant changes in the average yield of vines, the productive increases of the last decades of the eighteenth century and first half of the nineteenth must be resulting, mainly, from the enlargement of the vines' area (Fig. 1).[14] This extension of vineyards only occasionally must have been assessed on land occupied by other crops, such as cereals, since in most cases the new plantations mainly benefited unproductive land, which gradually, according to winegrower's possibilities and markets demand, were planted with vines. This must have been the practice followed by small and medium growers who hardly could renounce the product of other crops to convert them into vineyards. And was, likewise, the case of the new vineyards sponsored by funds transferred from other sectors (commercial or financial), as happened in the Douro, Bairrada and Extremadura regions.[15]

The, comparatively, low rate of the wine branch throughout the following years proceeds from the deep and lasting drop in production over the years 1850–1870, due, mainly, to the *oidium* crisis and to the long and difficult process of recovering the production in the following years (see Fig. 1). This slow process of recovery stemmed from the delay in finding the most effective treatments for this disease, its cost and the ones connected with the extra labours in the vineyards, needed to attack and prevent the disease (digger the vines more often, apply

[13]The Douro district would produce about 16,000 barrels (pipas) in the sixteenth century; 30,000 in the seventeenth century; 60,000 in the eighteenth century; and more than 100,000 by the mid of the nineteenth century, i.e., before the oidium and phylloxera diseases. Arquivo Nacional da Torre do Tombo, MR., maço 641.

[14]Wine production more then doubled between 1772/1773 and 1848/1849. It grew from 1.5 million hectolitres to 3.4 million.

[15]About this subjects see, Soares, 1873.

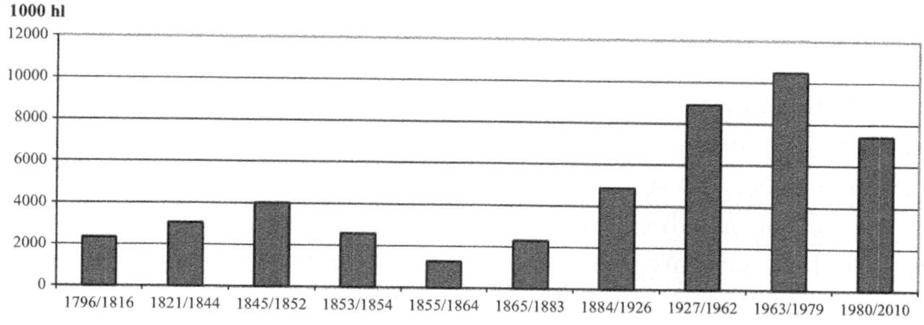

Fig. 1 Historical growth of Portuguese wine production 1796–2010 (average in 1000 hl) (*Sources* Martins, Conceição Andrade, *Vinha, Vinho e Política Vinícola em Portugal do Pombalismo à Regeneração*, op.cit.; Lains, Pedro e Sousa, Paulo Silveira e, "Estatística e produção agrícola em Portugal, 1848–1914", *Análise Social*, n° 149, 1998, pp. 935–968; *Estatística Agrícola* 1967–2010, Lisboa, INE, 1968–2011)

sulphur,...) and, last but not least, the emergence and spread of the *phylloxera*. Politically, this deeply depressing situation of viticulture and national economy encouraged the liberalization of the sector, accomplished between 1852 and 1865: reform and extinction of the Douro's wine company, abolition of the Douro's demarcated region and of the restrictive regime.[16] That is, a century after Pombal had imposed protectionist measures to a specific branch of economy, Port wine sector, its production and trade were, finally, released from all constraints. As well as, all other wines were permitted to come into Douro's wine district and into Oporto "barriers", and also to be exported through its harbour.

The *phylloxera* disease reached sooner and with higher strength the Douro wine country, whose vineyards were attacked and destroyed by the insect since the late 1860s, and later and less intensely the other wine regions, where preventive actions were implemented by the end of the 70s and the replacement of old and/or infected vines by American varieties began earlier. Like on the surroundings of Lisbon, where one

[16]The so-called "restrictive regime" was a set of protectionist laws on the production, transport and trade of Port wine established since 1756. Besides the wine crisis, the 1850s has been a time of general crisis: huge floods, crop failures and epidemic outbreaks (cholera morbus, yellow fever).

of the larger and richer landlords of the country, José Maria dos Santos, shaped by then (mid 1870–1880) the "greatest vineyard of the world": around 6 million grapevines planted on unproductive sandy soils, precisely the most resistant to phylloxera, and producing, by the mid 1890s, between 10 million to 15 million hectolitres/annually. A huge wine production which, in the midst of a global crisis of overproduction, had the advantage of been situated face to the main "commercial centre" of the country (Lisbon) and being drained through a net of taverns supported by that winegrower.[17]

Therefore, in the late 1870s, when the phylloxera was still confined to Douro wine region, vineyards already covered about 200,000 ha of the mainland (more than 4% of agricultural surface); wine production, although still 30% below the pre-oidium average values, accounts for almost 25% of agricultural production and for about 68% of its growth; and country's wine cartography already showed deep changes (see Fig. 2).[18] The "southern provinces" (Centre South and South) were harvesting almost 50% more wine than the Northern ones, while before the "1852 disease" their production was 32% inferior to that. At the turn of the century, their share almost reached 50% of national wine production while the share of the northern' provinces slumped to less than 30%.

The recovery, since the 1880s, of the pre-*oidium* flows of production, and the high growth of the following years (rate of 1.3% per year until the 1920s) will be at the heart of the turn of the century overproduction crisis (see Fig. 1). In fact, when the country's politic regime changed to a Republic (1910) the extent of vineyards had already reached 300,000 ha (7% of agricultural surface); wine production had climbed to 6 million hectolitres, which in value accounts for almost 16% of agricultural gross product, less than in the 1870s, it's true, but not so much considering the growth of agricultural production throughout this period (70% between 1870s and end 1900s).[19] Once more, this crisis of overproduction and fall of prices gave place to state intervention in this branch

---

[17]About this landowner see, Martins, 1992, pp. 367–404.

[18]See Fig. 2. About these subjects see, Pery, 1875; Lains, 1990.

[19]See, Castro, 1908; Lains, 2003, pp. 253–255.

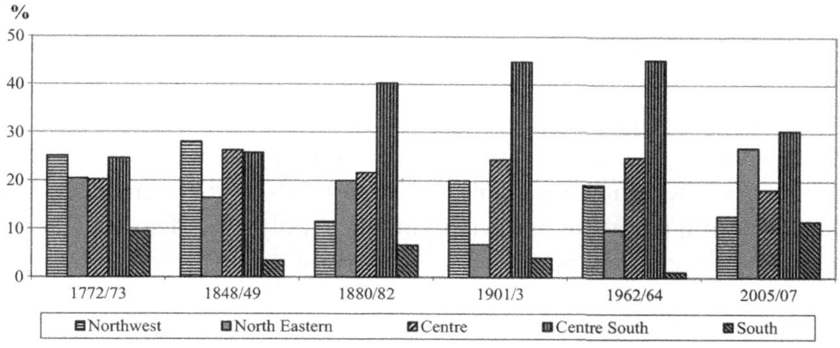

Fig. 2 Regional distribution of Portuguese wine production (%) (*Sources* Martins, Conceição Andrade, *Vinha, Vinho e Política Vinícola em Portugal do Pombalismo à Regeneração*, op.cit.; INE, *Estatísticas Agrícolas*, several years; IVV, *Anuários*, 1994–2007)

of the economy in order to regulate and "control" it. Whether restoring, in 1907/1908, the old Douro Demarcated Region, extinguished in the 1860s, or creating new ones: the green wine demarcated region, in the North-West, the Dão wine demarcates region, in the centre of the country, the Colares wine, Carcavelos wine and Moscatel of Setúbal wine demarcated regions, nearby Lisbon (see Map 1). Either restricting vine plantations, or regulating, once again, the Port wine trade and production, namely establishing a Port Wine Shippers' Guild and an Agricultural and Commercial Port Wine Association (both in 1908). Or, as well, taking actions to foster the growth of wine trade, namely by granting exportation premiums.

Under the Corporative regime (1933/1874) the wine sector control tightened further, particularly concerning the wine production of the demarcated regions, and particularly the Port wine production and the Port wine shippers' activities. The control of Port wine production was done through the "benefício", i.e. the amount of Douro's grape must production annually "approved" to be fortified ("transformed" into Port wine) by the Casa do Douro. Established in 1933 together with the Port Wine Institute (IVP) and the Exporters' Guild, the first of these institutions (Casa do Douro) was set up to "protect" and monitoring growers activities; the second (IVP), was supposed to control the "quality" of the wine and warrant its origin by granting certificates of origin; and the third, to oversee the exporting firms' activity and, eventually, establish minimum export prices. A few years later (1937) it was decided to set up another organization expressly concerned with ordinary wines, the Junta Nacional do Vinho (JNV), whose main purpose was regulating this wine market balancing supply with demand. During almost half a century of existence, it actively contributed to the modernization and organization of this wine sector, for the dissemination of knowledge about wine and for the promotion of cooperative wineries. Dissolved in 1986, when Portugal joined UE, it was replaced by the Institute Of Vine and Wine (IVV)

If, historically, the wine branch played such an important role in economic policies it was not only because, as Salazar used to say in the 40s, drinking wine helps to feed a million Portuguese, but mainly because of this sector's weight, as a whole, in Portuguese economy and in the balance of trade (see Table 2). But also for its role in the agro-industrial economy and, recently, in the development of inner's country land, helping to mitigate rural depopulation and its negative effects by the revitalization of local economies.

Table 2 Wine in Portuguese balance of trade

Weight of wine in Portuguese special trade			Imports coverage rate by wine exports		
	Port wine (%)	Portuguese wines (%)		Port wine (%)	Portuguese wines (%)
1776/1808	13	18	1800/1819	14	16
1809/1886	33	45	1820/1899	21	30
1887/1940	20	35	1900/1939	8	14
1941/1986	4	8	1940/1984	2	5

Source Martins, Conceição Andrade, *Memória do Vinho do Porto*, op.cit., pp. 238–240

Port Wine, the Locomotive of Portuguese Wine Economy

It was throughout the eighteenth century that Port wine imposes itself as a first quality wine, whose characteristics allowed it, when well manufactured (vinified), to age well and even improve its flavours. The process of making Port has been modified and improved since then, but its key features are a good maturation of the grapes, and precise rules of vinification and ageing, including the addition of varying proportions of wine spirit at Douro's wine cellars and during its "stage" at the warehouses of Gaia and Oporto (the so-called refreshments).[20] "*Manufactured*", first of all, to answer the British demand and taste for "*full-bodied, strongly coloured and strong tasting*" wines (i.e. "*dark, strong and sweet*"), the share of Port wine in Portuguese wine exports to the UK quickly rose from less than 1/5 to more than half in the first two decades of the eighteenth century, and to ¾ thereafter (see Table 3). Thus, Port wine won all other wines' competition in the UK, including ordinary Portuguese wines, and put these in its orbit, both in the foreign and domestic markets.[21] The Port wine was, by the way, the only wine that had a positive overall behaviour in eighteenth-century England, and most of its success was due to the British wine trade firms established at Oporto since the second half of the seventeenth century (Warre in 1670, Croft in 1678, Dawson and Harris in 1680, Bearsley in 1692, Offley Forrester in 1729, ...) as well as to the British Factory (Feitoria), whose regulation dates back to 1727.[22]

Therefore, since the eighteenth century that Port wine trade, as well Madeira's wine, was the driving force of Portuguese wines trade overseas, specially to the United Kingdom until 1831, when it was decided

---

[20]The process of making Port wine includes fermentation, fortification and ageing, to allow the wine to mellow, develop its flavours and mature, in cool dark warehouses at Oporto and Gaia where the temperate climate of the coast ensures that the wines will age slowly and harmoniously. One of the unique properties of Port is its ability to gain in richness and flavour over very long periods of ageing in wood, partly because it is fortified and partly because it is a wine of extraordinary concentration and aromatic potential (http://www.croftport.com/en/).

[21]Regarding Portuguese wines competition in the British market see Public Record Office, *Accounts and Papers*, XXXIV.

[22]Croft is, nowadays, the oldest firm still active in Port wine business.

to level tariffs on all foreign wines, thus ending the preferential conditions that Portuguese wines had enjoyed under the Methuen Treaty (1703).[23] Although this measure was, on its own, less crippling for the port wine trade with England than those implemented by Gladstone in 1860 and 1861, the truth is that, between 1830 and 1859, Portuguese wines lost some 15% of their share of the British market, and the drop became even more accentuated after the changes to customs duties introduced by Gladstone in 1860 and in 1861. Indeed, once tariffs were generally lowered, though progressive charges introduced on wines in accordance with their alcohol content, Port wines were included in the highest category (over 26° Sykes) and had to pay over a shilling more per gallon than less alcoholic wines.

That is to say, the differential duties that encumbered the product made it much less competitive on the British market.[24] Moreover, the prohibition upon exporting wines to Britain that had not been properly approved and qualified for that destination meant that, according to Forrester, a third of the Upper Douro production was "condemned" to be consumed on the domestic market.[25] Not precisely because these wines were defective in any way, or of lower quality, but rather because they were pure (i.e. made only from unblended fermented grape juice) and/or produced outside the demarcated area. Far more than this geographic fluke, what irritated Forrester was that both the law and the export trade rejected those wines on the grounds that they were not good enough quality and were not to the English taste (i.e. not "dark, strong and sweet").

[23]From 1831 on, foreign wines had to pay 5 shillings and 6 pence per gallon, approximately double the amount paid by wines from the British Empire (2 sh and 9 d). It will be recalled that Article II of the Methuen Treaty stipulated that "from henceforth" Portuguese wines would pay lower import duties than French wines, and, in fact, for a long time they enjoyed an even better advantage than the third less agreed in the 1703 Treaty. See Martins, 2003, pp. 111–130.

[24]At that time, Port wine shipped to the United Kingdom paid more per barrel in export duty than the same product sent for other European countries or to America. On this matter, see Forrester, 1850.

[25]Those measures were implemented in 1822, 1825 and 1833. Between 1833 and 1852, the portion of Douro production that was not approved for export and therefore destined for home consumption vastly exceeded the portion approved (over 70%). %). Cf. Martins, 1990, p. 202 and pp. 322–325.

Table 3 Port wine share in the main Portuguese wine markets[a] (nineteenth and twentieth centuries)

	UK (%)	Nordic countries[b] (%)	France (%)	Benelux (%)	Brasil (%)	USA (%)	Pt Colonies and PALOPs[c] (%)
First half nineteenth century	90	59	18	66	24	41	42
Second half nineteenth century	91	94	3	70	22	80	1
First half twentieth century	88	57	19	30	10	7	2
Second half twentieth century	67	29	83	59	9	4	0.3

Notes
[a]Average of the quantities exported during each period
[b]Denmark, Norvege and Sweden
[c]PALOPs means African countries whose official language is Portuguese
Source Martins, Conceição Andrade, *Memória do Vinho do Porto*, op.cit., pp. 248–253

Thus, the law and the merchants effectively conspired to encourage the widespread practice of adulterating port. Not only demanding that wine separated off for sale to the United Kingdom should have particular qualities that the wines themselves were unable to produce, but also insisting that the English preferred wines that were "full-bodied, strongly coloured and strong tasting". So, while port had traditionally been laced with 4 to 5 gallons of brandy per barrel, now most of the wine exported to the United Kingdom received five times that amount, and even had elderberries and mistelle added to it. In opposition to merchants' believe, this did not appeal to the English, whose tastes were now inclining more towards lighter younger cheaper wines (such as sherry and French wine). And worse, it also meant that the supply of Douro wines could not keep up with the increased demand from Britain. Those adulterations practised (or instigated) by the merchants had yet another perverse effect, since it not only damaged the reputation of port among the more wealthy classes, but also led to its disqualification, in 1859, by a wine jury. His members alleged that the Gaia warehouses were full of wines unsuitable for export and, thus, deserving to be burnt, and requested for measures to restore the "licit and legal" trade with foreign markets.[26]

Even if Port wine sector was highly regulated and constrained, either by a restrictive system as by heavy taxes on foreign trade, it was also quite protected from other national wines competition both in the domestic or international markets. For that purpose, since the 1750s until the 1860s it was forbidden to export any other wines by the Oporto Harbour, as well as their access to that city, its surroundings and Douro's wine district. Besides, among other privileges, the Douro Wine Company had the exclusive of supplying the taverns of Oporto and surroundings, of providing wine to some Brazilian captaincies and of distilling grape spirit in the Northern provinces. The supply of brandy to fortify Port wine, as well as of darker, stronger, and full-bodied wines to blend with Douro wines and improve their quality, or increase the quantity of Port wine stored in the warehouses of Oporto and Gaia, encouraged winegrowers from the Northern provinces to enlarge their vineyards. Furthermore, the demographic growth, the raising of Europeans' standard of living (and also of the Portuguese's, although more moderate), and the consequent increase of international, domestic and colonial demand (Brazilian, first, and African from the end of the 19th) urged the winegrowers of the Centre and South Centre provinces to extend their vines, trusting that the capital proximity and the extinguishing of Douro's protectionism (in the 1850–1860s) might ensure new exits for their wines.[27]

This process of vineyard acreage enlargement was particularly intense between the last quarter of the 19th and the 1960s, reacting to the increasing demand for ordinary and cheap domestic wines. As show Tables 4 and 5, the foreign demand for this type of wines grew quicker than those of Port through these years, especially in Northern

[26]On these matters see, Forrester, 1844, 1859.

[27]It was, in fact, this expansive conjuncture, add to the progressive abolishment of the "restrictive regime", eventually accomplished in 1865, that urged winegrowers to expand their vines area, a crop, after all, more profitable than many others, including grains.

and Central Europe and in the colonial markets, even if the growth rate of the first period (1776/1859—1860/1904) might reflect the gap between Port wine exports and those of all the other Portuguese wines, which was particularly high until the1830s.

The winegrowing expansion of the last quarter of the eighteenth century and the first decades of the 19th is, therefore, straight connected with the growth of domestic and foreign demand for wines, both stimulated by Port wine production and trade.[28] So it's not surprising that, before the phylloxera, the Douro wine country was the larger and most important Portuguese wine region. With around 100,000 ha of vineyards producing an average of 450,000 hl of wine (22% of all national production), more than half of this region's wine production was transformed into Port wine, commodity that contributed to 2/3 of national wine exports, around 30% of Portuguese overseas trade and covered 1/5 of imports. But the importance of Port wine in Portuguese economy can be measured by many other indicators, namely its share in the national wine trade, and its weight in the balance of trade (see Tables 2 and 6; Fig. 3).

The Turning Point of Portuguese's Viticulture: Nineteenth-Century Vine Diseases

In the "collective imaginary" *phylloxera* is the "most terrible scourge" that reached Portuguese viticulture. First of all, due to the devastation it caused in the most important viticultural *terroir* (Douro's wine country), where the aphid destroyed thousand of vineyards and left large spots of land covered with dead vines (known as mortórios).[29] Secondly, owing

---

[28]The first great expansion of vineyards dates back, however, to the last decades of the seventeenth century, and is straight connected to the benefits then granted to Portuguese wines in the United Kingdom and reinforced, a few years later, by the Methuen Treaty (1703). See Martins, 2003.

[29]Native to North America, the plylloxera is a disease induced by an aphid (insect) with wings that feeds on leaves and roots, causing nodules and eventually killing the vine. It came to Europe, with vines imported from North America and quickly "attacks" the French vineyards since early 1860s. In Portugal the phylloxera appeared in the Douro's valley by the end of the 1860s and the crisis reached its climax in 1881/1885. About the evolution and effects of this disease in Portugal see, Martins, 1991.

Table 4 Main overseas markets for Portuguese wines[a] (nineteenth and twentieth centuries)

		First half nineteenth century (%)	Second half nineteenth century (%)	First half twentieth century (%)	Second half twentieth century (%)
UK	For Port wine	81.8	60.8	57.8	19.9
	For the other Portuguese wines	17.2	3.5	3.7	3.0
Brasil	For Port wine	9.3	22.4	6.0	0.4
	For the other Portuguese wines	58.3	47.4	25.4	1.2
Nordic countries[b]	For Port wine	4.3	3.5	8.7	7.4
	For the other Portuguese wines	5.9	0.1	3.2	5.5
France	For Port wine	0.03	1.9	11.4	35.6
	For the other Portuguese wines	0.3	34.0	22.8	2.2
Benelux	For Port wine	0.5	1.9	5.7	19.0
	For the other Portuguese wines	0.5	0.5	6.3	4.0
USA	For Port wine	1.8	0.7	2.3	1.1
	For the other Portuguese wines	5.0	0.1	0.3	9.1
Portuguese Colonies and PALOPs[c]	For Port wine	1.3	0.2	0.9	0.4
	For the other Portuguese wines	3.4	10.5	27.2	48.9

Notes
[a]Average of quantities exported during each period
[b]Denmark, Norvege and Sweden
[c]PALOPs means African countries whose official language is Portuguese
Source Martins, Conceição Andrade, *Memória do Vinho do Porto*, op.cit., pp. 248–253

Table 5 Growth of the foreign demand for Portuguese wines

Annual average growth rates		
Periods	Port wine (%)	Other Portuguese wines (%)
1776/1859 and 1860/1904	3.3	5.2
1860/1904 and 1905/1949	0.4	0.9
1905/1949 and 1950/1989	0.5	1.5

Sources Martins, Conceição Andrade, *Memória do Vinho do Porto*, op.cit., pp. 248–252; Id., *Vinha, Vinho e Política Vinícola ...*, op.cit., vol. 3, anexo 5

to the inefficiency and high cost, either of most of the treatments tried (in particular sulphide injections), or of its cure (American grafts, and replantings), which considerably rose the wine costs of production.[30] And thirdly for its social and economic effects, once it caused a decrease in wines quality and its depreciation, which jointly with higher costs of production ruined thousands of winegrowers and promoted emigration and rural depopulation; gave rise to socio-economic crises and to the wine crisis of the late nineteenth century (of overproduction and prices depreciation); and reduced wine revenues with negative effects on public finances and the trade balance.

Table 6 Port wine share in Portuguese wine trade

	Port wine quantities (%)	Port wine values (%)
1775/1814	72	77
1815/1879	62	79
1880/1939	35	58
1940/1974	18	45
1975/1989	34	61

Source Martins, Conceição Andrade, *Memória do Vinho do Porto*, op.cit., pp. 233–254

[30]The first attempts to treat this disease employed vine's ash, soot, arsenic, cupric acid, soda nitrogen, ammonia, potassium sulphate and Peyrat insecticide, but the only ones that proved to be truly effective were submersion in water, carbon sulphide injections and American vines grafted in local grape varieties, or planted as direct producers. These managed, eventually, to put Phylloxera under control, but the price of this disease was very high, especially for Douro's wine country... See Martins, 1991.

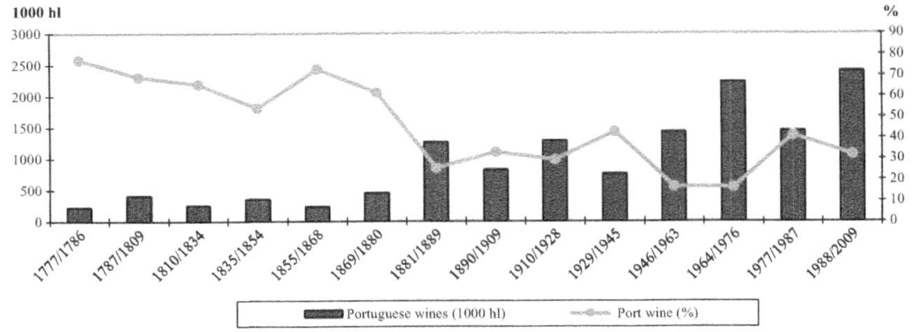

Fig. 3 Portuguese wine exports 1796–2010 (in 1000 hl and % of Port wine) (*Sources* Martins, Conceição Andrade, *Memória do Vinho do Porto*, op.cit.; Instituto Nacional de Estatística, *Estatísticas do Comércio Externo*; Estatísticas do IVP, do ICEP, do IVV/IVDP e do IVM)

Yet, if we take into account the effects of this disease not only at the wine production level but also into all the viticultural process, excluding in Douro's wine district phylloxera was not as devastating or innovating as *oidium* (powdery mildew) (see Fig. 1 and Table 7).[31] Indeed, the era of "viticultural progress" of Portuguese winegrowing and winemaking began with the *oidium*, once it has been then that: (i) increased the process of vineyards renewal and extension, either because the disease spread better in weakened vines, or because some grape varieties were more resistant than others to powdery mildew[32]; (ii) the new plantations began being made in line and with greater spacing between the newly planted vines; (iii) were intensified and improved some cultural practices and techniques, particularly those

[31]During the peak of the oidium crisis (1856/1860) wine production fell to almost ¼ (from near 4 million hl in 1845/1852 to 1 million) and remained below the average of the 1840s until the 1880s. Douro wine district was deeper affected by the phylloxera, that completely destroyed a huge amount of its vineyards as it was already said. About the impact of this disease in that region, see Martins, 1991.

[32]Since 1856/1857, the agronomic revues argued in favour of the replacement of old vines with new ones. The sudden increase of the French demand for Portuguese wines in the 1870s also incited winegrowers to extend their vineyards area. Remember that the plylloxera "attacked" the French vineyards since early 1860s, spread rapidly to all winegrowing regions and in a few years infected and destroyed more than 600,000 ha of vineyards and caused production losses of about 50%.

related with digging, pruning, grafting and fertilization, this one still "restricted" to natural fertilizers, but already considered the "preservative treatment" of *oidium*, while sulphur was taken only as a palliative; (iv) the winemaking processes were improved to remove from wine the taste and smell of sulphur[33]; (v) were carried on studies on vine's phytonomy and on vine diseases pathology, allowing to set which grape varieties were more resistant to oidium (moscatel, malvasia, etc.) and more suited to the geomorphologic and climatic characteristics of each region; (vi) was pushed the transfer and concentration of vineyards[34]; and (vii) and the national wine map began showing its future configuration (See Fig. 2).

A famous wine-cropper from Azeitão (nearby Lisbon), José Maria da Fonseca (1804/1884), is a good example of this "openness" to improvements that spread through the vineyards and the wineries. The innovations and improvements he introduced in the commercial area were also extended to the vine culture and the manufacture of wine. He developed, in his vineyards, the plantation in line and with spacing; used farming with plough and mule cattle; and introduced grapevines varieties from other regions or imported. In his wine cellars he practised the "desengaço" of the grapes (remove them from the bunch); manufactured the wine by the system of open waterspout; acquired new filters and modern filling machines; and fortified his must and wines with less graduate spirits.[35]

It was, indeed, all those changes and innovations introduced at different steps of the productive process to combat the oidium and to clarify the wine that lead us to reinforce the idea that it was, in fact, the first of the vineyard's diseases cycle (oidium) that started the turning point of Portuguese's viticulture. Thus, the major grape diseases that hit out European wine countries from the 1850s (powdery mildew, *phylloxera*, mildew, *maromba*, anthracnose, etc.) acted simultaneously

---

[33]Namely, with the introduction of new techniques of fermentation and "clearing" of the must which involves fining and filtration. See, Matos, 2013, pp. 165–189.

[34]As illustrate the cases of Dona Antónia Adelaide Ferreira (in Douro) and José Maria da Fonseca (in the surrounding area of Lisbon). The first one has been studied by Pereira, & Ollazabel, 1996; the second by Martins, 2000, pp. 35–54.

[35]See Martins, 2000.

Table 7 Wine production and exports during *oidium* and *phylloxera* crises (averages in 1000 hl)

Years	Wine production	Wine exports
1845/1852	3911	402
1853/1855	2357	340
1856/1860	1006	192
1861/1865	1430	252
1866/1872	2059	324
1873/1883	2385	575
1884/1890	4825	1415
1891/1899	4171	785
1900/1910	5265	868
1911/1921	4528	1238

Sources Martins, Conceição Andrade, *Vinha, Vinho e Política Vinícola em Portugal*, op.cit.; Lains, Pedro e Sousa, Paulo Silveira e, "Estatística e produção agrícola em Portugal, 1848–1914", op.cit.

as constraint and progress factors of the wine sector. In the first case, due to its negative effect on production quantities, costs of cultivating and of wine manufacturing, and on farmers' income. And in the second case, because they helped to the rise of wine prices, to the introduction, dissemination and generalization of new cultural practices, to the establishment of new and more accurate winemaking practices and techniques, and to the general modernization of all wine branch's.[36] From all the changes that occurred on Portuguese viticulture between the *oidium* crises (1850'decade) and the spread of phylloxera outside the Douro's district (1880'decade), the most determinants were, no doubt, those connected with the need to fight and control the effects of the first of those diseases (*oidium* or powdery mildew). On one hand, due to the innovations and improvements introduced in the soil management at different stages of the productive process: reinforcement of the digs, top-dressings and fertilizers, changes in the planting and pruning systems, introduction of chemical disinfectants. On the other hand, as a result of the innovation and improvements in the fields and at the wine cellars and wine presses to clarify the wine. And also due to the

[36]About this innovations and tranfer of technology see Madureira and Matos, 2005.

modifications introduced, since then, into the country's wine cartography, as shown in Fig. 2.[37] That is, the supremacy of Centre South wine districts over the Northern provinces, in opposition to what happened previously, which endured until the EU integration, in 1986.

Besides, if we compare the Portuguese wine regions of the Douro, Bucelas, Carcavelos or Setúbal with those of Bordeaux, Bourgogne (France) or Jerez (Spain), its clear that in any of them the profitability of the wine culture, on the one hand, and the succeeding attacks of cryptogrammic diseases of the second half of the nineteenth century, on the other, acted as additional incentives for the modernization of this economic sector. As did, recently, the EU, through financial support to the replanting or modernization of vineyards in some wine districts, namely in Douro's where competing with the powerful multinational Port wine firms, quite a few old wine families have been investing in vineyards at theirs Quintas, using the latest vineyard landscaping techniques and the finest traditional Port wine grape varieties, but also preserving the old terraces and vines. So, recovery was achieved during the nineties after uprooting aged and unprofitable vineyards, in return for indemnity payments and gradual replacement of old and less productive grape varieties.

From Productive Fragmentation to Wine Cooperativism

Historically, wine productive structure was based, overwhelmingly, on small and very small production and producers, as show data available to the county of Arcos in 1820: 53% of the parishes harvest less than 3 casks of wine (lower echelon); 47% between 3 and 10 casks (*medium* echelon); and none above 10 casks (upper echelon).[38] However, what

[37]See Fig. 2 in page 29 of this chapter.

[38]Capela, 1984.

most sticks out in this case is the relatively small amplitude of the farming exploitation sizes—minimum of 0.7 barrels/pipas (in Sistelo) and a maximum of 6 barrels/pipas (in Aboim)—as well as the fragmentation of the productive structure also quite evident in a 1842 study on the statistics of wine production in Portugal.[39]

Prior to the oídium crisis (around 1850), harvests average in the "wine growing country" (Douro wine district) rose to 80,000/100,000 barrels/pipas of wine. But, although its productive structure was based on small estates and farming—vineyards producing around 1 to 2 pipas—what weighed most in the total production of the region were the farms (Quintas) whose harvests went up dozens and even hundreds of pipas. Such was the case of the Vesúvio Quinta, situated far upriver in the Upper Douro, where in the late 1840s the average harvest rounded 700 pipas.[40] In the post-oídium (the mid-1870s) wine productive structure has been characterized as follows: the main production came from the "small and medium estates" and most of the winemakers harvest between 1 and 2 barrels (pipas) of wine, despite they were not uncommon producers of more than 500 barrels (pipas).[41] So, only exceptionally "medium-sized" and smallholders had enough economic strength to labour their vineyards according to the most appropriate procedures, or financial resources to store and age their wines, although they could raise its value "at least" 10% per year.[42]

More then half a century later, in the 1940s there would be 336.876 winegrowers in Portugal (mainland), just over half of which (52%) in the area of activity of the National Wine Board (Junta Nacional do Vinho—JNV) and close to 1/3 (30%) in the Green Wine region (Região do Vinho Verde—RVV) (see Map 1). In decreasing order stood the wine

[39]This study is based on data on the production of wines, brandies and vinegar provided by the registers of the literary subsidy (wine tax created in 1772 to finance Minor Studies and abolished in 1857). See Costa, 1842.

[40]See Pereira, 1990.

[41]*Breve Notícia*, 1874.

[42]Either by applying to the vineyards all appropriate cultural operations (digging, pruning, re-routing, etc.) or the manures, chemical fertilizers and correctives most indicated. See Menezes, 1891; Rasteiro Júnior, 1892.

regions of Dão (11%) and Douro (6%), followed by the remaining wine regions of Bucelas, Carcavelos, Colares and Moscatel of Setúbal, each one representing less than 0.5%. Regarding the approximately 21,600 winegrowers of the world oldest demarcated region, the Douro wine district, almost ¾ (72%) were very small vintners/laborers harvesting less than 5 barrels (pipas) of wine and 12% small producers of 5 to 10 pipas. The larger winegrowers (of more than 50 pipas) accounted for about 2% and the remaining medium-sized producers (14%) gathered between 10 and 50 pipas. In the distribution of the benefit, i.e. the authorization to convert their wines into Port wine and, consequently, sell it at higher prices, the most fortunate were, however, the medium and large producers, since the lower echelons (less than 5 pipas) that produced about 1/5 of the region's wine contributed only 1% to 2% of the total benefited. The productive structure of the JNV area was, however, still more fragmented, once more than 80% of its winegrowers produced less than 5 pipas of wine and 10% between 5 and 10 pipas. The medium size producers (between 10 and 50 pipas) did not exceed 8%, and the big ones (50 to 500 pipas) and greater producers (of more than 500 pipas) together little over 1%. Two decades later, the situation remained virtually unchangeable, except concerning the winemaking that profited from the establishment of more than 50 cooperative wineries in the JNV area.[43]

Since the end of the nineteenth century that the formation of associations among winegrowers was spreading, directed, primarily, to the unification of winemaking processes and to the homogenization of ordinary wine types through the establishment of social wineries and commercial companies. However, the lack of legal framework and of technical and economic support restraint their establishment and/or survival until 1935/1942, when were established the wine cellars cooperatives of Muge and Almeirim (in the Centre South region). Slowly until 1952, and in a more planned way, later on, established on "technical-economic bases" that would lead to the undeniable success this structure would come to have in the years 1960 and 1970.[44] At the

[43]See Martins and Monteiro, 2002.

[44]Leónidas, 1971.

beginning of the 1970s, the 109 cooperative wineries sited in the mainland had the capacity of "manufacturing" 28% of the average annual wine production and integrated about 9% of the country's winegrowers. This movement profited, firstly, the winegrowers, especially the smaller ones who could more easily drain their production and have access to credit. But it also benefited consumers, by supplying the markets with greater regularity and with better wines.

Conclusion: The Challenges of the Globalization

In the wine branch, the process of merging began later than in the beverage industry (which included tea and coffee) and its aim was to deal with both the concentration in the distribution and retail sector and the growing globalization of the wine industry. In other words, to enable it facing up the control of international distribution networks by large multinational companies and adapt the industry to an increasingly globalized market. In Port wine sector, mergers and acquisitions (M&A) grew importance in the early 1960s, when Harvey's (Allied Domecq) bought Cockburn and Martinez Gassiot (1961) and Sandeman acquired Offley Forrester (1962). This process of M&A also involves national companies, such as Sogrape, that bought A. A. Ferreira in 1987; Offley Forrester (in 1996), previously sold to Barcardi-Martini; and Sandeman (in 2002) acquired by Seagram in 1980. These acquisitions carried out by Sogrape also result from the decreased weight of its main brand—Mateus Rosé—on the firm's sales, which compelled to diversify its portfolio.

This transfer of "national" and multinational Port wine companies[45] to great transnational economic groups is connected with the evolution of the international commercialization and distribution channels for alcoholic beverages, and with the consequent need to increase substantially the investments in those areas. Teresa Silva Lopes studied the

---

[45]Many of the so-called "national" Port wine companies aren't, in fact, once they had been founded out of the country (United Kingdom, Ireland, Spain, etc.) and/or belonged to foreign families. Such is the case of Sandman's, established in London at the end of the eighteenth century by a Scottish wine merchant, and now a multinational Port wine company.

dynamics of the changes that occurred on the distribution channels used by Port wine firms during the twentieth century, and concluded that until the 60s the commercialization structures of those firms changed slowly comparatively to what happened in other segments of alcoholic beverages, namely in those of whisky and champagne where great changes had already taken place both on consumers' preferences, competition and new administration practices, mostly related to investments in new brands and in bottled wines at the origin.[46] This explains their subsequent vulnerability to the competition of the great beverage firms and of international distribution, where the concentration was already high as a result of "several waves of mergers and acquisitions",[47] as well as the tendency to reinforce the vertical integration. In this context, many Port wine companies were integrated into multinational groups, or established partnerships or alliances with other companies, and only a few kept up its independence.

To face the challenges of globalization, in 1992 seven of the ten largest Portuguese wine companies—Aliança, Bacalhôa Vinhos de Portugal/JP, Finagra/Herdade do Esporão, José Maria da Fonseca, Messias, Quinta da Aveleda e Sogrape[48]—joined as a task force to promote internationally their wines. This cooperative strategy of companies, which together account for more than 75% of bottled wine exports, has enabled the Group of Seven (G7 of wines as it is known) to act jointly on two areas. Firstly, in emerging markets (China and Japan), but also in the traditional ones (Europe, the United States, Brazil and PALOPs), to where are exported more than 90% of Portuguese wines.

[46]See, T. Lopes, 1998; T.S. Lopes 2001.

[47]Teresa, 2000.

[48]The oldest is José Maria da Fonseca. Established in the late 1820s in the Setúbal Península (Azeitão, 30 km South of Lisbon) its firm is famous for the international projection gave to the Moscatel of Setúbal since the first half of the nineteenth century, and for its pioneering either in the vineyards, the wine cellars or the wine trade. José Maria da Fonseca's was one of first wine companies to "create" a trade mark, to favour shipping its wines bottled rather than in bulk and, outside Port wine branch, to win gold medals and/or first class ones in almost all nineteenth century International exhibitions its wines were presented. Founded in 1942, Sogrape is well known thanks to its Mateus Rosé wine. Following its restructuration, in the 1980s, the company made strong investments in the main Portuguese wine regions, especially in Douro's. About José Maria da Fonseca, see Martins, 2000; about Sogrape, see Pereira, 2003.

But the formation of large economic groups and the increasing globalization of the sector led to the re-evaluation of the company's distinctive symbols, straight linked to their history and tradition. That is why Sogrape, one of the main Iberian wine groups, makes a point of presenting itself as "the first family wine company in Portugal", and Aveleda wishes to be seen as "a family business managed and guided, far over three Centuries, by generations of the same family" (!) This strategy is global and does not apply only to companies from the old continent. Take, for example, the cases of Gimenez Mendez, from Uruguay, who presents itself as "a family company committed to the excellence and quality of its wines", or Muratie, a small family business in South Africa boasting about being one of the first in that country to produce Port Wine (!)

References

Books

Alves, Á. da M. (1943). *Subsídios para a História do vinho na cidade do Porto*, Porto.

Breve Notícia. (1874). *Breve notizia da Viticultura Portugueza ou Resumo dos esclarecimentos indispensáveis para se avaliar a colecção dos vinhos de Portugal apresentados na Exposição Internacional de 1874 em Londres*. Lisboa: Imprensa Nacional.

Capela, J.V. (1984). *Produção e Comércio do Vinho dos Arcos 1750–1850. Alguns Dados e Problemas*, Arcos de Valdevez, Braga: Gráfica da Editora Correio do Minho.

Castro, D. Luís de. (1908). *Alguns aspectos económicos do projecto vinícola*. Lisboa: Separata da Revista Agronómica.

Coelho, M.H. (1977). *O Mosteiro de Arouca do século X ao XII*, Coimbra.

Coelho, M.H. (1983). *O Baixo Mondego nos finais da Idade Média*, Coimbra.

Costa, C.A. da. (1842). *Estatística da Produção dos Vinhos em Portugal no Anno de 1840, Extrahida do Arrolamento do Subsidio Litterario do Mesmo Anno, e a Sua Relação Com a Instrucção Primaria do Reino*, Lisboa.

Forrester, J.J. (1844). *Uma ou duas palavras sobre vinho do Porto: dirigidas ao publico britannico em geral, e com especialidade aos particulares: mostrando como, e porque he adulterado, e apontando alguns meios de se conhecerem as adulterações*. Porto: Typographia Commercial Portuense.

Forrester, J.J. (1850). *A Short Treatise on the unequal and disproportionate imposts levied on Port-Wine, shipped from Oporto to Great-Britain; compared with the imposts levied on wines, of the same character, shipped to America and other countries*, London.

Forrester, J.J. (1859). *Provas de verdade contra provas de vigho*. Porto: Typographia Commercial Portuense.

Francis, A.D. (1972). *The Wine Trade*, London.

Lains, P. (1990). *A Evolução da Agricultura e da Indústria em Portugal (1850–1913). Uma Interpretação Quantitativa*. Lisboa: Banco de Portugal.

Lains, P. (2003). *Os Progressos do Atraso. Uma Nova História Económica de Portugal, 1842–1992*. Lisboa: Imprensa de Ciências Sociais.

Lencastre, J. de. (1953). *A vitivinicultura através de alguns documentos medievais de arquivos portugueses (secs IX a XX). Subsídios para um estudo*, Porto.

Leónidas, V.R. de P. (1971). *As Cooperativas e o Fomento da Vitivinicultura*, Lisboa.

Lobo, A. de S.S.C. (1903). *História da Sociedade em Portugal no Século XV*, secção I. Lisboa: Imprensa Nacional.

Martins, C.A. (1990). *Memória do Vinho do Porto*. Lisboa: Instituto de Ciências Sociais da Universidade de Lisboa.

Martins, C.A. (1998), *Vinha, Vinho e Política Vinícola em Portugal do Pombalismo à Regeneração*, vol. I, Chapter 3, pp. 100–150, Évora.

Martins, C.A., & Monteiro, N.G. (Eds.). (2002). *A Agricultura, vol III de História do Trabalho e das Ocupações*. Oeiras: Celta.

Menezes, A.C. de. (1891). *5ª Região Agronómica*. Viseu: Typographia da Folha.

Pereira, G.M. (1990). *O Douro. O Vinho, a Vinha e a Região. De Pombal a João Franco*. Porto: CENPA.

Pereira, G.M. (2003). *Sogrape uma história vivida*. Campo das Letras.

Pereira, G.M., & Ollazabel, M.L.N. de A. de. (1996). *Dona Antónia*. s.l.: Edições Asa.

Pery, G. (1875). *Geographia e Estatística Geral de Portugal e Colónias*, Lisboa.

Rasteiro Júnior, J. (1892). *Esboço de uma Memória Sobre a Economia Agrícola da 4ª região Agronómica*. Lisboa: Typographia e Stereotypia Moderna.

Shillington, V.M., & Chapman, A.B.W. (1988). *The Commercial relations of England and Portugal*. London: s/d.

Silva, M.J.B. (1994). *Esgueira. A vida de uma aldeia do século XV*, Cascais.

Soares, R. de M. (1873). *Relatório da Direcção-Geral de Comércio e Indústria àcerca dos Serviços dependentes da Repartição de Agricultura desde a sua fundação até 1870*, Lisboa.
Soares, R. de M. (1874). *Breve Notícia da Viticultura Portugueza ou Resumo dos esclarecimentos indispensaveis para se avaliar a collecção dos vinhos de Portugal apresentados na Exposição Internacional de 1874 em Londres*. Lisboa: Imprensa Nacional.
Soares, R. de M. (1878). *Mémoire sur les vins du Portugal*. Lisbonne: Imprimerie Nationale.
Sousa, F. de. (2006). *A Real Companhia Velha. Companhia Gerald a Agricultura das Vinhas do Alto Douro (1756–2006)*. Porto: CEPESE.
Teresa, T.S. (2000). *Brands, Mergers and Acquisitions in the Alcoholic Beverages Industry*, Working Paper, The University of Reading.
Villa Maior. (1868). *Relatorio sobre a Classe LXXIII da Exposição Internacional de 1867*, Lisboa.

Paper in Journals

Barreto, A. (1988). O vinho do Porto e a intervenção do Estado. *Análise Social*, nº 100, 1º.
Barros, A.J.M. (2003). Tombo do mosteiro de Ancede (séc XIV). *Douro—Estudos & Documentos*, vol. 16, pp. 217–308.
Brito, E. De. (1889). A propósito da crise vinícola. Memória apresentada ás commissões de fazenda e de agricultura, pelo deputado Elvino de Brito. *Boletim da DGA*, nº6, pp. 450–469.
Carvalho, A. M. Lopes de. (1890–1891). *Portugal Agrícola*, p. 229.
Durand, R. (1972). La vigne et le vin dans le bassin du Mondego au Moyen Age (XII-XIIIe siécles). *Arquivos do Centro Cultural Português*, vol. V, pp. 13–37.
Gonçalves, I. (1987). Entre o campo e a cidade na segunda metade do século XIV. *Estudos Medievais*, pp. 73–97.
Lopes, T. (2001). A evolução das estruturas internacionais de comercialização do vinho do Porto no século XX. *Revista de História Económica e Social*, nº 1, pp. 91–132.
Lopes, T.S. (1998). Internacionalização e concentração no vinho do Porto: 1945–1995: uma abordagem pelos custos de transacção. *Cadernos da revista Douro. Estudos & documentos*, nº 3.

Martins, C.A. (1991). A filoxera na viticultura nacional. *Análise Social*, nº 112–113, pp. 653–688.

Martins, C.A. (1992). Opções económicas e influência política de uma família burguesa oitocentista: o caso de São Romão e José Maria dos Santos. *Análise Social*, 116–117, pp. 367–404.

Rodriguez, J.I. de la T. (1997). A viticultura nos mosteiros cistercienses do vale do Douro português (séculos XII–XIII). *Douro—Estudos & Documentos*, vol. 3, pp. 17–28.

Santana, M.O.R. (2003). Da vinha e do vinho na documentação foraleira manuelina do vale do Douro. *Douro—Estudos & Documentos*, vol. 15, pp. 11–24.

Trindade, M.J.L. (1974). A utilização agrária do solo em torno de Lisboa na Idade Média. *Boletim Cultural da Junta Distrital de Lisboa*, nº 39–40, pp. 3–10.

Paper in Books

Castro, A. De. (1971). *Balança Comercial*. In Serrão, Joel (Ed.), *Dicionário de História de Portugal*, vol. I, Lisboa, pp. 274–276.

Madureira, N.L.M., & Matos, A.C. de. (2005). *A tecnologia*. In Lains, P. & Silva, Á.F. da (Eds.), *História Económica de Portugal, 1700–2000*, vol. II, *O Século XIX*, Lisboa, Imprensa de Ciências Sociais, pp. 189–218.

Martins, C.A. (2000). *Survival and renewal of Portuguese family wine firms in front of internationalisation, 1820–1999, Fourth Convention of the European Business History Association*, EBHA, Bordeaux, pp. 35–54.

Martins, C.A. (2003). *O Tratado de Methuen e o crescimento do comércio vinícola português na primeira metade de Setecentos*. In José, L.C., & al. (Eds.), *O Tratado de Methuen (1703) diplomacia, guerra, política e economia*, Lisbon, Livros Horizonte, pp. 111–130.

Matos, A.C. de. (2013). *Matemático por formação, químico por paixão: Júlio Máximo de Oliveira Pimentel, um "politécnico" no Portugal Oitocentista*. In Pina, A.M., Maurício, C., & Vaz, M.J. (Eds.), *Metamorfoses da Cultura, estudos em homenagem a Maria Carlos Radich*, Lisboa, CEHC-IUL, pp. 165–189.

Matos, A.C. de, & Martins, C.A. (2003). *As primeiras universais e a internacionalização da economia portuguesa na segunda metade do século XIX*, papper to the XXIII *Encontro da APHES*, Coimbra.

History of a Vineyard in Champagne: From Eighteenth to Twenty-First Century

Serge Wolikow

Introduction

This contribute illustrates the history of the vineyard of Champagne in interaction with the invention of sparkling wine in an area of ancient viticulture. The socio-geographical configuration of this vineyard has been transformed over a period of several centuries, associating crises and expansions, at the end of which emerges in the twentieth century a vineyard very different from that at the beginning of the eighteenth century, when the sparkling wine is invented in the Champagne region. Heritage and innovation are interwoven throughout this evolution during which emerges a new Champagne vineyard whose territory is still experiencing significant changes for 70 years (Map 1).[1]

[1]About the history of vines and wines in Champagne see, among others, Chappaz (1951) and S. Wolikow and C. Wolikow (2012). If there are not different indications, the following paragraphs are referred to these references.

S. Wolikow (✉)
University of Burgundy, Dijon, France
e-mail: serge.wolikow@u-bourgogne.fr

S. A. Conca Messina et al. (eds.), *A History of Wine in Europe, 19th to 20th Centuries, Volume I*, Palgrave Studies in Economic History,
https://doi.org/10.1007/978-3-030-27772-7_3

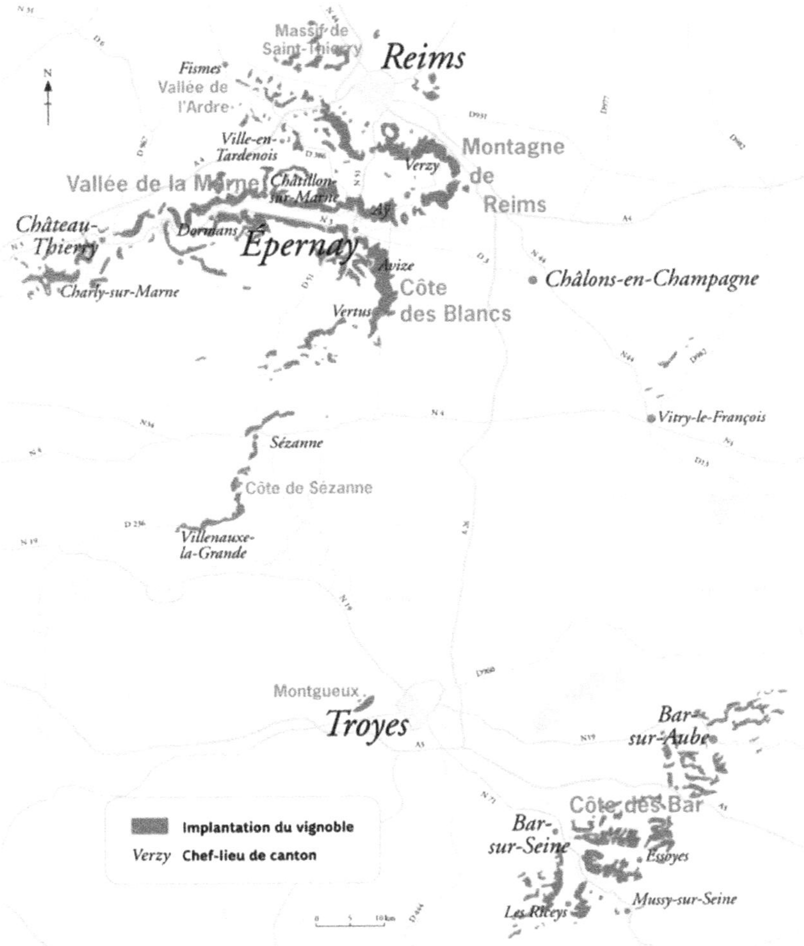

Map 1 La Champagne Viticole (*Source* https://www.champagne.fr/fr/terroir-appellation/terroir-champenois/vignoble-champenois-geographie)

This paper is organized around three historical sequences that mark a profound transformation of the vineyard despite the permanence of the vine in this geographical area.

In the eighteenth century, the old winegrowing economy of Champagne remained largely dominant: the vineyard of effervescent wine was still very minor in a heterogeneous vineyard with respect to grape varieties, producing fine white wines for export and red wines more common for local consumption even if a significant share of these wines arrive in Ile de France. During the eighteenth century, the Champagne vineyard experienced a strong geographical expansion reaching an extension of more than 50,000 ha over four departments: Marne, Aube, Aisne and Haute-Marne.

Then the Champagne vineyard of sparkling wines becomes a specialized vineyard, more concentrated geographically and also based on a generalized technical dissociation.

The separation between viticulture and winemaking is characterized by an economic system characterized by strong social contrasts between three different groups of actors: the manufacturer's trade, its employees and grape growers. This dissociation takes place during the nineteenth century in correlation with the decline of the vineyard of quiet wine and the expansion of the vineyard of sparkling wine. This determines a contraction of the surfaces and the modification of the whole economic organization.

From then on, export became the driving force behind a strong expansion that only slowed down at the end of the nineteenth century. Then the vineyard of Champagne underwent a major economic and social crisis from 1908 to 1911: touched in turn by the phylloxera, marked by the competition of wines from the south of France, this vineyard completes its recomposition around sparkling wines but it is up to this moment that the conflicts around the supply broke out with the confrontation between winegrowers and traders. The difficulties are lasting, as evidenced by the stagnation of production and areas until after the Second World War. This multi-decennial recession is linked to the crisis in markets after 1914, but also to the upheaval of viticulture caused by the late post-phylloxeric reconstitution in Champagne in the aftermath of the war, aggravated by the severe destruction suffered by the vines during military operations.

It is in this difficult context that the Champagne appellation, the first in France, was born in 1927, implying a precise delimitation with criteria and indications relating to viticulture and winemaking—the grape varieties, the size, the elaboration, for as only 1/3 of the appellation is planted, a sign of the economic difficulties of the sector at that time.

After 1945, the economic and professional organization of the Champagne vineyards is evolving so much that it can be considered as a new Champagne system whose keystone is an interprofessional organization based on parity between wine producers and traders within direction. In fact it is a new organization of the wine economy—associating the general union of winemakers (SGV) and business houses (UMC). The growth of production is based on a balance between producer-winemakers, cooperatives and the developing traders. Thus, in the vineyard, a fragile balance is noticeable between the price of grapes, yields, but also control of the land.

The expansion of planted areas is considerable, tripling in four decades from 1960 to 2000. At the same time, higher yields and higher productivity leads to an eightfold increase in final output. For all that the vineyard remains paradoxical with its smallholders—owner, the important weight of cooperatives, the intertwining of the winegrowing trade and winegrowers in the context of an economy where the sharing of added value generates a prosperity which concerns all operators. However, today in 2017, the uncertainties and new problems linked to the globalization of markets and the economic recession in Europe are fueling uncertainties about the sustainability of this prosperity.

The Transformation of Champagne Vineyards from the Eighteenth to the Nineteenth Century

Character and Persistence of the Old Champagne Vineyard

The continuity of the culture of the vineyard from the Middle Ages to the present day should not hide strong transformations sometimes ignored if not denied in the name of the vines' antiquity. Certainly, most of the areas cultivated today were already planted with vines in the seventeenth and eighteenth centuries, and even before. But the vines were very different from what they became. Above all, they were more extensive and less concentrated. In 1692, an investigation by the intendant of Chalons recorded no less than 646 viticultural localities throughout the generality of Champagne, the boundaries of which corresponded largely to the present-day Champagne-Ardenne.

The areas planted with vines experienced notable variations from the Middle Ages to the eighteenth century, without it being possible to quantify the phenomenon precisely. The Hundred Years War and the Wars of Religion had weakened the vineyard. The vineyards of Epernay and Mardeuil rose from about 1000 hectares in the 1560s to 450 in 1599, before returning to its original level in 1645.[2]

It was not until the eighteenth century to have a precise overview of the vineyards. In 1726, the vineyard of Reims had about 6000 hectares. Its distribution is very similar to that of today, with large vineyards in the Montagne de Reims and the Montagne de Saint-Thierry. The same map for the year 1773 shows a very important increase of the vineyard, of the order of 50%. Because of the low yields and the impossibility of increasing them, plantations, although banned since 1729, are the only way to increase production in response to consumption that increases during the eighteenth century. Benoit Musset indicates that in the region of Reims, it would have gone from 33 litres per inhabitant in the years 1690 to 71 litres in 1772–1784. In the city of Reims, it would have even gone from 134 to 200 litres per year in the second half of the eighteenth century. It is in this context that the Champagne vineyard reaches in the 1780s its widest historical extension. If we consider this time the vineyard of the generality of Champagne, it reached thus, according to a survey of 1773, about 50,000 ha that is to say much more than the delimitation of today limited to about 33,000 ha.

[2]These data are summarized in the book by Benoît Musset (2008).

Some Large Farms and Many Small Winemakers

The old vineyard of the eighteenth century was the domain of the winemakers. If the vineyards of the early Middle Ages were largely controlled by the Church and the aristocracy, through a highly supervised work, independent winegrowers appeared in the documents from the eleventh and twelfth centuries. Until the Revolution, the large religious exploitations were numerous and the largest. Largely a result of donations and legacies, they were integrated into true mixed farming enterprises, alongside the vast grain estates, supplemented by real estate income to support the vagaries of wine production on a large scale. In the eighteenth century, the largest winegrowers were the abbeys Saint-Pierre d'Hautvillers (29 hectares), Saint-Pierre-aux-Monts Châlons (19 hectares), Saint-Remi Reims, Saint-Martin d'Epernay (7 hectares), but also the archbishop of Reims, the chapters of Reims and Châlons (7 hectares) or the Hôtel-Dieu de Reims (18 hectares). These domains disappear, with the Revolution, from 1790 to 1791, bought in small lots by an overwhelming majority of winegrowers.

However, large lay farms were formed in the seventeenth and eighteenth centuries, exceeding 3 hectares, threshold, at that time, the large vineyard. On the eve of the Revolution, the domain of Sillery came in first with 40 hectares, in front of those little nobles, officers and bourgeois of Epernay, Reims and Chalons. However, the accumulation of vines was limited by the importance of operating costs and irregular income. The vines almost never counted for more than a quarter of the property and real estate patrimony of the aristocratic and bourgeois property. About 150–200 proprietors have been at the base of the production of bottled wines, sparkling wines and fine wines until the second half of the nineteenth century, when traders are land estates by buying in large numbers parcels ruined by phylloxera. However, most of the vineyard was owned by the winemakers: between 70 and 80% of the vineyards, with the exception of the area around Reims and Epernay where city dwellers were more present.

From the Middle Ages to replantations in post-phylloxeric lines from the 1890s to 1900, and especially until the partial mechanization of the years 1950–1960, the works of the vine were of a remarkable stability which contrasts with the strong modifications at the level of the vines and the wine production.

The Construction of a New Specialized Vineyard Within Champagne

The increase of planted areas is general but does not concern only the vineyards producing great wines. The differentiation of the vineyard is increasing, as in the vineyard of Reims for which there are many documents that attest to it. At the end of the eighteenth century, the vineyards of Aube and Haute-Marne experienced a strong extension, reaching 15,471 ha and 11,847 ha, respectively, compared to 20,354 ha for the Marne territory in 1790. This expansion despite the old royal prohibitions, reflects a movement of funds caused by the increase of markets and popular consumption of wines. This evolution is related to the stagnation of yields and the rise in consumption. Yields increase little and remain below 20 hl per ha. Yields, however, vary quite strongly depending on the vineyards. They appear higher in large farms where they can reach 25 hl per hectare. But they remain much lower in the new lands gained by small farms from the vineyard, which explains why the expansion of surfaces was the answer to the rise in demand. This is mainly a demand for proximity based on local consumption, in the rural world, and in nearby towns.

In the Reims region, per capita consumption nearly doubled during the eighteenth century. This popular consumption concerns red wines for everyday consumption. In short, on the eve of the Revolution, the production of great white wines and sparkling wines is only a very small part of the Champagne vineyard and contributes only very locally to its growth. The sale of red wines, provided by the innkeepers or directly by the bourgeois owners, without forgetting the sale of the winemakers themselves to the villages outside the vineyard, thus constitute currents of exchange which relate to wines of current consumption, in margin of the other currents of exchange which concern the red wines conveyed towards Flanders and the Paris region, partly by the river transport on the Marne. On these different markets, they collide at the end of the eighteenth century with the products of the vineyards of the South of France, even if the red wines of the Marne continue to do well on the Parisian market, as Sébastien Mercier attests it: "the red wine of Champagne seems to me preferable in Burgundy: opinions have long been divided. My voice with red champagne."[3] On the eve of the Revolution, the Champagne vineyard continues to produce mainly red wines. If the expansion of the vineyard is based on the growth of popular consumption, the rise of white wines, sparkling or not, concerns the vineyards of Epernay and Reims whose specialization is gradually affirmed and is driven by the sale in markets outside the region. The geographical differentiation of the vineyard is completed by a differentiation according to the farms. Only a small number of farms supply grey wines and sparkling wines. The technical means and the necessary surfaces were discriminating in order to be able to produce these wines, which required fine grape varieties of lower yield and particular winemaking methods, starting with pressing requiring facilities that small winegrowers, although numerous, did not possess or to which they did not have access.

During the Revolution and the Empire, the evolution, begun in the Marne at the end of the eighteenth century with a first shrinking of cultivated areas, extends to all the departments of the region, before increasing in the second half of the nineteenth century (Table 1). This mutation modifies, for a time, the balances between the departments: the retraction of the cultivated areas is more asserted in the Marne than in the Aube or even in the Haute-Marne. The vineyard of the Aube reaches its maximum with 23,000 ha in 1852 while that of the Marne has only 17,844 ha, which is slightly more than the Haute-Marne whose vineyard still represents 16,097 ha. These contrasting evolutions express an increased differentiation of the vineyard. The expansion of vineyards of red wine for current consumption continues, except in the Marne where this type of vineyard decreases sharply due to a different economic situation. There is of course the existence of a vineyard

[3]Mercier (1781–1788 [1994], pp. 403–405).

Table 1 Bottles sent by winemakers and Maisons de Champagne (1844–2016)

Champagne			
Years	France	Other countries	Total
2016	157,954,272	148,082,097	306,036,369
2015	161,822,697	150,708,747	312,531,444
2014	162,266,302	144,870,262	307,136,564
2013	167,333,600	137,640,110	304,973,710
2012	171,379,813	137,380,575	308,760,388
2011	181,644,194	141,323,261	322,967,455
2010	185,098,656	134,514,530	319,613,186
2009	180,954,333	112,360,384	293,314,717
2008	181,209,546	141,244,306	322,453,852
2007	187,785,100	150,922,092	338,707,192
2006	181,129,602	140,660,196	321,789,798
2005	178,360,043	129,304,879	307,664,922
2004	178,358,541	123,056,432	301,414,973
2003	174,231,485	119,273,475	293,504,960
2002	175,000,710	112,671,711	287,672,421
2001	164,522,817	98,172,497	262,695,314
2000	149,626,415	103,583,131	253,209,546
1999	190,449,776	136,589,287	327,039,063
1998	178,965,956	113,453,974	292,419,930
1997	165,154,959	103,884,679	269,039,611
1996	160,677,346	95,194,229	255,871,575
1995	157,908,136	91,386,052	249,294,188
1994	157,085,789	89,839,159	246,924,948
1993	152,669,094	76,420,634	229,089,728
1992	142,648,795	76,764,123	219,412,918
1991	136,225,162	77,014,335	213,239,497
1990	152,318,711	84,787,098	237,105,809
1989	157,999,199	94,315,560	252,314,759
1988	149,352,381	89,967,042	239,319,423
1987	136,349,116	81,449,242	205,159,283
1986	133,126,140	72,033,143	204,920,108
1985	125,099,323	69,852,198	194,951,521
1984	116,723,599	71,469,415	188,193,014
1983	101,950,525	59,096,834	161,047,359
1982	95,070,384	52,571,920	147,642,304
1981	98,731,809	57,327,484	156,059,293
1980	116,721,579	63,577,147	180,298,726
1979	114,971,960	68,150,693	183,122,653
1978	112,199,925	75,624,747	187,824,672
1977	97,552,430	73,546,922	171,099,352
1976	81,839,363	70,421,491	152,260,854

(continued)

Table 1 (continued)

Champagne			
Years	France	Other countries	Total
1975	71,692,317	54,846,599	126,538,916
1974	59,336,954	43,688,448	103,025,402
1973	76,352,157	47,569,429	123,921,586
1972	71,245,063	50,820,590	122,065,653
1971	66,012,349	51,330,098	117,342,447
1970	71,169,802	31,054,288	102,224,090
1969	67,086,841	26,896,979	93,983,820
1968	59,982,335	26,514,567	86,496,902
1967	68,562,592	24,498,455	93,061,047
1966	64,847,515	22,040,429	86,887,944
1965	58,192,955	20,428,081	78,621,036
1964	52,050,368	18,154,327	70,204,695
1963	46,831,453	17,186,806	64,018,259
1962	42,484,190	15,435,536	57,919,826
1961	38,658,873	15,528,976	54,187,849
1960	35,356,579	13,908,922	49,265,501
1959	28,731,117	13,538,956	42,270,073
1958	27,587,354	13,114,937	40,702,291
1957	35,705,008	12,717,111	48,422,119
1956	31,278,718	13,025,479	44,304,197
1955	25,773,214	11,933,612	37,706,826
1954	22,153,428	10,824,352	32,977,780
1953	19,477,929	11,100,079	30,578,008
1952	18,651,060	12,076,452	30,727,512
1951	20,750,839	15,507,435	36,258,274
1950	17,178,971	13,960,362	31,139,333
1949	16,184,132	11,041,034	27,225,166
1948	17,125,003	10,220,974	27,345,977
1947	12,380,470	9,284,708	21,665,178
1940–1946	No data for WWII		
1939–1940	17,003,788	10,680,122	27,683,910
1938–1939	21,610,935	10,149,673	31,820,608
1937–1938	23,772,427	11,957,420	35,729,847
1936–1937	28,297,501	11,735,287	40,032,788
1935–1936	25,327,283	7,854,962	33,182,245
1934–1935	20,302,324	7,377,526	27,679,850
1933–1934	21,961,249	8,466,325	30,427,574
1932–1933	20,902,169	4,370,667	25,472,836
1931–1932	16,238,524	6,603,448	22,841,972
1930–1931	15,207,429	9,419,415	24,626,844
1929–1930	13,146,057	14,238,159	27,384,216
1928–1929	11,307,691	12,513,670	23,821,361

Champagne			
Years	France	Other countries	Total
1927–1928	8,169,248	13,046,690	21,215,938
1926–1927	17,527,436	14,688,853	32,216,289
1925–1926	20,537,877	15,629,408	36,167,285
1924–1925	15,514,036	14,685,604	30,199,640
1923–1924	17,877,017	14,072,407	31,499,474
1922–1923	9,465,717	9,078,383	18,544,100
1921–1922	5,884,377	6,659,496	12,543,873
1920–1921	8,361,571	12,746,808	21,108,379
1919–1920	9,433,636	13,582,381	23,016,017
1918–1919	10,687,628	5,067,671	15,755,299
1917–1918	10,679,116	6,936,618	17,615,734
1916–1917	7,565,602	8,436,214	16,001,816
1915–1916	4,680,398	6,725,159	11,405,557
1914–1915	3,126,833	7,235,177	10,362,010
1913–1914	8,134,196	18,410,436	26,544,632
1912–1913	9,151,110	20,946,534	30,097,644
1911–1912	9,084,936	20,288,963	29,373,899
1910–1911	15,517,879	23,066,523	38,584,402
1909–1910	13,120,946	26,173,580	39,294,526
1908–1909	12,713,024	19,992,314	32,705,338
1907–1908	11,522,272	22,212,346	33,734,618
1906–1907	10,114,548	23,056,847	33,171,395
1905–1906	11,714,404	23,876,731	35,591,135
1904–1905	8,864,947	19,845,852	28,710,799
1903–1904	9,808,774	21,084,881	30,893,655
1902–1903	9,335,412	22,523,746	31,859,158
1901–1902	7,894,212	20,311,228	28,205,410
1900–1901	7,426,794	20,628,251	28,055,045
Champagne and sparkling wine (vin mousseux)			
1899–1900	6,680,923	21,773,513	28,454,436
1884–1885	2,822,601	18,189,256	21,037,655
1879–1880	2,266,561	16,524,593	19,191,134
1874–1875	3,517,182	15,318,345	18,835,527
1869–1870	3,628,461	13,858,839	17,487,300
1864–1865	2,801,626	9,101,441	11,903,067
1859–1860	3,039,621	8,265,395	11,305,016
1854–1855	2,552,743	6,795,773	9,348,516
1849–1850	1,705,735	5,001,044	6,706,779
1844–1845	2,255,438	4,380,214	6,635,652

Sources Author adapted from 1844 to 1945: G. Chappaz (1951), tome II. Following Years: Comité interprofessionnel du vin de Champagne (CIVC website https://www.champagne.fr/)

of fine wines that is consolidating, and whose dimensions are growing even though there are still a majority of red wine producers around 1860. But, in the face of lower prices of wines. In the beginning, small-scale winegrowers are experiencing greater difficulties, resulting in emigration to the cities and reconversion of booming industrial activity, especially in textiles. Jules Guyot notes it to deplore it: "in all the extent of the Marne, the vines are done with the task and the day, without the least interest granted to the winegrower in the production: also it results there a great difficulty of workforce".[4]

If the movement begins in the middle of the century, it is only in the last third of the nineteenth century that it rushes. The regression of areas under vines is evident, the share of champagne production in the domestic production is declining relative, while the overall volumes are also decreasing. The weight of all the vineyards of northern France decreases compared to those of the Midi, whose production and areas are growing steadily during the last decades of the nineteenth century. The diseases of the vineyard, powdery mildew, mildew then phylloxera, aggravate the situation of vineyards whose production costs are higher compared to southern wines which, resulting from high-yield mass production, are now transported by rail to major urban centres of consumption with preferential rates.

This new situation affects the vineyards which, in the Paris region or the North-East, provided a production destined for popular consumption. The collapse is all the more brutal as it corresponds to a period of general economic difficulties, the effects of which are felt massively in the 1880s and 1890s. This coincides with the development of phylloxera, which then reaches the Champagne vineyards, when the complete reconstitution of the vineyards of the south of France allows them to produce massively wines whose prices, in spite of the transport costs, are well below the red wines of Champagne. While the vineyards of Haute-Marne, whose outlets were local, collapse, that of the Aube recedes very strongly, finding a solution only in the promotion of its fine wines which, for a long time, were exported but who find themselves

[4]Guyot (1876, p. 428).

in difficulties on the Paris market, while they obtain compensation towards the Marne.

In this last department, part of the vineyard disappears, on the side of Vitry-le-François, Sainte-Ménéhould or Fismes. In these different vineyards where high-yield grape varieties dominated, competition from cereal crops and livestock contributed to this decline. If we take into account the overall production of the Marne in 1862, red wine still accounted for 5/7th of production and, for all Champagne, 9/10th. In 1890, the Agricultural Statistics of France estimates that ordinary quality wines represent 80.8% of the production, in 1908, they represent only 57 and 17% in 1913. The production of the vineyard of Haute-Marne rose from 346,000 hl in 1882–1884 to 11,500 hl in 1910–1913, while for the Marne, the corresponding figures were 412,000 and 129,000 hl.

The vineyards of Champagne have therefore undergone a complex evolution throughout the two centuries (Table 1), at the end of which a major upheaval has come to transform overall viticulture due to the combination of economic factors and phylloxera. Within this general evolution, special attention must be paid to vineyards which are gradually specializing in the production of sparkling wines. The viticulture devoted to the production of white wines, then sparkling wines, of course participates in traditional methods, but it allows the development of techniques which constitute the principles of a viticulture turned towards the production of quality wines, thanks to which Champagne viticulture finds a positive outcome to the closure of its local outlets in favour of export markets.

The modification of the grape variety accompanies the evolution of the vineyard according to a process still little known and little studied in the detail. However, the question of grape varieties deserves a careful but very difficult history due to the diversity of species and the extreme variability of local names as well as the poverty of the nomenclature. It should be added that the same plots were for a long time often planted in several grape varieties, in order to mitigate the risks related to climatic hazards, against which different species react differently. Jules Guyot considered that the choice of grape varieties was the essential factor to explain the quality of the new Champagne wines: "Without the careful choice that the inhabitants of the Marne have made the most perfected vines in their climate and soil, they would have produced and produced only very common wines".[5]

The uncertainty of denominations makes it uncertain to precisely identify the grape varieties and their distribution. From one village to another, the designations change, but the diversity of terms echoes, very often, a mixture of grape varieties. At the beginning of the nineteenth century the ampelography (study of grape varieties) is constituted as a more rigorous knowledge. Evolutions are, however, recognizable during the eighteenth century. After the great winter of 1709, large replantings seem to have favoured the extension of black grape varietals with white juices, the morillons, at the expense of white grapes, spruces or golden white.[6] The winemaking treaties of the first half of the eighteenth century praised black grapes, as Canon Godinot calls them, for producing grey wines or red wines. White grape varieties such as the Gouais, are criticized and considered together as incapable of producing quality wines. "In order for the wine to be finer, we must remove all the vines that give white grapes and those that give coarse black grapes".[7] However, both are often mixed and coexist in plots, even in the Marne valley and the Montagne de Reims. In fact, during the eighteenth century, the rise of popular consumption, the extension of wine-growing areas, despite the prohibitions, often mean the extension of high-yielding grape varieties planted by small winemakers whose horizon remains the market local. The movement seems to continue in the revolutionary period. However, other developments are also changing the *encépagement* (planting) of the vineyard: it is in particular the extension of white grapes in the Montagne de Reims and especially in what will become the Côte des Blancs.

At the beginning of the nineteenth century, the *encépagement* is thus far from being uniform what Jullien and Jules Guyot raise successively. However, it seems that confusion is decreasing. Already in the 1780s, we can locate a grape variety, especially in large farms marketing

---

[5]Ibid., p. 389.

[6]Godinot (1722, p. 4).

[7]Bidet (1759, p. 230).

white as red. The first agricultural surveys and directories of the early nineteenth century show a vineyard of the Marne of 15,000 ha, roughly divided in two from the point of view of *encépagement*: 9000 ha in "seedlings", representing 60% of the areas, and 6000 ha of "fine vintage".[8] But the grape variety will evolve fairly quickly during the nineteenth century, depending on the demand, but also the ability of wine producers to adapt to the price movement. Jules Guyot notes a turning point in the years 1850–1860: "I began to study the districts of Châlons, Epernay and Reims, in 1845, and I saw at that time, vineyards of gouais providing wine of drink to 30 en the barrel, where are today planted fine grapes, black or white, which give a wine of 200 fr. It is impossible to find any more indisputable proof of the enormous influence of the grape variety on the quality of the vine products".[9] The *encépagement*, among the fine plants, also depend on the climatic factors and the progress of the methods of elaboration. Thus, during the nineteenth century, the cultivation of white grapes hitherto limited progresses, especially in the area that becomes the Côte des Blancs.

The question of *encépagement* is even more crucial with the reconstitution of the vineyards in the twentieth century to cope with the calamity of phylloxera. The phylloxeric destruction has led to some standardization of grape varieties at the national level, but the diverging solutions adopted here and there for the grape variety choices may vary depending on local situations, professional interests but also advice from agricultural professors. In this case, in Champagne, the reconstitution systematizes the use of Pinot and Chardonnay in the vineyards of the Marne while it brings to foreground, in the Aube, the gamay recommended if not imposed on the winemakers by the representatives of the Minister of Agriculture. The reason given is that this variety, more productive and rustic than pinot, would correspond to the objectives of a diversified production and intended for a wide consumption on the Parisian markets. The democratic dimension of this variety is at the centre of an argument that suggests the possibility for the Aube winemakers

[8]Guyot (1876, p. 390).

[9]Guyot (1876, p. 389).

to retain their customers, including champagne merchants.[10] This choice is quickly unfortunate because at the moment when asserts the extension of pinot in the Marne, the producers would have more difficulty to assert their belonging to the Champagne vineyard and to the making of sparkling wine.

This crucial issue of grape varieties is still at the heart of the 1927 legislation, which defines the Champagne appellation by providing for the disappearance of the gamay, particularly in the department of Aube, after a lapse of 18 years. This one will be prolonged and arranged until 1962, the date on which gamay is excluded from the authorized grape varieties for the elaboration of the sparkling wine of Champagne. Even if some old grape varieties, such as arbanne or meslier, have been approved, in the residual form, the construction of the Champagne in the twentieth century, has prolonged and systematized a transformation of the vines *encépagement*. Of course, from this point of view, it is also necessary to take into account the improvement and control of the plants which, in the framework of the reconstitution of the vineyard after the phylloxera, benefit from the constant and fundamental action of the Champagne Wine Association (AVC) created in 1898 by 24 business houses to save then French vines and "plants champenois" by promoting the grafting and the selection of plants.

Be that as it may, the vitivinicultural production system, linked to the development of sparkling wine, is progressively modifying all the vineyards of Champagne, according to a logic dominated by the international markets and the wine operators that are the trading houses. The development of the sparkling wine causes, parallel to the extension of the vines which are intended for it, a transformation of the status of the winegrowers who abandon the winemaking and become exclusively winemakers whose remuneration depends on the sale of their grapes to the merchants. These, holding the technical means and controlling the markets, strengthen their economic position within a vineyard whose prosperity results mainly from a product, the sparkling wine, whose export is during the nineteenth century the main outlet.

---

[10]Guicherd (1905).

Construction and Evolution of Champagne Champagne in the Twentieth Century

The revolt of the champagne winegrowers at the beginning of the century signals the beginning of an evolution marked by the affirmation of their role and their place. It is part of a national crisis but has specific forms in Champagne.

The major crisis then developing in Champagne takes place on the basis of the social relationship built throughout the nineteenth century. The dependence of winegrowers on business houses had been steadily increasing with the transformation of the vineyard. At the beginning of the twentieth century the winegrowers must sell their harvest without delay to the traders since they are deprived of wine material. When, in the first years of the century, climatic hazards and the collapse of national wine prices combine, the economic and social crisis is explosive because it appears that traders to maintain their level of production are refuelling outside the vineyards of the Marne. It was at this time, as early as 1908, that the first attempt at administrative delimitation was implemented. The events of the spring of 1911, marked by violent demonstrations in the north of Champagne and massive demonstrations in the south of the region, will permanently mark the vineyard.

How to interpret the popular mobilizations of the years 1910–1911? Are they a parenthesis, an accident of history where they a notable moment in a long-term evolution. They are often isolated and considered in themselves.

Yet current research shows that these movements are part of a long phase of social conflict and mobilization winemaker that extends over several decades. Indeed the long duration is the right dimension to estimate the impact of these revolts which had a social dimension but also political. This implies to consider the organization of the viticultural system of Champagne Champagne to the present day. When we do this, we are able to appreciate the current singularity, at the beginning of the twenty-first century, of the Champagne vineyards, by connecting it to these revolts of the beginning of the twentieth century, whose shadow marks as well the early existence of the appellation as early as 1927 as the interprofessional organization with its exceptionally wide sphere of activity.

In the French winegrowing territories of the "Belle époque", tensions and conflicts have been recurring for at least two decades and Champagne is no exception. Yet it lives them in a specific and differentiated way in the departments of Marne and Aube, to the point that we can advance the hypothesis that dominates two different political cultures.[11]

The revolts of the Marne and the mobilizations of the Aube in 1911 take place according to very different repertoires of action which lead to major clashes. Each one draws on different experiences and situations.

In the Marne, the economic and social conflictuality is already old and structured in a vineyard where traders dominate winemakers entirely at their mercy, while an abundant labour wage is employed in business houses. The poor harvests, the fall in grape prices, are causing a decline in the income of many winemakers who no longer have the resources to make wine for everyday consumption whose market has collapsed. The denunciation of fraud, as in Languedoc is the leitmotiv that appears as the main explanation of the difficulties of both, winegrowers as traders, even if they maintain their production and sales figures. Radical solidarism and social Christianity constitute competing political references that share the political scene while references to the themes of the labour movement are still marginal in a vineyard yet marked by the proximity of the urban world of the textile or transport industry. In the Aube, where the vineyard is reconstituted by the majority replanting of gamay, the world of independent winemakers is quite different since the weakness and the uncertainty of the incomes of the vineyard maintain in these winegrowers a strong pluriactivity agricultural, or artisanal. The share of far-left political ideas is important in the face of a conservative camp made up of notables rooted in village territories. From the Dreyfus affair to the separation of the churches and the state, politicization has been strong in a department where the *Libre pensée* is strongly rooted.

[11] S. Wolikow and C. Wolikow (2012, p. 132).

The tempo and the course of the clashes in the two departments express differences but also interweaving in the spring of 1911. In the Marne valley, the scale and violence of the crisis which affects the winegrowers leads to exasperation, when they feel that they have been betrayed by the trade and the notables who promised them a delimitation which would enable them to sell their grapes. The fear of proletarianization combined with the misery of trading employees leads to the destruction of cartons that feed the fraudsters, but also the cellars and cellars of large houses spotted for their suspicious transactions. The violent overflow is both an expression of accumulated resentment, but also a settlement of accounts with the partisans of moderation and of the agreement with the trading. Far-left political ideas are important here to a conservative camp composed of notables anchored in village territories. From the Dreyfus affair to the separation of the churches and the state, politicization has been strong in a department where free thought is strongly rooted.

In the face of the traders, the winemakers of the Marne are organizing to negotiate the purchase price of the grapes while the winegrowers of the Aube affirm their desire to belong to the champagne vineyard. On this point it is only after nearly two decades of debate and political and judicial clashes that a solution is found, in 1927. At this date is defined by the law the Champagne appellation which defines the area geographical area of the vineyard that can produce the sparkling wine. It can be noted that the vineyard of the southern champagne is incorporated there, but what is also to specify the *encépagement*, elements on the management of the vine, the definition of the places of elaboration. In the immediate future it pacifies the situation and reflects the acceptance of a compromise since the winegrowers of the Aube, fully integrated into the appellation accept the obligation to replace in the long term, within twenty years, the gamay by the pinot. But because of the economic crisis, the defined geographical area which includes more than 30,000 ha remains underutilized since only one-third of the surfaces is then planted. This situation lasted until the mid-1950s. Although the vineyard configuration changed legally, the economic situation remained poor. It is only in 1955 that we find the level of production of the 40 million bottles reached on the eve of the 1914 war (Table 1).

The Birth of the First Appellation: An Area That Delimits the Wine Terroir but Also the Development of Champagne

With winegrowers' revolts the place of the winemakers has now been affirmed without any immediate change, but the differences with the vineyards of the Marne persist when, after the 1914–1918 war, the Champagne economy faced too many challenges: the closing of many international markets, the reconstitution of the vineyards of the Marne after the destruction of the war and the multiplication of legal proceedings against the communes of the Aube who claim their reinstatement in the Champagne region. In the national context of a parliamentary activity to guarantee the quality of the wines, the law of 1927 explicitly specifies the creation of the Champagne appellation, whose territorial delimitation now includes the vineyard of the Aube and which specifies the incoming grape varieties in the making of sparkling wine. This delimitation was the subject of a compromise prepared and negotiated at the Champagne level at the instigation of the deputies of the Beverage Commission, notably its president, the socialist Edouard Barthe and the communist Marmande Renaud Jean. These parliamentarians, from wine departments of the Midi, came to the field and encouraged the various actors of the vineyard to agree. The first wine appellation acquired, the Champenois vineyard has an interprofessional organization. Recognition by the Syndicate of winegrowers in the economic field, materializes in 1935 when the Special Commission of Champagne Champagne Châlons, charged with discussing annually the fixing of reference prices of grapes and authorized yields. The deep and lasting economic recession that then affects the vineyard, recurring overproduction and lower prices explain partly that a significant fraction of the trading houses accepted what they had always refused.

Champagne Vineyards After 1945: More Than a Renewal—A Boom and an Unprecedented System

At the end of the 1940s the economic situation of the Champagne vineyards is still very fragile. The misery of the winemakers is the common lot of most of them, even in the department of the Marne where most of the vineyard is concentrated, while the vineyard of the Aube is further reduced. Production is difficult to recover because of the limited opportunities in a destroyed Europe, as well as shortages and ageing of the winemaking equipment. The revival of the vineyard is inseparable from the emergence of new actors whose role asserts itself in the 1950s and consolidates during the next two decades. At the instigation of the union and with the support of the public authorities, the cooperatives develop, which put the winegrowers in more favourable conditions to negotiate the price of the grapes sold to the traders.

Soon, these cooperatives are launching into champagnization, allowing many winemakers to acquire a know-how in the field of winemaking and venture soon into the marketing of Champagne on the French market, at a time when consumption sparkling wines are developing, while that of wines for everyday consumption is beginning to decline. From the 1960s, production increases, yields increase, planted areas also. The vineyard, whose production area had stagnated since 1927 since it remained limited to 11,000 ha, is therefore experiencing a steady geographical progression, in a context where the land structure is preserved because the winegrowers' union has managed to control the distribution of planting rights according to criteria that consolidate the small farm, that of winemakers owners against the property of traders. The proportion of 90% for the winemakers is ensured throughout the forty years that see the vineyard to more than 30,000 ha in the early 2000s. We must emphasize the contractual arrangement that the union of winemakers managed to impose during thirty years, from the end of the 1950s to the 1990s. The establishment of four-year contracts defining reciprocal commitments in terms of the delivery and purchase of grapes, linking winegrowers and traders, accompanies an unprecedented development of the vineyard and guarantees to the winegrowers a remuneration which allows the investment and the development of the cooperative sector like that of the independent winegrowers who produce Champagne themselves. The face of the Champagne vineyard is also experiencing a notable geographic transformation with the rapid development of the southern vineyard of champagne, in the Bar coast, which represents in the late 2000s about a quarter of the Champagne vineyards (Map 1). This extension of the Champagne vineyard is, in many respects, exceptional when compared to the overall evolution of most vineyards in France.

In the 1990s, the breakdown of the contractual system, the loss of autonomy of many trading houses in conjunction with the assertion of a dominant group, but also the rise of the brands worn by cooperatives, changed the situation of a vineyard whose production, after having continuously progressed until the mid-2000s, then knows a plateau around 320 million bottles.

When the European Commission adopts a directive in 2008 that provides for the liberalization of planting rights, the wine world reacts only slowly. However, the issue of planting rights in the Champagne vineyards is stronger than in other vineyards, certainly, because it remains in many respects dependent on a regulation whose progressive implementation since the end of the years. 1920 produced its beneficial effects in the second half of the twentieth century. This is proof of the growth of cultivated areas, given that the entire area defined and revised marginally for 80 years is now planted. The number of winemakers, far from decreasing, has progressed. The limitation of yields, the regulation of the purchase price of grapes, the trade union weight in the interprofessional organization as well as the role of the latter constituted so many responses to the erratic situation of the beginning of the twentieth century and the recession between two wars.

Conclusion: At the Dawn of a Systemic Crisis?

Since 2008, the Champagne vineyard has known an apparent stability that masks evolutions likely to change the economic and technical system set up after WWII (Table 2). While the international markets for sparkling wines are expanding steadily even after the crisis of 2008–2009, shipments of champagne wines

Table 2 Statistics about Champagne (2016)

People involved	4461 sender winegrowers, 39 cooperatives vineries, 300 Maisons (companies of wine producers)
Surface of vines	33,805 hectares: 22,454 (Marne), 7992 (Aube and Haute-Marne), 3359 (Aisne and Seine-et-Marne)
Encépagement (grape planting)	Pinot noir, 38%; Meunier, 31%; Chardonnay, 31%
Grape harvest and yields	9164 kg/hectare; 268 million of bottles
Stock	1478 million of bottles including the *réserve* (31/07/2016)
Turnover generated	4.7 billion euros (2.1 for the French market, 2.6 for the export)
Shipments (number of bottles)	France: 157,954,272 (52%)—89,836,252 sent by the Maisons de Champagne (57%), 68,118,020 sent by *récoltants* and cooperative vineries (43%) Export: 148,082,097 (48%)—129,559,093 sent by the Maisons de Champagne (87%); 18,523,004 sent by *récoltants* and cooperative vineries (13%) Total: 306,036,369—219,395,345 sent by the Maisons de Champagne (72%), 86,641,024 sent by *récoltants* and cooperative vineries (28%)
Main foreign markets (number of bottles)	United Kingdom—31,189,753 USA—21,805,677 Germany—12,486,572 Japan—10,948,555 Belgium—8,331,410 Australia—7,835,968 Italy—6,632,788 Switzerland— 5,700,367 Spain—3,994,176 Sweden—2,966,876

Sources Author adapted from CIVC website

have remained stable overall for a decade, but only exports out of Europe have increased significantly. The French market, which for a long time has been very buoyant, is falling apart. The first affected are the independent winemakers, harvesting-manipulating whose market remains mostly located at the national level. The major Champagne houses, through their brands, however, benefit from new international markets to Asia and America. Cooperatives that have engaged in a branding policy are part of this evolution, thus offering winegrowers not to be absent from these expanding markets.[12] However, the position of the major groups tends to strengthen within the appellation thanks to a policy of long-term contracts, services offered to small farmers now permanently linked to their buyers of raw materials. If the management of the interprofession remains parity, the influence of the big trading houses increases all the more that the differentiation within the world of the winegrowers also evolves so that the interests of the wine world are not always convergent. In short, the history of the Champagne vineyard is far from over while the question of planting rights, expansion of the production area and the evolution of the world market remain very uncertain!

References

Books and Publications as Sources

Anonyme. (1712). *Recueil de poésies latines et françoises sur les Vins de Champagne et de Bourgogne*. Paris.

Banque de France. (1969). *Le vin de Champagne*. Paris: études de la BDF.

Bidet, N. (1759). *Traité sur la nature et sur la culture de la vigne, sur le vin, la façon de le faire et la manière de la bien gouverner; à l'usage des différents vignobles du royaume de France*. Paris: Savoye.

[12]About the winemakers ability to further improve the quality of their wines during the first decades of new Millenium see, for example, S. Wolikow and C. Wolikow (2018).

Chappaz, G. (1951). *Le Vignoble et Le Vin de Champagne*. Paris: Éditions L. Larmat.

Courtépée, C. (1785). *Description générale et particulière du Duché de Bourgogne*, Dijon, 7 vol., t. 7.

Gabriel, P. (1913). *La viticulture dans le département de l'Aube*. Paris: A. Rousseau.

Godinot, J. (1722). *Manière de cultiver la vigne et de faire le vin en Champagne, et ce qu'on peut imiter dans les autres provinces pour perfectionner les vins*. Reims: B. Multeau.

Guicherd, J. (1905). *Monographie des cépages de l'Aube*. Troyes: P. Nouel.

Guyot, J. (1876). *Étude des vignobles de France pour servir à l'enseignement mutuel de la viticulture et de la vinification françaises*. Paris: Georges Masson.

Le vin de Champagne. (s.d.). Paris: Comité interprofessionnel des vins de Champagne de la ville d'Épernay.

L'Exposition de Troyes illustrée. Journal du Concours régional de l'Aube et des départements de l'Est (Yonne, Côte d'Or, Marne, Haute-Marne, Meuse, Ardennes). (1860). Troyes, Bi-weekly, 16 numbers.

Menon. (1749). «Du Vin – Observations». In *La Science du maître d'hôtel cuisinier*. Paris: Chez Paulus du Mesnil.

Mercier, L.-S. (1781–1788 [1994]). *Tableau de Paris*. Paris: Mercure de France.

Moreau-Bérillon, J. C. (1925). *Au pays du champagne: le vignoble, le vin*. Paris: Lahure.

Serres de, O. (1600 [1804–1805]). *Le Théâtre d'agriculture et mesnage des champs*. Paris: Mme Huzard.

Books and Papers

Dion, R. (1959). *Histoire de la vigne et du vin en France. Des origines au XIXe siècle*. Paris: Dion.

Garcia, J.-P. (2017). «Des "petits" vignobles en émergence en Bourgogne». In Le Bras, S. (dir.). *Les Petits vignobles*. Tours: PUR-PU François-Rabelais, pp. 141–154.

Garrier, G. (1998). *Histoire sociale et culturelle du vin*. Paris: Larousse.

Lachiver, M. (1988). *Vins, vignes et vignerons. Histoire du vignoble français*. Paris: Fayard.

Musset, B. (2008). *Vignobles de Champagne et vins mousseux (1650–1830). Histoire d'un mariage de raison*. Paris: Fayard.

Parker, T. (2017). *Le Goût du terroir. Histoire d'une idée française*. Tours: PU Rennes-PU Tours.
Wolikow, S., Wolikow, C. (2012). *Champagne! Histoire inattendue*. Paris: Éditions de l'Atelier.
Wolikow, S., Wolikow, C. (2018). *Rosé des Riceys. Tradition et exception en Champagne*. Les Riceys: Éditions du syndicat des producteurs de Riceys.

The Development of Winegrowing, Winemaking and Distribution of Wine in the Lower Moselle (Eighteenth–Twentieth Centuries)

Thomas Schuetz

Introduction

Research on the history of the scientification and mechanization of winegrowing and winemaking has only just begun. The following chapter illustrates some of the relevant aspects for the development of winegrowing, winemaking and distribution of wine through a case study of the Lower Moselle in the time from the late eighteenth century until the end of the twentieth century.

Apart from the Dissertation of Alexander Maringer (2014), a work that is devoted to legal questions, many relevant aspects haven't been subject to a profound historical analysis. Neither is it possible to investigate all aspects of the relevant discourses, social groups or events in the preferable length and depth. The development of wine production

T. Schuetz (✉)
History of the Impact of Technology, University of Stuttgart,
Stuttgart, Germany
e-mail: Thomas.schuetz@hi.uni-stuttgart.de

S. A. Conca Messina et al. (eds.), *A History of Wine in Europe, 19th to 20th Centuries, Volume I*, Palgrave Studies in Economic History,
https://doi.org/10.1007/978-3-030-27772-7_4

and wine marketing wouldn't be described in an appropriate manner, if limited on the mere narrative of events or explained with an internalistic approach by describing "the single correct path" (Dosi 1982). From the perspective of the history of science and technology it is necessary to include the historical background and its consequences on the development and reception of innovative technologies (Bijker 1995) in the vineyard and the cellar in its specific economic, social and political constellation to explain the creation of different wines and thus gaining the possibility of comparing (Hentschel 2003; Bloch 1994) the different regional studies that have been collected here.

Today's Wine Production at the Moselle

The Moselle wine production at the end of the millennium, as portrayed in advertising and the local popular and consumers' reception, was mainly famous for its aromatic white wines made from the Riesling grape with smaller partitions of other varieties (Pilz 2016; Dippel 2005). The comparable high prices have been justified by the difficult natural conditions and the high quality. These characteristics have been formalized in regional, national and European regulations and provisions, which claim to protect a traditional regional product. A look at the homepage of the Episcopal Wine Estates of Trier shows exemplary the essential narratives (Heßler 2012) that have been used in this context:

> [...] The centuries-old winemaking tradition is maintained until today. It is seldom that culture, tradition, and nature are so closely interwoven as in the steep slopes along the Mosel, Saar, and Ruwer. The inimitable creation of Riesling wines with finesse, elegance, and depth are the primary goals of the Bischöfliche Weingüter Trier. The necessary capital is an incredible diversity of core plots in legendary steep slope sites [...]. (Verwaltung der Bischöflichen Weingüter Trier GbR 2016)

This is just one example out of numerous comparable medial representations of the images associated with these products. Since the last reform of the relevant wine law in 2006 the German part of the Moselle valley is actually an independent wine region (Weingesetz, § 3). And in the latest applicable laws the utilization of traditional images is as well detectable, like in the case of the relatively new categories called "Classic" and "Selection" that have been created to protect "*quality wines from classical grapes varieties, which are typical for a region*" (Deutsches Weinbauinstitut 2015).

A look backward in time reveals, that this perception is not based on historical facts. "Meyers Konversations-Lexikon" in the edition from 1852 described the wines from the Mosel as follows:

> [...] They belong, after the wines from the Rhine, to the most pleasant and praised wines and are especially recommended as light table wines, there are red and white varieties [...]. (Meyer 1852)

While the edition from 1888 claimed this:

> [...] Almost only white wines are produced [...] in common years when the late ripening Riesling grape isn't completely ripe the wines are often gallized [...]. (Meyer 1888)

Already this quick glance shows that wine production changed profoundly in the nineteenth and twentieth century. To understand this development, it is necessary to take a look at the discourse among the relevant experts (Bijker 1995) in a time when the Moselle was a mere peripheral Prussian province and Prussia a backward country that struggled to keep up with the scientific, technological and economic changes (Greten 2005). The transfer of knowledge, the imitation of established educational institutions and the development of the local wine into a viable product in the second half of the nineteenth century generated social structures and institutions that enabled the winemakers to react to changing customer demands and production conditions later on. The parallel development of scientific knowledge and technical practises allowed winemakers to react to the changing perceptions of administrators, experts and consumers about wine from the Moselle.

Natural Condition at the Lower Moselle

The river Moselle determined the way wine was produced and traded since pre-industrial times, it flows in numerous loops from southwest to northeast and cuts through the soil of the Rhenish Massif, a low mountain range basically consisting of slate, thus not only creating the natural border between the highlands of the Eifel and the Hunsrück but as well numerous steep slopes in good exposition. The terroir is very suitable for winegrowing, because the poor soil forces the vines to grow deep roots and so the plants and the grapes show significant high degree of minerals (Jackson 2014; Bacon 2004). The region lies comparable far in the North (Ashenfelter and Storachmann 2010). As a result of the relatively short growing season, wines from the Mosel have been known for their high acidity (Bellinghaus 1924).

Even though it is necessary to note the difference between a high acidity in the must because the grapes have been harvested too early, before the synthesis of the fructose has been completed (Jackson 2014, p. 99f), and the high degree of malic acid, which is a common phenomenon in northern wine regions, like in the Moselle or in the Champagne region. The malic acid not only gives the wines a fresh hint of green apples it also enhances the ageing potential. The deep cut valley of the river furthermore bears the risk of early frosts, because fog can't dissolve easily (Meyer 1934). These difficult conditions for the growth of wines with good structure also meant that the labour in the vineyards had been rather demanding. The work was not only dangerous because of the height and the unsafe ground of slippery slate it was as well labour-intensive, complicated and more expensive to mechanize. The geological situation is comparable to other wine producing regions, like the Middle Rhine Valley or parts of the Neckar Valley, even though, the Moselle is characterized by the dominance of steep slopes and the lack of level eras. A situation that is nowadays used for advertising purposes, in the past this created harsh conditions for the pre-industrial production. The steep slopes are difficult to cultivate and there is almost no alluvial rich soil in the river banks or in the hinterland, a situation that made a mixed agriculture impossible and limited the economic possibilities of the winegrowers (Bellinghaus 1924; Maringer 2014; Christoffel 1926).

The Historic Development Since the Late Eighteenth Century

For the Moselle region, as for large parts of Central Europe, the time of the French Revolution and the following Napoleonic Wars were the time when the outdated and in many aspects inefficient feudal system had been challenged and in many cases superseded (Meyer 1934). The territorial reform of 1798 created a new administrative unit under French rule called *Département Rhin et Moselle* while the City of Koblenz became its capital. Even though this new stately structure wouldn't last further than 1815, when the Moselle became Prussian (Treue 1984), the agricultural and administrative structures have been changed fundamentally and these basic structures remained even under Prussian rule (Maringer 2014). In particular, it meant that the feudal institutions have been abolished, the church lost its control through ownership and levies, and civil law replaced the obsolete feudal law (Treiling 2009; Greten 2005).

As a result, the established forms of ownership structure and the organization of production saw fundamental reforms. Based on the freedom of the individuum the French economic politics introduced freedom of trade and capitalism (Klein 1934; Meyer 1934). Before 1798 the time of harvest was determined either by the feudal lord or by an account of local dignitaries of a village (Phillips 2000). The following work steps of grape harvest and pressing reflected the established division of labour typical for the regions. This "Villikationssystem"—still showed elements of pre-Carolingian feudalism, with a manor house to which belonged large, expensive or maintenance-intensive technology, like mills or winepresses. While large parts of the actual labour in the vineyards were organized in subordinated plots by serf- or tenants-families (Gönnewein 1963, p. 163ff; Simpson 2011).

Under French rule these established practices ended and vineyards have been auctioned in the course of secularization. Many favourable sites have been bought by prosperous bourgeoisie, who followed the aristocracy and the church as owners (Phillips 2000; Clemens 1996,

p. 129ff). This change not only increased the meaning of money as tool for social negotiation processes but as well left the responsibility for the economic success in the hands of the respective owners (Nordblom 2012). Under these new conditions the popularity of the Riesling grape grew considerably (Mahlerwein 2012). Under feudal law, the security and quantity of the harvest were of greater importance than the quality of the wines (Matheus 1980; Laufner 1987) because the repressive economic system rather diminished the field for personal initiative and creativity (Simpson 2011). Mixed planting, the harvest of grapes of differing ripeness and careless maintenance in the vineyard as in the cellar have been quite common when compulsory labour offered no rewards for increased efforts (Meyer 1934).

The Riesling grape was known before and had even been supported regionally (Maringer 2014). The variety appeared at the Moselle at first only in comparable small quantities planted in the better exposed vineyards on the upper slopes, in Trarbach-Enkirch and Piesport (Meyer 1934). Certain characteristics made this grape variety interesting for the Moselle-vintners. The plant is comparably resistant to frost. But apart from the durability of the plant, the wines from Riesling had a further advantage for the vintners and merchants, because they were much more storable (Jackson 2014). While the established production methods crafted wines that had to be drunk during the following year. Winemakers with slopes in good exposition tried to produce sweet white wines, following the examples of the international successful wines from Sauternes or Tokay (Phillips 2000). And these producers also started to emphasize the local origin as an alternative to the mere categorization according to the region (Christoffel 1979). The common phenomenon of alternation of years with mediocre quality or even no harvest at all and other years with very good yields, thus low prices due to excess supply, could be compensated by storing surpluses and blending them with wines from inferior, later vintages (Simpson 2011; Simon 1920).

With the Prussian taxation reform of 1818, Moselle wine found a large exclusive market in the Kingdom of Prussia, protected from foreign products (Meyer 1926). Even though the wines from the Moselle had to compete with the production from the Prussian part of the Rhineland. As a result of the demand the area under cultivation grew considerably. As Monz had shown on the example of Trier, where the land with vines almost doubled from 559 to 1028 ha between 1819 and 1841 (Monz 1981). This meant, that large properties with second-rate exposition, have been planted with vines. During this phase of growth former traders tried to participate in the production and bought vineyards and land for the future cultivation of wine. This social group hoped to participate in the future revenues and was willing to pay rising prices for land through long-term loans or loans above market conditions (Nordblom 2012).

But the time of a protected market was rather short. With the creation of a Custom Union between the Kingdom of Prussia and the Grand Duchy of Hesse in 1828 and the German Customs Union in 1834 wines from the Moselle had to compete with wines from the South (Phillips 2000). With the increasing importance of railway transport in the second half of the nineteenth century the number of competitors even grew (Charters 2006; Phillips 2000; Klein 1934).

These changed conditions resulted in a fundamental crisis in the whole region. The wines couldn't be sold with the desired revenues and this made it impossible to service the debts that have been taken during the boom phase. Even worse a lack of available capital made it difficult to participate in the scientific and technological developments since the 1840s. The crisis was explained, with the neglect of quality and the emphasis of quantity. The traditional segmentation of property, the weak market and the difficult financial situation because of taxation and debts made the smallholder to the typical form of agriculture on the Moselle. They couldn't participate in the contemporary developments and tried to find an income through the production of quantity (Meyer 1934). A phenomenon that has been described as a so-called "subsistence trap" (Bohler 2007), a common occurrence of the nineteenth-century agriculture, even though more commonly caused by the continuously diffusion of estates through succession (Grabmayer

2012), then by the natural conditions, as in the case of the Moselle. On the other hand, advocates of quality rather than quantity like the wineries van Ellinkhuisen in the former Cloister of Machern, Bücking in Trabach or Hayn in Trier soon realized that the labour intense wine production in the steep slopes of the Moselle valley held the possibility to produce outstanding wines (Meyer 1934). These and comparable other wineries concentrated on the continuous advancement in the vineyard as in the cellar. The planting of Riesling and the systematic vine training with single post rather than in lines or the utilization of scientifically substantiated technique—as for the determination of the sugar content in grapes or must (Jenemann 1990, p. 20f)—are some examples of the scientific and technological innovations available for winemakers in that time. In the second half of the nineteenth century their high-priced wines of outstanding quality have been sold not alone in the traditional foreign markets of the Netherlands and Great Britain but also in Northern America and Russia. A development that resulted in the practice of commission trading and thus the establishment of an urban social group of traders (Nordblom 2012, p. 288ff; von Bassermann-Jordan 1975, p. 182ff).

Gallization

The political debate concerning the poverty of a large number of smallholders has been far too complex to be adequately described here. It ranged from fundamental questioning the structure of the capitalistic society to rightwing anti-Semitic propaganda (Pelger 1973). Among the many voices Ludwig Gall (1791–1863) is probably the most important and his approach to the problem is of great interest to the subject in question. Gall was a Prussian civil servant, who was interested in the contemporary scientific and technologic innovations. He believed that the problems of the Moselle could be solved if the winemakers would not only improve the quality of their must by adding sugar but by adding water as well. As a result, the high acidity of the must would be tempered, the degree of alcohol in the later wine would be higher, and this would make the wine stable for transportation and give him longer durability. As a surplus the quantity of the production could be increased as well and more and more vintners would be able to earn a satisfactory income from their work without having to resort to social benefits. He started to experiment with this improvement of must as soon as 1827. Diverted by other interest and projects he wouldn't publish his results before 1851, inspired by a very bad harvest of 1850 (Bellinghaus 1924). He soon got a broad reception and managed to establish the nomenclature of "Gallization" for dulcifying diluted must in correspondence to the term of "Chaptalization" for sugaring of must after Jean-Antoine Chaptal (1756–1832) (Charters 2006). But the reactions of the public and of experts was rather ambivalent and an argument began concerning the question of its legality, because the dilution of must or wine was traditionally a prohibited practice (Maringer 2014, pp. 10, 15, 49ff, 62ff, 143, 146, 148f, 162, 192, 248ff, 253). A consensus concerning the question of whether the practice was fraud or a mere process technology couldn't be found. Because legislation in the different German states differed and the food and health laws of the time had been rather indistinct in these aspects (Bauer 1877) it could occur that the dispute was brought before the court (Greten 2005; Monz 1981). Gall and his supporters have been unified in an unshaken belief in progress, in their world view the utilization of science and technology would improve the living condition of the population and they believed in the responsibility of the educated citizen to participate in the promotion of research and the diffusion of knowledge among the population. This meant at the same time that critics were decried as enemies of civilization (Anonymous 1854). Obviously, scientists were among his supporters, such as Carl Georg von Siemens (1809–1885) who obtained a professorship at the agricultural college in Hohenheim. He wrote about his experiments with gallized wines the following:

> After the made experiences it can't be doubted that the treated wine (that without difficulty can be doubled in value) really shows certain advantages, among which its cleanness and higher durability are salient. (Anonymous 1854)

At this point it is relevant to observe that wine—apart from the local consumption—was and is mainly a cash crop. Investors in the first half of the nineteenth century have been interested in quantity and neglected the quality of the grapes (Simpson 2011). Their business model was to further process basic wines into sweet liquor, fortified wine, sparkling wine and brandy. Gall claimed that the practice had been known to the wine merchants and that this "*small but rich party*" would suppress this knowledge with the aim of oppression and consequently control of the smallholders (Anonymous 1854). The opponents of Galls' method feared that the dilution of must would receive a negative public reception and hence limiting their sales opportunities. Their approach was to defame the method and they claimed that Galls' wines would be hazardous to the human health and would be distinguished by a taste of "disgusting sweetness" (Anonymous 1854). Even though the debate cannot be outlined in all detail here, it is relevant, that the dispute couldn't be resolved and in consequence the artefact "wine" didn't gain the status of closure in the social-constructivist meaning (Bijker 1995). All the ensuing wine laws are reflections of this social process of negotiation; while the legislation of 1879 simply forbade the adulteration or imitation of wines without determining what ingredients would be seen as adulteration (Gesetz betreffend den Verkehr mit Nahrungsmitteln … ect., § 10). The reformed law from 1901 made it clear what ingredients were allowed. The fining of the wine with egg white, gelatin, Isinglass or comparable substances, the blending of wine with wine, the chemical deacidification with lime carbonate and the addition of sugar, whether or not in aqueous solution, was legal. The only limitation was, that the wine was not supposed to be altered through the gallization, so that its character wouldn't fall below the "typical wine of the regional standard" (Gesetz betreffend den Verkehr mit Wein … ect., § 2). An obscure phrasing that already bore the need for further reforms. Even though it should be noted, that after such processing the wine couldn't be sold under the label of "Naturwein" (Gesetz betreffend den Verkehr mit Wein … ect., § 4). A direct hint to the influence of the contemporary *vin naturell*—movement in France among German politicians and experts. The legislation tried to satisfy the interest groups of smallholders, merchants and respectable vintners all at once. Especially the vintners of a higher social status, who knew of the elaborate French systems to categorize wines (Simpson 2011) and who produced renowned wines, didn't feel that the new law had the desired depth and complexity. Inspired by this desideratum, regional elitist societies of winegrowers occurred. At the Moselle the "Trierer Verein von Weingutsbesitzern von Mosel, Saar und Ruwer"[1] was founded in 1910 (VDP. Prädikatsweingüter 2016). The mechanization of cellar technology was predominantly utilized in their wineries (Klein 1934). The central concern of their association was the promotion of wine auctions, an approach that was aiming at increased revenues for the vintners and weakening the economic power of merchants through a fair and public negotiation of wine prices.

Diffusion and Implementation of Knowledge

The research of Paul and others has shown, that, as a result of the problems with genuine and false mildew and most prominent phylloxera and the attempts of scientists to solve these problems, the nineteenth century saw the alteration of wine production from craft to science (Paul 1996). The Moselle was a region that was infested relatively late with phylloxera. It was not until 1907 that there were the first documented cases, while the scientific investigation of the problem in France already began in the 1860s. So, it was possible to learn from the experiences made in France. In the case of the Moselle, it became obvious that the new developments in science and technology that have been available to the wealthy winemakers and merchants weren't available to the smallholders. To educate the sons of smallholder and consequently enable them to produce more efficiently a viniculture school was founded in Trier in the Year 1893 (Müller 1898, p. 3ff). Where the methods that had been developed in the fields of agriculture, chemistry and biology were diffused among the population. The established view of historians of wine is that these developments gave winemakers the capability

[1]Trierer Association of Vineyard Owners of Mosel, Saar and Ruwer.

to produce quality wine, like the established wineries already did. The older practices, where tacit knowledge and the verbal transfer of knowledge between generations characterized the production of wine, were questioned by the advance of theoretical knowledge transferred through schools, publications and model vineyards. But again, the Moselle was a latecomer, other German states had founded agricultural colleges and viticulture schools much earlier: Krems in Austria was founded in 1875, Weinsberg in Württemberg 1868 and Geisenheim in Hesse in 1872—to name but a few. A circumstance that can be explained by the fact that the region was only a peripheral part of Prussia and that in Prussia the focus of the state agricultural policy was quite clearly on the Junker and on large estates in the east of the country.

But the established historiographic narrative doesn't recognize all relevant aspects of this change. The capability of the winemakers wasn't limited to the production of better quality and higher durability than ever before, they also gained the possibility to alter central characteristics of their wine through the utilization of the advanced technologies, as the example of filter technology can show. To produce a clear wine, the remains of the fermentation process needed to be removed. Since the second half of the nineteenth century the fining of the wine, even though it never completely vanished, was increasingly replaced by different precoat filters (Hofbauer 1929). Textiles, paper or even asbestos have been used as filter material. The development came to its crucial point with the Universal Fast Filter of Enzinger from 1888 (Troost 1986)—which already showed the multi-layer filters that still can be found in cellars today. It combined the idea of using multiple layers of filter material with the possibilities of contemporary pressure pumps (Anonymous 1889). The demand that inspired this innovation came from the problems with not properly cleaned alcoholic beverages, when remaining sugar and remains of yeast led to a clouding of the beer through a secondary fermentation (Briggs et al. 2004). When the technology was transferred to the production of wine, the winemakers since the 1890s could choose the moment when to stop the fermentation. It was up to their decision whether they wanted a wine with a higher degree of alcohol and less sugar, or a sweet and light wine (Lea and

Pigott 2003). Keeping in mind that the chaptalization and gallization and the biological and chemical deacidification had been common, it is easy to understand the increasing possibilities to design a wine according to the costumers' expectations (Simpson 2011).

Apart from the utilization of science and technology in the cellar, the industrialization had also a remarkable influence on the work in the vineyard. The utilization of ploughs in the vineyard wasn't a common practice before the 1920s in the Moselle valley. Even though well-established in other regions the soil was basically manually treated with hoes and rakes (Bellinghaus 1924). Only when the industrial production of ploughs had displaced the older practice of the local production by craftsmen, a process that started in the last decades of the nineteenth century, and companies specialized in the production of agricultural machinery tried to diversify their range of products, the application of ploughs on steep slopes was considered. Before the First World War, the company Scherf in Saarburg-Trier produced electric winch-systems to pull small carts on rails through the slopes. It is not surprising that the costumers who could afford this technology have been the stately domains and larger private wineries (Mahlerwein 2012). In 1921, the domain of Serrig ordered a mobile winch propelled by an engine from Scherf. At first this technology was only used to disperse fertilizer but soon the flexibility of the system made other applications expedient. In the year 1926, a motor-winch was used for the first time for ploughing at the Saar. And in the following years the Maschinenfabrik Franz Clemens Söhne started with the serial production of motor-winches for winegrowers, thus lowering the prices and making the technology available to a broader part of the winegrowers. The engines from Franz Clemens Söhne have been designed not only to propel winches and thus transporting heavy materials in the vineyard, like fertilizer, earth or even automatic crop protection sprayers but could also be applied to propel further machineries needed during the processing of the grapes, like grape mills. Even though the multiple applications made these machines quite effective the industrial production of horse-propelled winches fell at the same time (Klein 1934).

The National Socialist Dictatorship

The Wall Street Crash of 1929 hit the wine production on the Moselle as well. The year 1932 showed that the dramatic economic and political developments in Germany didn't spare the wine trade. The land was governed without the participation of the parliament by emergency measures and large parts of the population have been affected by mass unemployment or the fear of losing their jobs. The demand for wine shrank almost completely to nil. Apart from very few highly regarded and internationally known wines, which haven't been affected, most wines had to be sold far below their production cost. With the National Socialists' ascent to power in Germany in 1933, anti-Semitism obtained a new, historically unique quality that had an impact on all parts of the society. After the appointment of Adolf Hitler as Reichskanzler in January 1933, the boycott of all Jewish business and the Law for the Restoration of the Professional Civil Service on in April of the same year made the situation for Jewish merchants in the wine business increasingly difficult. Without any resistance from their former customers, business partners and colleagues, all Jews have been displaced from the organizations concerned with viticulture. The Jewish merchants and commissioners haven't been banned from their trade jet. Since about 60% of the wine traded in Germany was in Jewish hands and between 800,000 and 1,000,000 people lived directly or indirectly from viticulture, the economic impact was too important for such measures. But already five years later Jewish merchants had been complete repressed when the state forbade the trade between Jewish merchants and the stately domains and invited all vintners to participate. Even though the legal successor of the VDNV, the VDP, prides itself by the claim that "[…] *no owner of a vineyard held an important or mediocre position in the Party*" (VDP. Prädikatsweingüter 2016), a serious scientific investigation of these questions is still pending (Buchheim 2010). The unrealistic ideal of a self-reliant nation of the National Socialist dictatorship can be traced in the limitations of wine growing as in other interventions by the state. In 1934 the plantation of new vineyards was heavily regulated. In the time wine was rather seen as a luxury product and among the members of the NSDAP older traditions of the temperance movement

Table 1 Land planted with wine (Mosel)

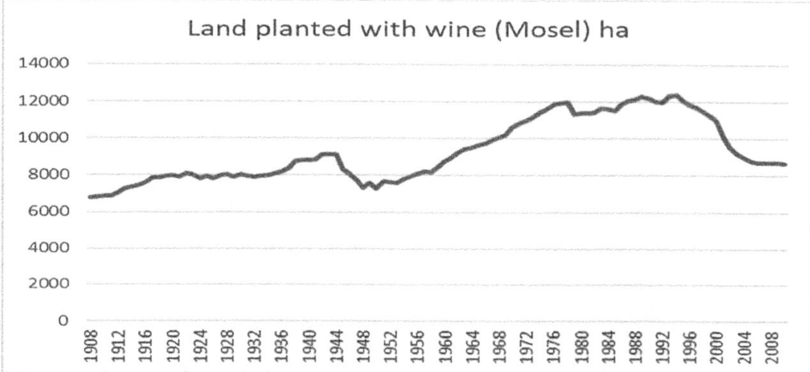

Source Dammers, D., *Historische Statistik*, 3rd Vol. of: Clemens, L., Felten, F. J., & Schnettger, M. (ed.), *Kreuz - Rad – Löwe / Rheinland-Pfalz: Ein Land und seine Geschichte*, Mainz, Philipp von Zabern, 2012, pp. 286–294

lingered on. To secure the food production no soil that could be used for the cultivation of grain or potatoes was allowed to be planted with wine (Koch 1993, p. 226f), and after the war the regional council of Hesse-Palatinate considered this law still valid (comp. Table 1).[2]

Sweet and Cheap—Moselle Wine in the Second Half of the Twentieth Century

After the Second World War, the region of the lower Moselle became a part of the new state Rhineland-Palatinate, in the Federal Republic of Germany this new state was special in a variety of aspects. With the lower Moselle and the Middle Rhine it held two regions famed for their wine, picturesque landscape and romantic castles, which both had a long tradition of tourism especially from England but also of many German holidaymakers who preferred to stay in their home country.

[2] *Amtliche Mitteilungen des OberReg.Präs. Hessen-Pfalz*, 1946, p. 117.

But apart from the sector of tourism the state of Rhineland-Palatinate became the largest wine producing state of the Federal Republic of Germany, while on the other hand the state had neither an established and accepted capital, nor larger cities—not to mention any significant industry (Nordblom 2012). Until 1991, the CDU[3] was the dominant party in Rhineland-Palatinate, which reflected the mentality of a conservative, rural state with a high share of Christian Churches, especially Catholics. From 1971 to 1987 she ruled there with an absolute majority. The paradigm of wine production of the following years was characterized by the growing utilization of science and technology as well as in the education of new generations of winemakers as in the implication of new technologies in the vineyards as means of rationalization. A development that can be explained by numerous factors which are all related to the phenomenon of the so-called *Wirtschaftswunder*. The practice of Equalization Payments in the Federal Republic of Germany gave the state of Rhineland-Palatinate the opportunity to make these innovative technologies available to smallholders by expanding the school system and promoting agriculture.

The 1950s were a time of excessive consumption after the experience of hunger and need during the last phase of the Second World War and the time until the reform of the monetary system in the three Western sectors in 1949 (Weinreb 2011). While the wages and income of the population grew considerable as a result of the very positive economic development, the prices for food and drink shrank. The excessive consumption and the resulting obesity became a visual symbol of a society that made almost no attempt to cope with its difficult past. Food had to be rich and plentiful and especially the taste of sweetness became very popular (Grigg 1995, p. 255ff). The upcoming convenient food industry was quick in the uptake of this preference for sweet, fatty and creamy foods and the resulting health issues have been serious social problem in all industrialized nations ever since (Cordain et al. 2004). The preference for sweetness didn't stop when it came to alcoholic beverages: sweet liquors, Brandies and Whiskies that have been flavoured and coloured with caramel and last but not least sweet wines have been

[3]Christliche Demokratische Union = Christian Democratic Party.

favoured by the consumers. The vintners and wine merchants tried to respond to this market demand, by the established and legal practices of gallization and chaptalization. The revival of the wine industry after the almost complete standstill, enabled by financial reconstruction aid of the Western Allies (Glöckner 2007, p. 195f), in connection with the growing import of French and Italian wines soon led to the problem of excess production. This worsened when the constitutional court declared that the limitations from 1937 have been unconstitutional. This verdict from 1958 resulted in a massive expansion of the planted area from 7500 ha in the 1950s to 12,300 ha at the beginning of the 1990s[4] and thus to a remarkable growth of the production since 1960, when the newly planted vines started to yield (comp. Table 1).

In this situation, the Franz Wilhelm Langguth Erben winery in Traben-Trarbach started to produce a wine under the brand name of "Himmlisches Moseltröpfchen" (Eng.: Heavenly Moselle Driplet). Hi-Mo, as the initiative had been called in a pejorative connotation among winemakers, proved to be successful: in 1963 ten million litres had been sold and the wines of 324 winemakers were processed and marketed. Inspired by this economic success blended wines distributed under a brand name without vintage appeared to be a lucrative market. The food industry giant "Alpenmilch" (Eng.: Alpine Milk) decided to create an affiliate in Bingen/Rhine in 1964 under the formation of "St. Ursula" winery. They produced four different types of wine, all with screw caps and all under one brand name called "Goldener Oktober".

Alpenmilch didn't venture into this new market segment before a profound consumer's survey. It showed that 60% of the German wine drinkers have been disgruntled by the different quality of vintages. The decision-makers at Alpenmilch, a global company with headquarters in Switzerland, wanted to get in line with this demand and invested five Million Deutsche Mark in "St Ursula" while opening their sales network, which delivered concentrated milk of the brand "Bärenmarke" to 140,000 retailers.[5] Among the first brand wines from "St. Ursula"

---

[4]http://www.weinland-mosel.de/de/die-region/historie.html (24 January 2017).

[5]Editorial, "Markenwein: Hilfe für Verstimmte" in *Der Spiegel*, 1964, n. 40, p. 60.

also a wine from the Moselle could be found, that was characterized as "sparkling and fresh". The results of Alpenmilch's consumer's survey not only had a significant impetus on the wine "St. Ursula" designed but also shaped the advertisement campaign. "Goldener Oktober" was advertised to be "flawless as a diamond" and especially known for its "salubriousness". Later laws strictly forbade the use of expressions that indicated health effects of any alcoholic beverages. In the 1960s that wasn't seen as problematic in the general public. An instance that is quite telling about the contemporary reception of wine as food and of food as an industrial product of unchanging qualities, constant availability and simple accessibility. The aspired retail price was 3 Deutsche Mark and even though it shouldn't be forgotten that 60% of the consumers are a considerable market share the dichotomy of this observations meant that on the opposite quite a large group of consumers wouldn't agree with the reception of wine as an industrial product. Even though it is hardly possible to detect their reception of wine ex negativo, the contemporary efforts of highly regarded wine producers might at least indicate the ambivalence and complexity of the contemporary discourse.

Among those vintners who produced highly regarded wines the general tendency to produce large amounts of cheap and sweet wines was seen as critical, because they produced small quantities of expensive sweet wines and feared that the general trend could be harmful for the reputation of the whole region. A legitimate fear considering the reception in the media, especially concerning the discourse about a reform of the German wine law. There had been a general consensus about the deficits of the existing legislation. Especially the lack of precise quantifications and nomenclature led to different implementary provisions in the respective federal states. The demand for legal security and standardization—also under consideration of the attempted standardization on a European level—resulted in numerous reformations of the wine law, of whom the most significant were from 1961, 1969, 1971 and 1994 (Koch 1993). The debate that accompanied these reforms showed the low reputation German, especially Moselle wines had at the time among German consumers. In 1967, 80% of the wines from the Moselle have been cut with wines from other German regions. Der Spiegel showed pictures of long lines of railway tankers with imported wines and the caption read: "mishmash instead of Moselle".[6]

The draft of the law from 1969 established three quality grades for wine; table-wine, quality-wine and special quality-wine. Even though this system has been altered and refined over time, it remained vitally important for the German wine production. The graduation only followed the degree of fructose in the must, wines with less natural sugar were perceived as of a lesser quality (Jenemann 1990). Even though the political decision-makers claimed that this solution would be the ideal way of combining French traditions with German practical demands, while still respecting the necessity of a future European solution the reception wasn't very favourable. The comparable lax laws with even less strict control of them—in 1971 there have been approximate 20,000 wineries at the Moselle while only five state inspectors had to control the legal requirements[7]—led to the odd phenomena of a quality wine flood. While in other European nations, notably France, Spain and Italy mainly produced wines of the respective lower categories, German wines of the middle grade of quality dominated the market.

But in the second half of the twentieth century the production of cheap wine in Germany became more and more difficult. The increasing consumption of European wines as a result of the economic unification of large parts of Europe and the rising productions costs in Germany resulted in the concentration on wines that could be sold with higher profits. As a result of changing costumer's expectations, the demand for sweeter wines shrank while drier wines became more and more popular during the second half of the twentieth century. While the utilization of science and technology in vineyard and wine cellar led to a democratization of quality wine (Charters 2006).

Wines from the Moselle until the 1980s have been characterized as very sweet, artificial wines and had a rather low reputation. Since the late 1980s the demand for such wines constantly shrank. In the consumers' reception, the linkage between the wines from the Moselle and the region as holiday destination, that had been beneficial for the wines sales

[6]Editorial, "EWG: Wein – Saure Front" in *Der Spiegel*, 1967, n. 11, p. 80.

[7]Editorial, "Wein: Zähne stumpf" in *Der Spiegel*, 1971, n. 45, p. 62.

since the 1950s, lost its attraction when more and more Germans could afford vacations in distant and more exotic locations (Cardello 1995). The image of the Rhine and the Moselle suffered heavily and the infrastructure originally designed for guided groups of tourists and bus tourism lost its attractivity in times of holiday flights and individual tourist.

The market for sweet and cheap wines, that had been serviced with Moselle wines from the 1950s till the 1980s, shrank as the connotation of sugar from a healthy and good tasting ingredient shifted towards that of a possible health issue. That didn't mean that cheap sweet wines disappeared from the market (Cardello 1995; Fleuchaus and Arnold 2011, p. 163ff) but the ever-increasing production costs made it impossible to produce them on the steep slopes of the Moselle valley. Those vintners who didn't give up the production once and for all[8] had to find a niche for their survival. From the approximate 8500 wineries in 1979 only 3200[9] have survived and the cultivated area shrank from 12,300 ha in 1990 to 8800 ha in 2012 (comp. Table 1).[10] The remarkable achievement of vintners, wineries and merchants in the late twentieth cntury was to cope with the negative image the wines from the Moselle had and change the public reception of their product. A goal that was achieved by the systematic utilization of integrated marketing strategies that ranged from the training of specialized communicators—for business-, tourist- and gastronomic-target groups, over the application of digital and traditional media (Stöckl 2011). A marketing strategy that became self-propellant, when the popular wine media accepted and diffused this narrative. As indicated at the beginning of this text, the promotional message that ensured the economic success under the conditions of the late twentieth century actively abolished the established image of Moselle wines—as sweet and cheap with dubious content, and promoted the image of high-quality wine produced in a traditional manner.

---

[8]Bartsch, M., "Kleines Tröpfchen" in *Der Spiegel*, 2013, n. 48, pp. 52–53; p. 52.

[9]Statistics from 2009 / Dienstleistungszentrum ländlicher Raum Rheinhessen-Nahe-Hunsrück, http://www.dlr-mosel.rlp.de (25 January 2017).

[10]www.weinland-mosel.de/de/die-region/daten-fakten.html (24 January 2017); Deutsches Weininstitut (ed.), *Deutscher Wein / Statistik / 2013/2014*, Mainz, 2013, n. P., p. 7.

Conclusion

The sociological investigation of consumer behaviour could show that promotional messages are successful when they confirm the fiction of rationality of costumers (Schimank 2006, pp. 57–81). The fact that the production of wine, that actually is quite scientific and technological advanced, is not advertised by the utilization of ideals of progressiveness and modernity is quite telling concerning the contemporary attitude towards science and technology. But apart from these aspects the example of the Moselle can show that this utilization of history was rather created than investigated and it is thus an example of the invention of a tradition as Hobsbawn has described (Hobsbawn 2013, pp. 1–14).[11] Because on the one hand wine as alcoholic beverage has manifold impacts on society, while on the other hand this invented tradition is used to legitimate legal regulations and provisions, the scientific deconstruction of it displays a twofold actual relevance.

References

Anonymous. (1889). Technische Neuerungen auf dem Gebiete der Brauindustrie. *Dinglers' Polytechnisches Journal*, 273, 101–113.

Anonymous (Gall, L.). (1854). *Des Ministers Grafen Chaptal und des Dr. Galls Weinbereitungs-Methoden vor dem Gesetz*. Trier: Verlag von F. A. Gall's Buchhandlung.

Ashenfelter, O., & Storachmann, K. (2010). Using Hedonic Models of Solar Radiation and Weather to Assess the Economic Effect of Climate Change: The Case of Mosel Valley Vineyards. *The Review of Economics and Statistics*, 92/2, 333–349.

Bacon, M. (ed.). (2004). *Water Use Efficiency in Plant Biology*. Oxford: Blackwell.

Bauer, M. (1877). *Die Verfälschung der Nahrungsmittel in großen Städten*. Berlin: Heymann.

[11] Hobsbawn, E., "Introduction: Inventing Traditions" in Hobsbawn, E., & Ranger, T. (ed.), *The Invention of Tradition*, Cambridge, Cambridge University Press, 2013, pp. 1–14.

Bellinghaus, H. (1924). Moselwein. *Rheinische Heimatblätter*, 1924/1, 66–73.

Bijker, W. E. (1995). *Of Bicycles, Bakelites, and Bulbs: Towards a Theory of Sociotechnical Change*. Cambridge, MA: MIT Press.

Bloch, M. (1994). *Für eine vergleichende Geschichtsbetrachtung der europäischen Gesellschaft* (Middell & Sammler, Ed., pp. 121–167).

Bohler, K. F. (2007). Historische Typen der Agrarverfassung und regionale Mentalitäten in Deutschland. *Sozialwissenschaftliches Journal*, 4, 11–24.

Briggs, D. E., Brookes, P. A., Stevens, R., & Boulton, C. (2004). *Brewing: Science and Practice*. Cambridge: Woodhead.

Buchheim, C. (2010). Der Mythos vom „Wohlleben": Der Lebensstandard der deutschen Zivilbevölkerung im Zweiten Weltkrieg. *Vierteljahresschrift für Zeitgeschichte*, 58, 299–328.

Cardello, A. V. (1995). Food Quality: Relativity, Context and Consumers Expectations. *Food Quality and Preferences*, 6, 163–170.

Charters, S. (2006). *Wine and Society: The Social and Cultural Context of a Drink*. Burlington: Taylor & Francis.

Christoffel, K. (1926). Die kurtrierische Weinbau- und Weinhandelspolitik seit dem 16. Jahrhundert. *Trierer Zeitschrift*, s.n.c., 109–144.

Christoffel, K. (1979). *Die Weinlagen der Mosel und ihre Namensherkunft*. Trier: Spee-Verlag.

Clemens, G. (1996). *Der „Moselkönig" Matthias Josef Hayn. Eine wirtschaftsbürgerliche Karriere in napoleonischer Zeit* (Burgard, Ed., pp. 129–141).

Cordain, L., et al. (2004). Origins and Evolution of the Western Diet: Health Implications for the 21st Century. *The American Journal of Clinical Nutrition*, 81, 341–354.

Dippel, H., et al. (2005). *Das Weinlexikon*. Frankfurt: Fischer.

Dosi, G. (1982). Technological Paradigms and Technological Trajectories: A Suggested Interpretation of the Determinants and Directions of Technical Change. *Research Policy*, 11/3, 147–162.

Fleuchaus, R., & Arnold, R. (ed.). (2011). *Weinmarketing: Kundenwünsche erforschen, Zielgruppen identifizieren, innovative Produkte entwickeln*. Wiesbaden: Gabler.

Glöckner, W. (2007). *Arbeit und Arbeitsmarkt* (Dreyer, Ed., pp. 195–242).

Gönnewein, O. (1963). Zur Geschichte des Weinbaurechts. *Zeitschrift der Savigny-Stiftung für Rechtsgeschichte*, s.n.c., 157–196.

Grabmayer, J. (2012). *Europa im späten Mittelalter 1250–1500: Eine Kultur- und Mentalitätsgeschichte*. Darmstadt: WBG.

Greten, V. (2005). *Ludwig Gall: moderner Ökonom seiner Zeit.* Hamburg: Dr. Kovač.

Grigg, D. (1995). The Nutrition Transition in Western Europe. *Journal of Historical Geography*, 21/3, 247–261.

Hentschel, K. (2003). Der Vergleich als Brücke zwischen Wissenschaftsgeschichte und Wissenschaftstheorie. *Journal for General Philosophy of Science*, 34, 251–275.

Heßler, M. (2012). *Kulturgeschichte der Technik*. Frankfurt: Campus.

Hobsbawn, E. (2013). *Introduction: Inventing Traditions* (Hobsbawn & Ranger, Ed., pp. 1–14).

Hofbauer, O. (1929). *Handbuch der praktischen Kellerwirtschaft*. Bolzano: Eichler.

Jackson, R. (2014). *Wine and Science: Principles and Applications*. Oxford: Elsevier.

Jenemann, H. R. (1990). *Zur Geschichte der Dichtebestimmung von Flüssigkeiten insbesondere des Traubenmostes in Oechsle-Graden*. Wiesbaden: Wiesbadener Graphische Betriebe.

Klein, J. (1934). *Der Wein und die rheinische Industrie – Ein Beitrag zur rheinischen Wirtschaftsgeschichte*. Köln: Druckerei des Studentenwerkes.

Koch, H.-J. (1993). Wechselwirkungen zwischen Weinbaugeschichte, Weinrecht und Weinkultur. *Geschichtliche Landeskunde: Veröffentlichungen des Instituts für geschichtliche Landeskunde der Universität Mainz*, 40, 223–243.

Laufner, R. (1987). *Weinbau, Weingenuß und Weinhandel im Trierer Land vom Jahre 1000 bis 1814* (Cüppers & Laufner, Ed., p. 55).

Lea, A. G. H., & Pigott, J. (ed.). (2003). *Fermented Beverage Production*. New York: Springer.

Mahlerwein, G. (2012). *Wirtschaftsgeschichte* (Clemens, Felten, & Schnettger, Ed., pp. 673–694).

Maringer, A. (2014). *Weinrecht und Verbraucherschutz: vom Alten Reich bis zur Gegenwart unter besonderer Berücksichtigung des Anbaugebiets Mosel*. Tübingen: Mohr Siebeck.

Matheus, M. (1980). Die Mosel – ältestes Rieslinganbaugebiet Deutschlands? *Landeskundliche Vierteljahresblätter*, 29, 161–173.

Meyer, F. (1926). *Weinbau und Weinhandel an der Mosel, Saar und Ruwer*. Koblenz: Verlag der Westdruckerei.

Meyer, F. (1934). Einführung und Verbreitung des Rieslings an der Mosel: Beitrag zur Wirtschaftsgeschichte des Moseltals. *Rheinische Heimatblätter*, 1934/1, 80–87.

Meyer, J. (1852). *Meyers Konversations-Lexikon*. Hildburghausen: Bibliogr. Inst.

Meyer, J. (1888). *Meyers Konversations-Lexikon*. Leipzig: Bibliogr. Inst.

Monz, H. (1981). Ludwig Gall: Retter der Moselwinzer oder Weinfälscher. *Schriften zur Weingeschichte*, 57, 3–32.

Müller, C. A. (1898). *Die Provinzial-Weinbauschule zu Trier*. Trier: Jakob Lintz.

Nordblom, P. (2012). *Wirtschaftsgeschichte* (Clemens, Felten, & Schnettger, Ed., pp. 259–328).

Paul, H. W. (1996). *Science, Vine, and Wine in Modern France*. Cambridge: Cambridge University Press.

Pelger, H. (1973). Karl Marx und die rheinpreußische Weinkrise. *Archiv für Sozialgeschichte*, 13, 309–375.

Phillips, R. (2000). *A Short History of Wine*. London: Allen Lane.

Pilz, H. (2016). In der Kostenfalle. *Weinwirtschaft*, 17, 16–20.

Schimank, U. (2006). *Rationalitätsfiktion in der Entscheidungsgesellschaft* (Tänzler, Knoblauch, & Soeffner, Ed., pp. 57–81).

Simon, A. (1920). *The Blood of Grape: The Wine Textbook*. London: Duckworth.

Simpsons, J. (2011). *Creating Wine: The Emergence of a World Industry, 1840–1914*. Princeton: Princeton University Press.

Stöckl, A. F. (2011). *Wein und Tourismus: Faktoren emotionaler Konsumentenbindung*. Diss., Kiel.

Treiling, T. (2009). *Mensch/Natur-Interaktion im Oberen Mittelrheintal: Komplexitätstheoretische Ansätze am Beispiel des Weinbaus*. Diss., Mainz.

Treue, W. (1984). *Wirtschafts- und Technikgeschichte Preussens*. Berlin: Walter de Gruyter.

Troost, G. (1986). *Zur Geschichte der Weinfiltration*. Wiesbaden: Wiesbadener Graphische Betriebe.

von Bassermann-Jordan, F. (1975). *Geschichte des Weinbaus*. Frankfurt: Frankfurter Verlags-Anstalt.

Weinreb, A. (2011). The Tastes of Home: Cooking the Lost Heimat in West Germany in the 1950s and 1960s. *German Studies Review*, 34/2, 345–365.

University Papers and Documents Online

Deutsches Weinbauinstitut (ed.). (2015). *Aktuelles Weinrecht.* Retrieved from https://www.deutscheweine.de/fileadmin/user_upload/.../Aktuelles_Weinrecht.pdf.

VDP. Prädikatsweingüter (ed.). (2016). *Die Geschichte des Bundesverbandes.* Retrieved from https://www.vdp.de/de/vdp/geschichte/geschichte-des-bundesverbands/.

Verwaltung der Bischöflichen Weingüter Trier GbR (ed.). (2016). *Bischöfliche Weingüter Trier.* Retrieved from http://www.bischoeflicheweingueter.de/en/wine-estate.html.

The Mountain Wine, 1800–1900: Case Studies from the Provinces of Sondrio and Trento

Claudio Besana and Andrea Maria Locatelli

Introduction

Grapes and wine of the Valtellina (Lombardy) and Trentino-Alto Adige area are fully integrated products in a polycultural economy (Lorenzetti 2012). It is useful to explain the path from a residual factor and self-consumption good to primary and quality crops. In the late Middle Ages and in the Modern Age the spaces dedicated to the oenology are linked to feudal and collective rules for land management. In both cases, up to the late nineteenth century, this winemaking system is an expression of the perpetuation of ancient customs, handed down between generations, and with a destination for local consumption. Moreover, especially in Valtellina, a niche production for the European markets becomes a peculiarity of the territory.

C. Besana (✉) · A. M. Locatelli
Università Cattolica del Sacro Cuore, Milan, Italy
e-mail: claudio.besana@unicatt.it

A. M. Locatelli
e-mail: andreamaria.locatelli@unicatt.it

S. A. Conca Messina et al. (eds.), *A History of Wine in Europe, 19th to 20th Centuries, Volume I*, Palgrave Studies in Economic History,
https://doi.org/10.1007/978-3-030-27772-7_5

Wine in this territory is an essential element to analyse the exit route from phases of long stagnation in the mountain area. With the eighteenth century, a strong reduction in production and a crisis of oenology takes shape with a dramatic slowdown in the mid-nineteenth century. There is another negative factor: the loss of substantial trade flows after that Valtellina and Trentino—Alto Adige become part of the Kingdom of Italy. During the long crisis in the nineteenth century, the Alpine territories seem incapable of generating processes of resilience and the reduction of the oenological activity feeds a financial and income crisis, that has its outlet in emigration. The condition of productive and qualitative regression remains until the 40s of the twentieth century and the two World Wars represent a further factor of perturbation. Only in the 50s in the two areas a product qualification appears with a stronger intensity in the Trentino area than in Valtellina.

"The land of Valtellina, surrounded by fearsome mountains, makes strong, heady wines" (Leonardo da Vinci, Codex Atlanticus) (in notes in the Introduction).

The Valtellina Viticulture

In 1858 Stefano Jacini described the vineyards in the territory of the province of Sondrio in this way: "What truly is a vineyard in Valtellina? Most of the time it is nothing more than a bare rock on which the farmer builds a little wall to hold the earth with which he has covered the rock, carrying it on his shoulders from the bottom of the valley" (Jacini 1858, p. 14). The cultivation of the vine in Valtellina has ancient origins. Certainly, the vast communication network within the Rhaetian Alps favoured the wine trade, but the cultivation of the vine was reinforced by the changes in landownership (Lorenzetti 2010). In the Rhaetian area of Lombardy, from the Visconti and Sforza lordships up to the Swiss domains, the wine trade became very important and its management acted as a factor of consolidation in the system of local government. During the sixteenth century the population increase pushed new land into use for the cultivation of the vine, even though such investment involved a heavy work commitment.

The sector's growth is also explained by the investment choices of some of the important families of Graubünden which, from the middle of the seventeenth century, acquired land in Valtellina and Val Chiavenna, strengthening a long-lasting productive and commercial tie between the two sides of the Alps. The commercial success of the Valtellina wines was mainly due to the high alcohol content, which increased their shelf-life (Besana and Locatelli 2019).

The cultivation of grapes was made possible by the particular east–west orientation of the Valtellina, the protection that came from the chain of mountains (Rhaetian and Orobian Alps), which gave shelter from the cold North winds and the humid winds from the South; while the nearby Lake Como, with its warm breeze, acted as a thermal controller (Locatelli and Tedeschi 2018).[1] In his 1859 illustrated guide to Lombardy-Venetia, Cesare Cantù described some wines from Valtellina which had an established reputation: "those wines of Sassella, Grumello, Inferno, Ronscio and Grigione, and all those around Sondrio; also those of Teglio, Bianzone and Villa; they are all rich in alcohol and carbonic acid gas, containing little colouring matter but much tartaric acid. The 'Sforzato' wines of Tirano, Villa and Bianzone have also been praised, as has the raisin wine, strong Chiavenna, made from dry grapes held in barrels that are never emptied, but refilled every year" (Cantù, 5/1, 1857–1861).

In the nineteenth century, the districts of Tirano, Ponte and Sondrio were the major wine producers in the province (Sassella-Sondrio; Inferno-Poggidirenti; Grumello—Montagna; Grigione—Castione Andevenno). In the Val Chiavenna, on the other hand, they cultivated vines that produced a white grape. In 1800 there were 81,113 vine canes producing 160,000 bunches (Rullani 1973). Half of what was produced was exported to Graubünden, to nearby Comasco, to the area of Milan and, through the Stelvio pass, to the Tyrol and Voralberg.

With the annexation to the Cisalpine republic and then to the Kingdom of Lombardy–Venetia, a potentially vast market was opened:

[1] The area has a consistent brightness, with a maximum of 70 cloudy days, constant breezes and low rainfall. The acid PH of the soils (3.2–3.5) gives a high level of acidity to the wines.

it could favour oenological specialization over against the importation of cheap grain. Between 1813 and 1817 a strong increase in wine prices was recorded, although that did not trigger structural changes, due to the widespread desire to remain faithful to the traditions of winemaking. This conservative attitude did not favour any growth in yield; the defence of tradition arose rather from the need to expand the workforce to respond to the continuous growth of the population (Besana and Locatelli 2019). The need for jobs among agricultural workers' families coincided with the desire of the landowners to extend their vineyards. In 1845, according to Habsburg statistics, production had doubled since the start of the nineteenth century. This growth was the result of the extension of terracing and the disappearance of the chestnut at the foot of the mountains on the right side of the Adda. It was a purely quantitative increase, accompanied by a deterioration in the quality of the wines, since the new land that was converted to vineyards was little suited to this type of cultivation.

The period of significant expansion of the vineyard was between the 1830s and 1840s (Besana 2001, pp. 349–351). However, at this point of maximum expansion, the sector was affected by a serious crisis. As in other winegrowing areas, between 1849 and 1859 the Valtellina vines were hit by a cryptogam (Romani 1957; Stranieri and Tedeschi 2015, pp. 173–180). The collapse in wine production led to a sharp decline in farm incomes, which had already been reduced by the increased land taxes as a result of the introduction of the new land register of the Kingdom of Lombardy–Venetia (see Table 1). The volume of wine produced dropped sharply, from 105,644 hl in 1838 to 2781 hl in 1854. The damage caused by the cryptogam was made worse by the anticipation of the expected

Table 1 Surface of vineyards (ha) and production of wine (hl)

Surface (ha)			
1828	4135	1939	4341
1900	5371[a]	1950	3800
Production (hl)			
1847	80,000	1900	205,303
1857	30,331	1950	88,436

[a]with restored vineyards, data is unreliable
Source Rullani 1973, vol. 1, pp. 108–109

grape harvest in the province of Sondrio and by the continuing inadequacy of the winemaking methods, which kept yields low. The tragic crisis was not properly dealt with, both in terms of the weak response of the local communities and of the broader institutions and the chronic lack of appropriate agricultural knowledge among peasant farmers. It was only from 1859 that more decisive state intervention, and the resulting campaign of rural education, succeeded in spreading practices capable of halting the scourge, especially the practice of vine sulphurization.[2]

This serious crisis was overcome in the early 1870s, when wine production reached 120,000 hectolitres, with exports abroad ranging from 30,000 to 40,000 quintals (Bozzi 1876, p. 32).[3] The new phase was related to the role of Società Enologica Valtellinese (Valtellina Wine Association), established in 1872. Production was admittedly limited, but the proportion exported was very high, certainly higher than that recorded nationally (Cova 1989, pp. 322–323).[4] The recovery was supported by wineries that were dedicated to the commercialization of their products, also in the foreign markets, and among these the Valtellina wine company stood out (Bozzi 1876, pp. 31–32).[5]

The overcoming the mildew crisis was not accompanied by any significant modernization in the techniques of vine cultivation; and for this reason, too, the sector suffered from the difficult endogenous and exogenous conditions. The splitting up of the vineyards, encouraged by the "rent system", did not favour the adoption of innovative techniques in vine cultivation and pest control. There were new outbreaks of disease in the second half of the 1870s, when the local vineyards were attacked by mildew and, above all, by phylloxera. The latter, in particular, led to a drop in land values. This was exacerbated by the need, as

[2]It should be noted that already by 1854 the Royal Imperial Lieutenancy had issued an instruction to combat mildew.

[3]In 1870s exports to the other provinces of the Kingdom of Italy reached a maximum of 3000 quintals.

[4]For example, in the first half of the 1890s, the national production was of about 31 million hl, exports abroad did not reach 2 million hl.

[5]Founded in the 1860s, the company was equipped with machines for the mechanical processing of the grapes; the two cellars of the oenological plant could store approximately 15,000 hl of wines.

in other places affected by the parasite, to effect the complete recreation of the vineyards, with the replacement of the traditional vines with American stock; the trunk was then grafted with traditional varieties.

As a result, there were further falls in production, which took place during a period of low prices. By the 1880s, even this corner of Lombardy fully experienced the national agrarian crisis, with the prices of all agricultural products falling. In this context the condition of the Valtellina and Chiavenna wine industry was further worsened, causing even greater unwillingness to invest and innovate. The falls in production and the low grape and wine yields combined to increase production costs, resulting in a sharp drop in income and widespread social distress.

Within this context, there was a significant increase in the indebtedness of farming families and the beginnings of a strong movement towards permanent emigration. The difficulties within the sector were aggravated by changes in the trading routes as a result of political events in the 1860s. Italian unification and the development of the railway network brought Piedmont wine to the Lombard market, as well as those of the South. The former was superior in quality to those of the province of Sondrio, while the latter were more appreciated for their very low prices (Cova 1989, p. 323).[6] By the 1880s, there were also changes in the trade with the Swiss Confederation (Lorenzetti 2005). The opening of the Gotthard tunnel alienated Valtellina from the markets of the Swiss hinterland, which for centuries had been important sales destinations for wines produced in the Lombard valley; while the upgrading of the European rail network favoured the arrival of French products on the Swiss market (Bonoldi et al. 2016).

Overall, in the first 50 years after Italian unification, winemaking in Valtellina saw periods of expansion in production and moments of great difficulty, experiencing also a strong decline in reputation.

[6]The unification of the national market placed the Valtellina vineyards within a context that was subject to hard competition. It should be remembered that wine production in Italy continued to grow in the final decades of the nineteenth century and in the first fifteen years of the twentieth century. While at the end of the 1870s, production was predicted to reach 20 million hl, on the eve of the First World War it exceeded 40 million hl in a year. A production that was "largely in excess of domestic consumption".

The difficulties in reforming production techniques and in aiming for a more refined product contributed to a decline in the entire sector. The problems in the industry, however, had a positive effect on farming families, to whom the cultivation of the vineyards and the grape production had always been entrusted. These years saw the start of a phase of social mobility, with smallholders becoming full owners of the land that they had worked for generations in return for the payment of a fee.[7]

In other words, Valtellinese winemaking seemed to be a long way from embracing new innovative processes related to crop mechanization and the introduction of chemical processes relating particularly to pressing, fermentation and ageing of the wine. The cellars of the landowners and peasants continued to be used for the production and storage of the wine; and both were unsuitable for mass production, which required large spaces. In a very few cases, crushers and destemmers were introduced, as well as presses driven by steam engines, which allowed a more careful selection and classification of the grapes. There was also little done to stabilize the wine, through pasteurization and the use of hydraulic pumps to speed up the flow of the liquid. More generally, among the winemakers of the Sondrio province there was little awareness of any link between the ageing potential and the essential character of the wine that allowed, among other things, storage in bottles. The latter quickly showed itself as the best tool for building a strong response to market demands.

From Crisis to Rebirth: Valtellina Wine in the Twentieth Century

The recovery of viticulture and the reopening of the markets for Valtellina and Chiavenna wine took place from the 1920s. After the First World War, there were 4500 ha in cultivation (see Table 1). The measures put in place by the various authorities and by the associations allowed the winegrowers to complete the reforms that finally led to a growth in

[7]The greater social mobility is more marked during the First World War and in the phase after 1918. It should be noted that in those years of high inflation the transfer was calculated according to the average prices of the previous decade.

production to 16,200 quintals of grapes in 1922, settling down to about 12,000 quintals per annum for the 1920s as a whole. The Valtellina vineyard returned again to the averages of the second half of the nineteenth century. The recovery came to a halt in 1925, but there were still several important achievements, including the completion of the reconstruction of the vines on American stock, organized by the President of the Provincial anti-phylloxera consortium. At the same time the winemaking and distribution structures were reformed—albeit modestly—by concentrating the two stages in cooperatives or with wholesalers. This coincided with the transfer to the farmers of all produce to be sold; but there were still problems, such as the low prices paid for the produce, considering the large amount of work required, as well as the small size of the farms. For a qualitative leap, it was also necessary to move away from the traditional reliance on the Swiss market, increasing the presence in the Italian market and renewing its performance in Germany. With the advent of the global crisis from 1929, the sector experienced difficulties for many years, causing production and trade to stagnate.

During the 1930s there was a net reduction in the extent of the vineyards. In 1939, 4341 ha were planted with vines, producing about 100,000 hl. Between the 1930s and 1950s wine production in Valtellina continued the system and production levels inherited from the long nineteenth century. In addition, the tendency to abandon agriculture in order to emigrate or to try to enter the manufacturing sector meant that viticulture was considered particularly arduous and passé. If one compares grape and wine production for 1897 and 1949, there are similar yields, indicating a qualitative improvement in viticulture. Indeed in 1949, 7380 quintals of grapes were produced and 13,300 hl of wine were put on the market. More specifically, a decline in arable land was recorded after 1945 in the Valtellina and Chiavenna regions, with the return of the predominant trade patterns and the disappearance of the last pockets of mulberry cultivation. On the other hand the conversion to pasture land expanded in line with national trends. Within this context, viticulture experienced a recovery, both in terms of the area under cultivation and in the yields produced, thus allowing a new start in winemaking. In 1950 the area under cultivation was still below that of the war period, with 3800 ha producing about 88,436 hl.

Table 2 Vine cultivation and wine production in the province of Sondrio

Year	Area (ha)	Grape (quintals)	Vinified (quintals)	Wine (hl)
1952	3827	152,100	153,700	104,500
1953	3856	204,600	206,500	142,500
1956	4016	183,200	182,800	118,800
1960	3915	248,100	248,100	148,800
1964	3900	215,000	213,600	160,400
1967	3820	247,900	246,800	181,100
1970	2702	266,100	264,100	184,900
1973	2812	290,000	288,000	201,500
1975	2798	272,200	272,200	185,100
1979	2811	258,400	258,400	180,900
1980	2330	228,000	228,000	159,600

Source Istat, *Annuario di statistica agraria*, Rome (1954–1981)

The data point to a structural problem in terms of the yield. This trend went hand in hand with the development of fruit growing. The revival in the cultivation of the vine, however, was marked by high-quality research in the product, while continuing to value the traditional outlets in the Swiss market.

In the early 1950s, Valtellina produced 230,000 quintals of grapes and 160,000 hl of wine on an average of 3900 ha (see Table 2). The average yield per hectare was 60 quintals, which was below the national average. Essentially there had been a contraction in the area planted compared to the beginning of the twentieth century, with some land abandoned; but above all, we see the conversion of many vineyards to other crops. The surveys carried out by the Chamber of Commerce show a shortage of labour, and at the same time a growth in the wages of workers, caused also by the difficulties associated with mechanization.[8] There were only a few wineries with adequate equipment for commercial winemaking, while there were major problems in vine cultivation. Many plants were very old, with very bent or twisted branches, and suffered

[8]In general, the cultivation of the vine was characterized by planting at a depth of about one metre, with the extensive use of manure; the cuttings were placed in rows 1.30–1.50 metres apart, with 1.40–1.70 metres between rows; the rows were laid out on the maximum slope line, with a north–south orientation; the system of training and pruning ranged from the simple Guyot to the multiple Guyot; the main grape varieties were Chiavennasca, Nebbiolo, Rossola and Pignola.

from over-topping, made worse by insufficient use of fertilizer. In 1953 the Chamber of Commerce, in consultation with the wine station of Conegliano, began to experiment with grape varieties from outside the valley such as Cabernet, Merlot and Sangiovese. The aim was to combine these grapes with local varieties to produce a wine for mass consumption.

Many areas claimed an increase in production, with an improvement in the cultivation techniques and more constant irrigation to counter the summer droughts. A reduction in the area planted with vines was also planned, in favour of the cultivation of nuts and/or fruit. The new techniques included using chemical fertilizer annually, as well as organic fertilizer periodically, together with a refinement of the pruning process. The mechanization programme involved investment for cableways, for piping networks for fungicidal treatments and for the distribution of motor pumps. An improvement in the quality of the ordinary wine was achieved, as well as with the introduction of new grape varieties, by using collective winemaking processes. For this, it was necessary to increase the number of winemaking cooperatives and reduce the excessive fragmentation of the cultivated land.

Between the mid-1950s and the early 1960s there was an increase in the area put under cultivation of the vine, and this was accompanied by an increase in grape production and especially in the quantities of wine made. This trend was particularly strong in the second half of the 1950s, which saw a significant increase in yields. From the second half of the 1960s there was a turnaround, with a reduction in the area under cultivation and in production levels; however, the relationship between the two variables indicates an improvement in the yield. A piece of legislation in line with the dictates of the EEC seemed to change the picture: the Presidential Decree of 1968 recognized the "Controlled Designation of Origin" status for wines produced in the most prestigious areas. Production was regulated with the demarcation of the production areas "Valtellina superiore" (c. 700 ha) and "Valtellina" (c. 1500 ha).[9]

[9]Valtellina Superiore DOCG Decree 11 November 2002–G.U. 27 November 2002. It replaced Decree 24 June 1998. Terraces of clay and silicon up to 600 metres above sea level. Nebbiolo is the vine that is cultivated according to the Guyot system. The wines have a ruby colour verging on garnet, and after a good period of ageing the tones fade towards orange. The aromas are intense

The Chamber of Commerce and the Agricultural Inspectorate, together with associations such as the Consortium for the Protection of DOC Wines of Valtellina, initiated programmes for promotion and development. At the same time, some cooperatives also allowed small farmers to market the product while larger enterprises were developed. As in other cases, the gaining of "designation of origin" status by the product led to foreign companies becoming interested; in Valtellina these took control of some of the largest wine producers. From 1968, with the legal tools in place to ensure its own production rating, the area started switching to mainly producing fine bottled wines, marketed always in Switzerland. The enhancement of the product followed a different path from that of associations looking after the dairy and fruit sectors, since it was able to attract private capital for the management of wine estates or of cellars for winemaking and distribution. In some cases, the entrepreneurial spirit in the winemaking sector, linked with the initiatives of wholesalers, has long been present in the territory. The Winemaking Company was absorbed by the Italian Federation of Agricultural Associations and there was a winemaking cooperative at Villa Tirano, but most of the production escaped the world of cooperatives and was done on private wine estates, where the commercial bourgeoisie rediscovered agricultural life.

All the private wineries that developed from the 1970s focused on the rediscovery and reappraisal of traditional grape varieties: Nebbiolo (Chiavennasca) for the production of Valtellina Superiore and Sforzato DOC, Rossola Nera, which was subsequently updated through cloning, and Pignola Valtellinese; but some entrepreneurial farmers introduced

and quite persistent, with hints of red fruit and jams, spices and leather. Following the path of the vineyards from west to east, about thirty kilometres along, you find the Sassella, then Grumello, the more structured and austere Inferno and finally the less complex Valgella Sforzato (DOCG recognized by Decree 19 March 2003–G.U. 7 April 2003). The "Sfurzat" is a special wine made from the harvest grape in October, from selection of the finest grapes-vine (Nebbiolo–Chiavennasca) and by drying on racks in dry and airy rooms, a process which takes more than three months. The traditional red vinification process is prolonged by a few weeks, and this leads to a wine of great structure, strong alcohol content and great softness: Valtellina Rosso (Decree 19 March 2003–G.U. 7 April 2003 replaced Decree 26 June 1998–G.U. 10 July 1998 and D.P.R. 11 August 1968).

Cabernet Sauvignon and Chardonnay. Some wineries that found new life with DOC status had a long history: an example is the Nino Negri, founded in 1897 to trade in the Nebbiolo grape, which was acquired at the end of the 1960s by the Swiss company Winefood, as a result of succession problems within the family. The Swiss experience was not particularly successful, and only cooperation between local winemakers allowed the business to continue.[10] Another example of entrepreneurship was the acquisition in 1969 of the so-called "La Gatta" estate by the Triacca family. In the sixteenth century the estate was a monastery of Dominican friars, and later became the residence of the noble De Gatti family, who in turn sold the property to the Mascioni's, a family of bourgeois merchants.

There was a further decrease in the cultivation of the vine from 1970, from an average of 3820 ha (1967) to 2811 ha (1979), while grape production and winemaking reached an average of about 271,000 quintals during the 1970s. In the province of Sondrio, 184,900 hl of wine was produced in 1970 and 180,900 in 1979, showing substantial stability in production levels (see Table 2). As already stated, from the 1970s various foreign wine companies invested in the acquisition of vineyards and in winemaking and the marketing of the product. In particular, many Swiss (from the Graubünden canton) and Germans (from the Meuse region) acquired plots of vineyards and made the Sassella and Sforzato wines, reinvigorating the traditions of these two typical wines of the valley through their techniques and commercial strategies. At the same time, local wholesalers like the Rainoldi family entered the world of winemaking. In the second half of the nineteenth century, Giuseppe Rainoldi ran a business trading grain before moving on to wine. In 1925 his son Aldo opened a winery for the sale of Nebbiolo wine in Switzerland, made in small chestnut barrels. From the mid-1950s, after the commercial difficulties of the 1930s, wineries concentrated on the bottling of the wines and on the expansion of the sales network in the European and North American markets (Stranieri and Tedeschi 2015, pp. 190–192).

[10]In 1986 the Swiss company sold the cooperative Vini Scaril, which itself had incorporated two other historic companies, Pellizzotti and Enologia Valtellinese. Later, these wineries entered the Gruppo Italiano Vini.

During the 1980s, some producers from Valtellina were faced with structural changes in the wine market. The application of the "controlled origin" status encouraged the development of production with a strong territorial focus, which at the same time responded effectively to the demands of the niche consumer. The recognition of the wine as a drink for refined taste palates, together with the success of the glass bottle as a sales tool, meant that the wine of Valtellina became a specialized product based on the identity of that particular area.

The process led in 1998 to the presentation of the Valtellina superiore DOCG to the public, with the first bottles appearing in Milan on 1 December 2000.[11] The DOCG is divided into four subzones, following the path of the vineyards from west to east for about thirty kilometres: Sassella, Grumello, Inferno and Valgella.[12]

On average in the first decade of the twenty-first century 2046 winemakers were registered 2046 with DOCG, DOC and IGT status, covering a total area of 1250 ha. The average age of the plants was 60 years, using a modified Guyot training system, while the average density of the crops was 4220 vines/hectare. Typically the farm was run directly, while there was only one wine cooperative (Villa di Tirano). There were 25 companies and/or wineries that produced Valtellina superiore, including those based in Valposchiavo in Switzerland. Indeed, the Valtellina DOC is the only Italian wine with a physical presence in foreign territory: there is a combined Italian-Swiss headquarters, and Swiss ownership of Valtellina vineyards. Most Valtellina DOC wines were sold in Italy (40%), while 25% was exported to Germany, Switzerland, USA and Japan; the remaining 35% was sold in the province of Sondrio. To manage the production system the Consortium of Valtellina wines was set up, the only one in Italy, which represented all the Italian and Swiss winemakers and bottlers.

---

[11]The first bottle was presented in Milan on 1 December 2000.

[12]Decree 24 June 1998 and DOCG with Decree 11 November 2002.

Trentino-Tyrolean Wine

Trentino and South Tyrol, like Valtellina, already boasted a winemaking tradition in the early modern period within a typical "ancien régime" economy characterized by multiple jobs. Feudalism came to an end in the seventeenth century, replaced both by large tracts of land which were often owned collectively and by fragmented landholdings, partly determined by the unbalanced relationship between the population and the available resources (Andreolli 1989; Alberti 1901).

It was an agricultural system determined in the first place by the goal to meet the consumption needs of the local population, based on the distribution of land among smallholdings that were directly cultivated and large collectively owned holdings (Leonardi 1996, pp. 15–28).[13] The situation changed in the second half of the eighteenth century, when the wine sector which, as mentioned before, boasted a centuries-old tradition, managed to raise production levels to not only meet local demand but also to contribute to the export economy. This was particularly evident in the valleys south of the Brenner Pass, where produce was sold in the Habsburg Empire and Bavaria. Even in these areas, however, the excessive ties with tradition led to low yields and to the packaging of poor quality wines (Zaninelli 1979, pp. 24–34).

Institutionally, between the eighteenth and nineteenth centuries the Trentino-Tyrolean area experienced profound changes, with the disappearance of the Episcopal Principalities of Brixen and Trent and then the establishment of the Bavarian and Italian-French domains in 1806–1815. In economic terms, it moved from a "war economy" to the so-called "Bavarian reforms", which aimed to reduce the hold of feudalism and to encourage trade in local products, especially silk and wine.

[13]The "*maso chiuso*" was an indivisible alpine farm handed down as a whole to the male firstborn. It was recorded in a land register called *libro fondiario*. In the German speaking area there was the principle of primogeniture covering all of the property owned by an extended family, and in this case the share of collective goods was reduced. More specifically, as in all the Alpine mountainous areas, a variety of crops prevailed, with specialized vineyards, where the "double pergola" was widespread, remaining relatively rare; while in the areas of the plains mixed cultivation prevailed. Vines and mulberry trees alternated with arable crops, mainly cereals or potatoes, while only small strips of land were planted for forage crops or with fruit trees. In terms of agricultural practices, the Trentino region was not different from other Alpine regions, with a lack of adequate fertilizers and rotation of crops.

An initial deployment of more advanced agronomic knowledge came during the period of French rule, thanks to the action of Filippo Re (Zaninelli 1998); later, with the return of the entire region to the Habsburg empire, the Society for Agricultural Reform was established (1838), which however had a very troubled existence (Gregorini 2003).

In the first half of the nineteenth century, the agricultural system as a whole suffered from a lack of capital, and manufacturing did not offer a serious alternative. The wine sector benefited from technical innovation less than other sectors, and wine production fluctuated (see Graph 1). In 1828, 323,931 hl were produced, while in 1832 it dropped to 244,086 hl; in 1847 estimates point to 447,085 hl (Leonardi 1996, pp. 65–75). From 1848, as a response to the attempted revolutions of that year, a new "neo-absolutist" government was formed to create the legal and administrative conditions for an economic take off, while also undertaking agrarian reform to finally undermine feudalism.

Trentino-Tyrolean viticulture suffered from the cryptogam crisis to the same degree as that of Valtellina. Between the 1850s and 1860s wine production in the Austrian Tyrol fell to almost 80%, from about 447,085 hl in 1847 to 89,417 hl. The initial response was the sulphur treatment promoted by Ludwig von Comini Sommerberg (Zaninelli 1979, pp. 172–178). Having overcome this crisis, the sector grew in the following years, thanks also to the associations beginning to take action to improve techniques: the Agricultural Society of Rovereto in 1869, the Trentino Agricultural Association in 1870 and the Agricultural Institute and Experimental Station of San Michele all'Adige in 1874 (Zaninelli 1979, p. 177). In line with the policies of the Viennese government of Taaffe, for the rationalization of agricultural resources and the modernization of techniques in the primary sector, the Provincial Council of Agriculture was set up in 1879. The creation of this institution was the beginning, in this region, of direct state intervention to instigate innovation in the rural world. The council began to reorganize and update the regulation of landownership and the *maso chiuso*. Initiatives were also provided for the development of viticulture and the wine trade, which led to a sharp turnaround for the crop; the area planted with vines, that had decreased to 1718 ha in 1874, climbed to 6250 ha in 1890 and then reached 16,353 ha in 1912 (Leonardi 1996, pp. 115–123).

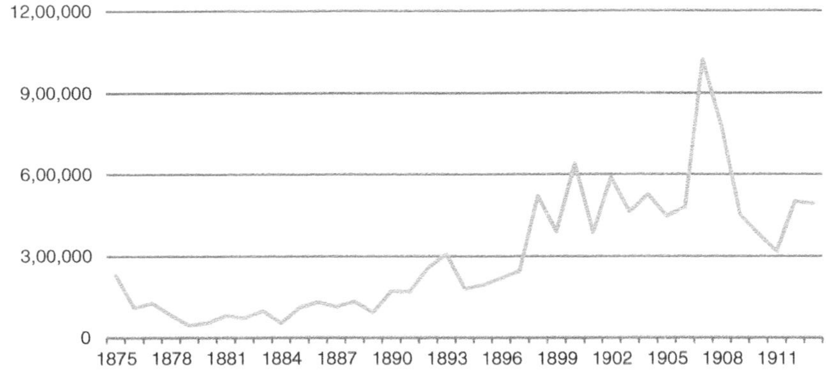

Graph 1 Wine production in Trentino—hectolitres (1875–1914) (Use dark colours) (*Source* Leonardi 1996, p. 173)

This growth was not linear. The spread of new parasitic diseases produced a decline in the harvests. As per the graph, wine production fell between 1875 and 1880, from 230,260 to 45,220 hl. In the 1880s it gradually recovers, thanks to institutional and entrepreneurial intervention, and it peaks in 1893 (307,310 hl) before levelling off in the following years at around 220,000 hl. A new period of growth began in 1898, lasting until 1907 (1,002,459 hl); then over the following years there was a substantial decline again, as a result also of the economic crisis that preceded the Great War (Leonardi 1996, pp. 169–172).

While the development of the railroad questioned the area's international role as a transit region, some organizations—and in particular the Agricultural Institute of San Michele directed by Edmund Mach, played an important part in combating the crisis by taking preventative action against phylloxera.[14] At the same time, the sector profited from the

[14]On 12 January 1874, the Tyrolean Regional Diet of Innsbruck decided to start an agricultural college with adjoining Experimental Station at San Michele all'Adige. Edmund Mach, the first director, is seen as the founder of the Institute. He came from the "Stazione sperimentale" (Experimental Station) of Klosterneuburg near Vienna and had a brief but intense career as a researcher in the field of agricultural chemistry and oenology. Mach was an excellent organizer and innovator, and he was instrumental in outlining the basic principles for an approach to activities both at school and in the laboratory. Mach, like other innovative agronomists, said that research and teaching should not proceed separately but rather constitute an inseparable pair upon which to build the foundations for

growth of the "cooperative movement". Indeed, since the late 1880s the cooperatives had contributed to the rationalization of the production process, to the improvement of wine storage practices and the strengthening of the sales network, operating particularly to reduce the competition of Italian wines in the markets of the Habsburg monarchy (Leonardi 1976; Del Fabro and Morelli De Rossi 1986).[15] It should be mentioned that the cooperative system gradually assumed a composite form, where the Tyrolean experience adopted the Raiffeisen model, with an emphasis on credit for the German area, while on the Italian side there was a concentration on consumer and agricultural interests (Leonardi 2002).

The founding of the cooperative cellar in Mezzocorona (1907) was something of a turning point. The process of founding the cellar brought together the wealthier proprietors and in 1912 recorded 50 members (Leonardi 2005). The initial aim was mutual support for the management of commercial activities, aiming to stabilize relations with customers (i.e. win their loyalty). Imitating this experiment, the League of Farmers was founded in 1911: based in Mezzocorona, it also aimed to manage the process of marketing the wine in an orderly way.

This system, now based on mutualism and cooperation and able to give a good account of itself in terms of the management of resources, was shaken up by the First World War. The financial crisis was particularly acute, with the failure of the rural bank of Mezzocorona and, as already noted, the prolonged fall in the price of grapes in line with the general decline in the prices of agricultural products (Leonardi 2002; Moioli 1987, pp. 19–46). The agricultural sector could not react to

the growth of the sector. The operational guidelines he drew up for the "Scuola" and the "Stazione sperimentale" would be continued with positive results by his successors until the transition to the Italian Institute, which took place after the First World War. In 1919, the Institute passed to the jurisdiction of the Province of Trento and in 1926 the Consortium took over the management of the institution with the Italian state.

[15]Among the more distinguished wine cooperatives were the "Associazione vinicola e viticola del Trentino" (Association of winemakers and growers of Trentino)—1888, the "Unione dei commercianti e produttori di vino del Sudtirolo Tedesco" (Union of traders and wine producers of the South Tyrol)—1890, the "Lega dei Consorzi agrari distrettuali di tipo viticolo del Sudtirolo Tedesco"(League of regional agrarian associations of winegrowers of the South Tyrol)—1893 to these should be added companies that had been operating for some time, such as the "Società Enologica di Trento" and the "Cantine Riunite di Roveret"o.

the economic downturn by reducing costs in terms of the work done, because this would mean losing income, and also capital, which was represented primarily by the workforce. The crisis was even more acute since the whole agricultural system of Trentino faced increasing difficulties in its commercial relations with the traditional Viennese markets. On the other hand, the new Italian trade routes were not a viable alternative, due also to a slowdown in consumer spending. The most dramatic time was in 1932 and 1933 with the failure of the Bank of Trentino and Alto Adige, following on from the national deflationary measures and the effects of the international crisis (Leonardi 2005).

The 1920s experienced a post-war reconstruction full of uncertainties. The period was also marked by the well-known question of the relationship between the Italian and German communities. Within this context, viticulture, fruit growing and animal husbandry became important elements of the agricultural economy in Tyrol south of the Brenner pass, within a largely new market situation. All these sectors had suffered heavy setbacks during the war years, and the preferred way, more or less, consciously followed, was to adapt the production systems inherited from the pre-war period without any particular innovative drive. Viticulture had to cope with a complete renewal of the vineyards, and in many cases the tendency was to replace the vines with fruit trees. There was also regression in that specialized vineyards became cultivated less—these fell from an average of 60 to 43.5 hl per hectare of cultivated land—and the more indiscriminate varieties recovered in favour.[16] Faced with the uncertain financial situation and stagnant consumer demand, the Piana Rotaliana tried to respond, despite increasing

[16]DOC: Casteller, Lago di Caldaro, Terodelgo Rotaliano, Trentino, Trento, Valdadige IGT (Decree 22 November 1995–G.U. 27 December 1995): Atesino delle Venezie, Vallagarina, Vigneti delle Dolomiti). Trento: Spumanti, Chardonnay, Pinot blanc and Pinot nero. Casteller is a pleasant wine with ruby red colours, not too intense and with quite delicate fruity aromas. Terodelgo Rotaliano: the land is fairly flat, with pebbly soils which support the forming of a generous and well-structured wine. The Trentino DOC (Decree 8 June 2002–G.U. 20 September 2002. It replaced the Decree 8 August 1996, the D.P.R. 4 August 1971 and subsequent amendments) is all one region. Vines are indigenous and imported. The red wines have a bright ruby colour, with fruity and floral aromas, sometimes of herbs and green peppers. Marzemino is a vine that is cultivated in Vallagarina.

difficulties, with joint action between the local authorities and the cooperative movement. In 1922 the Cantina of Mezzocorona producers was founded, which brought together another group of landowners who were not part of the catholic and cooperative sentiments of the winemaking cooperative of Mezzocorona. Common to all these initiatives was a clear enough commitment to the specific characteristics of the wine. For this reason, to maintain its market position, the Consortium of local Teroldego wines of the Piana Rotaliana was tentatively set up in 1932.[17]

The situation did not change in the years leading up to the Second World War. These years experienced stagnant production across the agricultural sector and particularly in viticulture (Agricoltura trentina 1976; Galizzi 1992; *Dossier vino* 2004). Undoubtedly the slowing down of the recovery process brought a crisis to the cooperative system, with the closure of many winemaking cooperatives. The deflationary crisis at the end of the 1920s had not severely impacted the wine sector, nor the cooperative movement in particular; however, in the 1930s, in the wake of the international economic crisis, the collapse was severe (Leonardi 2000).[18]

After the end of the war, the sector experienced a significant recovery during the 1950s. The area planted with specialized vines rose from 6667 ha in 1952 to 11,198 ha in 1960, while the production of

---

[17]The Piana Rotaliana includes the towns of Mezzolombardo, Mezzocorona, San Michele all'Adige, Roverè della Luna, Nave San Rocco and Faedo, encompassing a broader area than the geographical and historical boundaries of the plain of Trentino Alto Adige. A famous local historian, Aldo Grofer, has included in the Piana Rotaliana only the towns of Mezzocorona, Roverè della Luna and Mezzolombardo. According to Grofer, Nave San Rocco and Grumo, as well as San Michele all'Adige and Faedo, are within the Adige valley. The Piana Rotaliana was part of the Principality-Bishopric of Trent from 1004 to 1803. In the region there was the Tyrolean jurisdiction of Mezzocorona, and in the northern foothills outside Trento the bishop's jurisdiction held sway, and this included Mezzolombardo. Recently the towns of Faedo and San Michele all'Adige, belonging to other parts of the region for geographical and historical reasons, have been included within the boundaries of the Piana Rotaliana. In the past they were part of the jurisdiction of Montereale/Königsberg, adjacent with that of Mezzocorona at the Adige river. At this purpose see Gorfer 1990.

[18]In South Tyrol 60% of the Raiffeisenkassen disappeared (81 out of 135). In Trentino the crisis of the rural banks was not as severe as in the South Tyrolean valleys, but it was still significant: 60 institutions were placed in liquidation.

Table 3 Vine cultivation and wine production in the province of Trento

	Area (ha)		Grapes produced (quintals)		Vinified grapes (quintals)	Wine (hl)
	Specialized	Mixed	From specialized cultivation	From mixed cultivation		
1952	6667	17,405	474,700	358,600	773,900	557,700
1953	9774	12,121	732,200	267,400	945,500	665,900
1956	11,067	11,351	853,600	302,700	1,008,100	763,300
1960	11,198	11,073	1,127,200	329,800	1,277,200	673,800
1964	11,080	10,801	944,450	323,850	1,268,300	780,100
1968	11,182	1990	936,400	323,850	1,268,300	780,100
1972	11,372	974	1,085,900	31,700	1,107,800	798,000
1976	11,042	494	1,062,900	17,300	1,073,700	755,900
1980	10,055	240	1,278,900	9400	1,283,300	914,200

Source Istat, *Annuario di statistica agraria*, Rome (1954–1981)

grapes for wine rose from 773,900 quintals in 1952 to 1277,200 in 1960 (Annuario di Statistica agraria 1954–1985; Faustini et al. 1993; Istat Censimento 1998). Likewise the volume of wine produced rose from 557,700 to 673,800 hl in the same period. From the 1960s to the early '80s, the area planted with specialized vines stood at 11,000 ha, while there was a sharp decline in the mixed varieties. The production of grapes for winemakers stabilized at one million quintals, while the volume of wine fluctuated between 750,000 and 990,000 hl, depending on the year[19] (Table 3).

The Exception of Teroldego

Trentino is associated with mountain scenery and terraced vineyards; in comparison, the Piana Rotaliana is the exception that proves the rule (Strada del vino 2007). The so-called "Campo Rotaliano" includes the area containing the municipalities of Mezzocorona, Mezzolombardo

[19]At this stage, the winemakers are unable to increase the wine production from the same grape harvest, both through refining the techniques and through imported grapes.

and part of San Michele all'Adige (Grumo). The land is fairly flat with gravel and stony soils that favour the development of a well-structured wine (Grofer 1990). During the 1870s the existing system of polycuture for domestic consumption in the Piana Rotaliana changed into a more market-oriented agriculture. The changes were supported, and to some extent coordinated, by the aforementioned Provincial Agricultural Institute of San Michele all'Adige and by the Provincial Council of Agriculture, an agricultural development body set up by the Tyrolean provincial government. On the alluvial soils either Noce river the winegrowers produced Teroldego; as already noted at the beginning of the twentieth century "the prosperity of the Noce plain depends on two factors: first of all on the quality of the soil, and second on the selection of the vines by the farmers" (Battisti 1905).

The commercial success of Teroldego in central Europe was accompanied by the continued cultivation of other less valuable grapes for domestic use. This new direction went hand in hand with the sharpening up of the winemaking techniques, and this happened particularly in Mezzocorona (Calò 2012; Girardi 1982, pp. 35–36). An extremely important step in the shift towards a viticulture with a higher yield, and market-oriented on the basis of quality, was the rooting of the cooperative movement among the winemakers with the birth of the winemaking cooperatives: the winemaking cooperatives of Mezzolombardo (1901) and Mezzocorona (1904), the Consortium of the winemakers of Mezzolombardo (1907), the League of peasant farmers of Mezzocorona (1911) (Leonardi 2005).

The period between the wars was a very difficult time for viticulture in the Piana Rotaliana, as a result of war damage and the spread of phylloxera. The wine trade with Austria and Germany suffered a heavy downsizing; but above all the high level of debt among financial agents, involving loans that had matured during the war years, led to many financial problems, with the closure of various businesses and the failure of the main local financial institutions. The serious economic uncertainties led to a strong pressure to emigrate. More generally, in agriculture there was a return of land to the wood, and at the same time a renewed trend towards the fragmentation of landownership. The crisis was confirmed by the return of the preference for cereal crops, while the retention of livestock became a secondary objective. The cultivation of tobacco was the main alternative to viticulture. Prices of agricultural products, in particular, those of wine, silk, livestock and timber, were still lower in 1930 than before the war; and a year later a further substantial drop was recorded, until prices fell below the cost of production, with wine dropping from 93 lire/quintal to 36 lire/quintal between 1928 and 1931. Prices of agricultural products continued to decrease in 1932 and 1933, resulting in a general fall in income, which led to the aforementioned failure of the most important local financial institution, the Bank of Trentino and Alto Adige.

On the eve of the Second World War, however, the production hub of Mezzocorona contained some signs of vitality. In fact, in response to the winemaking crisis of the mid-1920s, the three cooperative groupings had initiated innovations in their winemaking methods and in their organization and sales strategies. All were committed to raising standards, with the planting of new vines using quality cuttings, and also investing a lot to improve the work in the wineries. They followed the principle that the winery did not set the price when the grapes of the members were picked, but that the remuneration was related to the results achieved at the point of sale. At the same time, the winery accepted grapes from external suppliers for processing. The failure of the local rural bank weighed heavily on the management of investments and on the financial situation more generally, while each winery was trying to build and manage its own winemaking plant. The producers of Teroldego, despite the shift in commercial outlets from Austria to Italy and the competition from Piedmont and Apulia wines, succeeded in retaining their commercial position during the 1930s. However, the different wineries had great difficulty in reaching agreement in the setting of prices and market shares. In the meantime, a new cooperative was founded.

Post World War II reconstruction highlighted the complexity of the problem of redefining the role of agriculture in the Trentino region (Trezzi 1998; Moioli 1980). The general picture showed a longstanding preponderance of small landholdings together with a surplus of labour, while production needed to become more specialized and to invest in mechanization.

On the Piana Rotaliana, in the context of the positive economic situation of the 1950s, a net population increase of 20% was recorded over the decade. At the same time the organization of production was changed as a result of new entrepreneurial and business experience. The scaling down of agriculture as a local source of income led to a profound reorganization of cultivation, with the expansion of orchards: viticulture, despite many difficulties and setbacks, recorded an increase in production and, above all, a new raising of qualitative standards. At the same time changes were made on the sales side, with a new focus on retail sales, no longer focusing just on wholesale. The reforms were hampered by lack of capital and by the continued use of a range of grape varieties: the latter, indeed, produced a low overall yield, made worse by the traditional preference for wholesale rather than bottling of the wine; and by the firm attachment to the use of rather basic equipment.

In this context of significant backwardness, the Mezzocorona winery stood out as a pioneering example. The cooperative model, after the great difficulties of the interwar years, now proved itself well able to organize the necessary human and material resources. Also in this alpine region, economic growth primarily depended on the spread of manufacturing; it involved the start of a difficult process of restructuring, marked by tension between the need to modernize for the market and the desire to preserve the traditional social values of the agricultural world. An ambivalent process got under way, that had to be supported by a system of grants and subsidized loans from public organizations, with the EEC then intervening to support the prices of agricultural products. In this situation there were many outside institutional factors that, from the end of the 1940s until the mid-1970s, impacted significantly on the changes taking place within Trentino-Tyrolean agriculture. The role of the regional and provincial autonomy movement should be mentioned in particular; also the influence of the "Green Revolution"; and finally the role of the Common Agricultural Policy, which supported agriculture through the European Agricultural Guidance and Guarantee Fund (EAGGF) (Casati 1996, pp. 23–30).

At the beginning of the 1950s, the wineries and cooperatives moved towards forming an association (Federation of cooperative associations), both to handle the ever-growing competition from Piedmont and Tuscan wines and to counter the spread of adulteration practices. Achieving such a goal was not easy, and it had to be approached in a structured way (Casati 1996; Provvedi 1959, pp. 15–20). In 1965 the Trentino consortium proposed the setting up of a large wine cooperative to centralize processing, bottling and marketing, but the winegrowers of Mezzocorona opposed it and instead wanted to create their own association to centralize bottling. The project did not go ahead as a result of the lack of agreement between private and cooperative interests. In 1966 supporters of the European Agricultural Guidance and Guarantee Fund (EAGGF) favoured a general renewal of vineyards, while continuing to allow competition from adulterated wine. This question of the adulteration of wine had been present for a long time, with cyclical periods of repression: many called for the enactment of a law that would protect the "designation of origin" not only at the level of the finished product but also at the point of origin.

During the 1960s market changes posed a series of questions. In the first place there was the shift from bulk sales to bottled wine, with its attendant challenges. The cooperative system foresaw a merger of the associations, and the targets were higher quality wine, continuing technological improvement and the application of the DOC specification (1971)(Saracco 1971; Istituto trentino del vino 1998; Convegno sui consorzi 1985). The cooperatives then aimed to replace the wholesalers in order to establish direct relationships with foreign importers. The path towards recognition of "designation of origin" had already begun in 1961, fully accepting the examples already in place at European level. The process required coordinated organization in terms of both the care of the vineyards and the winemaking. In particular, it was essential to refine the cultivation of the vine in order to diversify, and to create a centralized sales system to support specialization with pricing policies and appropriate contracts. All these objectives are linked quite naturally to the introduction of the DOC after the cooperatives of the territory had independently set up a specific consortium for Teroldego (Tomasi 1971).[20] At the same time the

[20]D.P.R. 18 February 1971 modified by D.P.R. 22 June 1987.

region provided for the establishment of a single structure for the sale of Trentino wines. It aimed at an organization involving all the winegrowers of the Plain, but the project floundered, not for economic or organizational reasons but because of irreconcilable differences concerning the location of the enterprise.

Between 1975 and 1985 the emergence of Spumante (sparkling wine) marked a new phase of development, aimed not only at the European market but also the American one, with a US company partnership, the Prestige Wine Imports Corporation. Growth suffered a heavy setback as a result of the discovery of a new widespread adulteration of the wine, the so-called methanol scandal, which undermined the credibility of the Italian product, both domestically and internationally.[21] The Piana Rotaliana reacted positively and made a further effort to raise standards, focusing also on an education programme in winemaking for the growers. At the same time the progressive integration of the wine crop was achieved within the context of a new appreciation of the oenological characteristics of the territory; this was accompanied by an increasingly clear use of trademarks that were tied to the identity of the territory.

These trends helped to build a sense of identity based on the cultural life and anchored in the characteristics of the territory. For that reason, the cooperatives were pushing for a renewal of the vines, on the basis of technical studies of the microenvironment and of the geomorphological composition; also as a result of the development of the scientific understanding of viticulture. The combination of scientific innovation and the new appreciation of the relationship between the territory and the cultivation of the vine led to an improvement in winemaking standards. This in turn enabled more remunerative prices to be set in the marketplace, with the expansion of commercial lines. The success of this initiative, upgrading the cultivation and production aspects, allowed the

---

[21]The most serious scandal in the wine industry dates back to 1986, causing 23 casualties, with several people injured (loss of vision) due to poisoning caused by the practice of increasing the alcohol content of the wine with methanol or methyl alcohol (a natural alcohol which is considerably toxic). The negative practice began in the province of Asti in Piedmont.

annual average production potential to reach more than 100,000 quintals by the end of the 1980s, while the cellaring capacity, the processing and storing of the wine by the cooperatives, reached an average of 125,000 quintals of grapes. This good outcome was made possible also by the development of the relationship with the Consortium of wine cooperatives in Trentino (CAVIT).[22]

Taking advantage of the cooperative system, and working well with the local institutions, Rotaliano agriculture experienced effective management of its viticulture to avoid overproduction; instead overproduction affected the fruit growing sector. At the same time cooperation between growers encouraged reduced yields per hectare. This was accompanied both by an in-depth study of the microclimate and of the systems of cultivating the vines, and by a deeper reflection on vinification and on the maturing of the wines. Finally, the local system, and specifically that of the plain, was fairly cohesive in the way it built and managed the facilities for the winemaking and storage: the use of advanced technology ensured that this part of the winemaking process was centralized in one place, the so-called "citadel of wine". The cooperation in winemaking therefore launched a management structure that included the whole supply chain.

During the last two decades of the twentieth century, the whole agricultural system in Trentino, including the agriculture of the Piana Rotaliana, faced many ups and downs in all its production sectors, above all in the area of exports—although several operators were encouraging moves to a more diversified market. The effects of the fall in agricultural prices during repeated negative economic cycles also weighed heavily. The reform of the Common Agricultural Policy (1992)

---

[22]CAVIT is a consortium of wine cooperatives formed in 1950, with the headquarters in Ravina di Trento (since 1964). In the first decade of the twenty-first century the membership reached 5400 winegrowers, with 7000 ha planted with vines. Initially the consortium was created to assist farmers in the use of new technology. Later it also had a commercial mission. The cooperative has reached out to the 10 associated cooperatives: Roverè della Luna (Valle dell'Adige); Rotaliana di Mezzolombardo; Tablino (Valle dei Laghi); Trento (Valle dell'Adige); Aldeno (Vallagarina); Vivallis di Villalagarina; Agraria Riva del Garda (Alto Garda); D'Isera; Mori Colli Zugna; Viticoltori di Avio (Vallagarina).

introduced a gradual shift from price support to the direct integration of income that was accompanied by constraints to limit surplus production. These EU policies reduced demand at times, although the expansion in foreign markets enabled the producers of the Piana Rotaliana (935 winegrowers) to buck the trend (Gios 1990, pp. 23–31).

In the mid-1990s the largest producer was a cooperative: the Mezzocorona Group was a company with an integrated network and an innovative role as a corporation with an effective market presence. This feature was made possible both by increased cooperation in cultivation and vinification and by the contribution of producers from outside the Trentino region in the marketing of the wines produced—this ensured adequate differentiation and openness to different market demands.

Almost all the DOC wines are concentrated in the area between Mezzolombardo, San Michele all'Adige and the plain to the south between Rovereto and Ala. One of the DOC is the Casteller, a wine with a ruby red colour, not too intense and with quite delicate fruity aromas[23]; but the most common "controlled designation" in the region is the Trentino DOC, which has some sub-areas: Sorni, Superiore Marzemino Isera, Superiore Marzemino Ziresi, Superiore, Superiore Vino Santo, Vino Santo and Marzemino.[24] The grape varieties are both indigenous and imported, including Marzemino, Schiava and Rebo, the result of the crossing of Merlot with Marzemino. Other red grape varieties cultivated are Pinot Noir, Cabernet and Merlot, which in cooler climates such as the area of Trentino and South Tyrol offer a good complexity of taste. The rosé and white wines are represented by imported varieties such as Chardonnay, Sauvignon, Riesling, Müller Thurgau, Pinot Bianco and Pinot Grigio. Nosiola is, in the opinion of many oenologists, a "little jewel" of the area. This grape grows in the Sarca valley where, thanks to the favourable microclimate due to thermoregulation generated by several small lakes, it is the basis of the production

[23]D.P.R. 3 May 1974, 3 November 1989, Decree 31 May 2002.

[24]D.P.R. 4 August 1971, and then 8 August 1996.

of Vino Santo.[25] At the commercial level, the most important products in recent decades have been the Trento DOC sparkling wines.[26]

Conclusions

The essay focuses on the long-term relationships existing between land properties and oenology. It is quite evident that wine is not only a product for local consumption but also a product for export that opens the door to the economic interaction between these areas and distant territories. The specialization offers an alternative resource to the workforce in agriculture and above all generates professional skills that integrate the mountain rural life with the artisanal and commercial initiatives in towns and villages. These experiences in the long nineteenth century suffered crises and lost some of their commercial assets (Switzerland and Austria-Hungary). Besides, the historical reconstruction focuses on two different paths for Valtellina and Trentino during the twentieth century. During these periods the crisis of traditional mountain agriculture strongly affects viticulture and wine. The identification of a new production paradigm is very complex, also due to the marginal position of these two regions in the Kingdom of Italy between the late nineteenth and the early twentieth centuries. Subsequently, the tragic human and economic cost of the two World Wars hits the socio-economic structures of these two areas.

---

[25]Wine grapes and production of wine have grown steadily from the 1990s. The most of output have been created in the North, with an average growth rate in the Veneto region of 9.3% between 2009 and 2015, 9.4% in Trentino and 5.8% in Lombardy over the same period; in the same period Piedmont recorded a figure of −0.8%. In 2009, the ranking of the DOC wines showed Montepulciano d'Abruzzo with 895 hl/1000, Chianti with 790, Asti with 675, Prosecco with 865 and Trentino with 513. In 2008, in Italy the DOC Trentino was the brand with the highest level of production in hectoliters. Data by Federdoc.

[26]The most famous Spumante (sparkling wine) of the area is the Ferrari—Lunelli. In 1902 Giulio Ferrari aimed to achieve a high-quality wine by introducing the cultivation of Chardonnay in Trentino. In 1952 Ferrari, having no direct heirs, passed the management to Bruno Lunelli, owner of a wine shop in Trento, who transformed the Ferrari wine estate into a wine company that aimed to produce sparkling wine for the domestic and foreign markets, Lunelli introduced and managed an intensive promotion of the corporate brand linked to the particular taste. Since the 1970s, Franco, Gino and Mauro Lunelli created a series of labels that became a "classic" of the sparkling wine industry: Ferrari Rosé, Ferrari Perlè and Giulio Ferrari Reserve.

In Trentino and Alto Adige, associations of farmers, and local institutions, feed innovation in technics and production. In this way new oenological paradigms are found with a qualification in wine standards and an adaptation in tastes for mass consumption. The convergence of men and resources on these objectives is also made possible by the action of innovative winemakers and by local institutions with synergies for professional training, infrastructures and credit. Thus a "milieu" first appears in Trentino and then in Valtellina. This area of excellence achieves a productive and technological intensification characterized by specialization and quality, also aiming at managing product brands.

References

Alberti, G. (1901), *Sull'antico commercio del vino trentino*, Trento: Ed. Trentina.

Andreolli, B. (1989), *Produzione e commercio del vino trentino tra medioevo e età moderna*, Florence: Accademia economico-agraria dei Georgofili.

Annuario di statistica agraria, Roma 1954–1985.

Battisti, C. (1905), *Guida di Mezzolombardo e dintorni*, Trento: Ed. Trentina.

Besana, C. (2001), *La vita economica negli anni della maturità dell'equilibrio agricolo-commerciale*, (Rumi G., Ed., pp. 58–76).

Besana, C., Locatelli, A.M. (2019), *Eine Bergökonomie im Wandel. Merkmale der landwirtschaftlichen Produktionssyteme des Veltlins in 19. Jahrhundert*, (Lorenzetti L., Decorzant Y., Head- Köňig A.L. Ed., pp. 58–76).

Bonoldi, A., Head-Konig, A.L., Lorenzetti, L. (Eds.) (2016), 'Transits: infrastructure et societè dans les Alpes de l'antiquité à nos jours', *Histoire des Alpes*, 26, Zurich: Chronos.

Bozzi, F. (1876), *Relazione presentata alla Camera provinciale di commercio e arti di Chiavenna dal proprio presidente sui lavori eseguiti nel biennio 1875–76, corredata da alcuni cenni sul commercio e sulle industri della provincia di Sondrio*, Chiavenna: 1876, (Rullani, 1, 1973, p. 111).

Calò, A. (2012), *Trentino*, San Michele all'Adige: Fondazione Edmund Mach.

Cantù, C. (1857–1861), *Grande illustrazione del Lombardo Veneto*, 5/1, Milan: Corona & Caimi, 1857–1861.

Carera, A., Taccolini, M., Canetta, R. (Ed.) (1998), *Temi e questioni di storia economica e sociale in età moderna e contemporanea. Studi in onore di Sergio Zaninelli*, Milan: Vita & Pensiero.

Casati, D. (1996), *L'agricoltura nella prospettiva della riforma della politica agricola comune e della crescente internazionalizzazione dei mercati*, (Falcetti 1996, pp. 23–30).
Convegno sui consorzi di tutela dei vini Doc: Verona 18 aprile 1985, a cura della Federazione nazionale fra i consorzi di tutela di vini a denominazione d'origine, Firenze, 1985.
Cova, A. (1989), *Problemi tecnici ed economici della produzione del vino in Italia tra Otto e Novecento*, (*Il vino*, pp. 322–383).
Del Fabro, U., Morelli De Rossi, G. (1986), *Il buon vino: Friuli Venezia Giulia e Trentino Alto Adige*, Udine: Lorenzini.
Dossier vino: la vitienologia trentina, il sistema di produzione, l'identità del territorio, Trento: Camera di commercio, industria e artigianato, 2004.
Falcetti, M. (Ed.) (1996), *Trentino, società, agricoltura. Riflessioni sulle prospettive dell'agricoltura del Trentino*, Trento: Acli Trentine.
Faustini, G., Lando, M., Magagnotti, P. (1993), *Volto di una regione di confine: storia, economia e cultura del Trentino-Alto Adige*, Trento: Regione Trentino Alto Adige.
Federazione nazionale fra i consorzi di tutela di vini a denominazione d'origine (1985), *Convegno sui consorzi di tutela dei vini Doc: Verona 18 aprile 1985*, Florence: Federdoc.
Galizzi, G. (Ed.) (1992), *Una politica per l'agricoltura della montagna alpina*, Milan: FrancoAngeli.
Garbari, M., Leonardi, A. (Ed.) (2003), *Storia del Trentino*, vol. V, *L'età contemporanea*, 1803–1918, Bologna: Il Mulino.
Gios, G. (1990), *Qualità e capitale umano*, (La qualità 1990, pp. 23–31).
Girardi, S. (Ed.) (1982), *Mezzocorona fra storia e cronaca*, Trento: Cassa Rurale di Mezzocorona.
Gorfer, A. (1990), *Trento e Valle dell'Adige. Piano rotaliano*, vol. 3, Trento: Arti Grafiche Saturnia.
Gregorini, G. (2003), *L'agricoltura trentina tra mercato, pressione demografica e regole agronomiche*, (Garbari M., Leonardi A. 2003, pp. 531–596).
Il Trentino e gli anni Ottanta. Verso una cultura della comunità, Trento: Publiprint, 1980.
Il vino nell'economia e nella società italiana medioevale e moderna, Convegno di studi, Greve in Chianti (21–24 maggio 1987), Florence: Accademia economico agraria dei Georgofili, 1989.
ISTAT (1954–1985), *Annuario di statistica agraria*, Rome, Istat, 1954–1985.
ISTAT (1998), *2° Censimento generale dell'agricoltura, 25 ottobre 1970, 2, Dati sulle caratteristiche strutturali delle aziende, f.11, Provincia di Trento, Dati provinciali e camerali*, Rome: Istat, 1972.

Istituto trentino del vino. (1998), *Punto trentino Doc*, Trento: Istituto trentino del vino.

Jacini, S. (1858), *Sulle condizioni economiche della provincia di Sondrio*, Milan: Crivelli.

L'agricoltura trentina: un'agricoltura di montagna nel contesto comunitario. Conferenza provinciale di agricoltura, Trento 23–25 gennaio 1976, Trento: Provincia autonoma di Trento, 1976.

La qualità integrale. L'esperienza dei produttori viticoli della Piana Rotaliana, Trento: Studio garfico G. & C. Nuova stampa rapida, 1990.

Leonardi, A. (1976), *Depressione e Risorgimento economico del Trentino. 1866–1914*, Trento: Società di studi trentini di scienze storiche.

Leonardi A. (Ed.) (1987), *Il Trentino nel primo dopoguerra. Problemi economici e sociali*, Trento: Società di studi trentini di scienze storiche.

Leonardi, A. (1996), *L'economia di una regione alpina: le trasformazioni economiche degli ultimi due secoli nell'area trentino-tirolese*, Trento: Itas.

Leonardi, A. (2000), *Risparmio e credito in una regione di frontiera: la Cassa di risparmio nella realtà economica trentina tra 19 e 20 secolo*, Rome: Laterza.

Leonardi, A. (2002), *Credito cooperativo e società locali: l'esperienza delle Casse rurali di Mezzocorona in un secolo di profonde trasformazioni, 1902–2002*, Mezzocorona: Cassa rurale di Mezzocorona.

Leonardi, A. (2005), *Collaborare per competere. Il percorso imprenditoriale delle Cantine Mezzocorona*, Bologna: Il Mulino.

Locatelli, A. M., Tedeschi, P. (2018), *The Disappearance and Rebirth of a Wine. The Sfurzat in Valtellina*, (Marache C., Meyzie P., Villeret M., pp. 71–83).

Lorenzetti, L. (2005), *Lo spazio insubrico: un'identità storica tra percorsi politici e realtà socio-economiche 1500–1900*, Milan: Casagrande.

Lorenzetti, L. (2010), *Destini periferici: modernizzazione e mercati in Ticino, Valtellina e Vallese 1850–1930*, Udine: Forum.

Lorenzetti, L. (2012), 'Ruralité, industrie et formes de pluriactivité: une approche comparative Valllais (Suisse) et Valteline (Italiè) 1860–1930', *Histoire, économie & societé*, 3, pp. 71–83.

Lorenzetti, L. (2016), *Transits: infrastructure et societè dans les Alpes de l'antiquité à nos jours*, redaction Andrea Bonoldi, Anne-Lise Head-Konig, Luigi Lorenzetti, Zurich, Chronos.

Lorenzetti, L., Decorzant, Y., Head-Kőnig, A.L. (Eds.) (2019), *Relire l'Altitude: La terre et ses usages. Suisse et espaces avoisi- nants, XII°–XXI° siècles*, Neuchâtel: Editions Alphil.

Marache, C., Meyzie, P., Villeret, M. (Eds.) (2018), *Des produits, entre declin et renaissance (XVI–XXI siecles)*, Bruxelles: Peter Lang.

Moioli, A. (1980), *30 anni di sviluppo economico nella provincia di Trento*, (*Il Trentino*, pp. 27–37).

Moioli, A. (1987), *Ricostruzione post-bellica e interventi dello Stato nell'economia della "Venezia tridentina"*, (Leonardi A. 1987, pp. 19–118).

Provvedi, F. (1959), *'La tutela dei vini tipici'*, *Economia trentina*, 1, pp. 15–20.

Rauzi, P.G. (1981), *Il Trentino e gli anni Ottanta. Verso una cultura della comunità*, Trento: Publiprint.

Romani, M. (1957), *L'agricoltura dal periodo delle riforme al 1859: strutture, organizzazione sociale e tecnica*, Milano: Vita e Pensiero.

Rullani, E. (1973), *L'economia valtellinese e la Banca Popolare di Sondrio in un secolo di vita dell'Istituto (1871–1971)*, 1, Sondrio: Banca Popolare di Sondrio.

Rumi, G., Mezzanotte, G., Cova, A. (2001), *Sondrio e il suo territorio*, Milan: IntesaBCI.

Saracco, C. (1971), *Vini a denominazione d'origine: leggi e norme di applicazione*, Bologna: Ediagricole.

Strada del vino e dei sapori della Piana Rotaliana, Trento: Trentino SpA, 2007.

Stranieri, S., Tedeschi, P. (2015), Producing and selling wine in Eastern Lombardy (19th–21st centuries), *Rises. Ricerche di storia economica e sociale*, 1, pp. 173–198.

Tomasi, L. (1971), 'I vini a denominazione di origine controllata nella provincia di Trento. Situazione e prospettive', *Economia trentina*, 2, pp. 16–40.

Trentino, società, agricoltura. Riflessioni sulle prospettive dell'agricoltura del Trentino, Atti del Convegno 14 maggio 1994 -San Michele Adige, a cura di Falcetti M., Trento, 1996, pp. 23–30.

Trezzi, L. (1998), *La Ricostruzione in provincia di Trento (1945–1950)*, (Carera A., pp. 561–588).

Zaninelli, S. (1979), *Un'agricoltura di montagna nell' Ottocento: il Trentino*, Trento: Società di studi trentini di scienze storiche.

Zaninelli, S. (1998), *Filippo Re e l'agricoltura trentina agli inizi dell'Ottocento*, Trento: Provincia autonoma di Trento Servizi beni librari.

"The Idea of Improvement": Theorized vs. Practised Vine Growing in Friuli

Andrea Cafarelli

Constraints and Opportunities

Vine growing is probably the sector that in the last two centuries has developed most by adapting to the profound changes that have characterized agriculture in Friuli.[1] Today, as in the mid-nineteenth century, although features, purposes and markets have changed, it has a strategic function and provides a significant contribution to the local and national economy. According to data from the 2010 general census, the regional agricultural area devoted to vineyards amounts to over

[1]This paper is based on sources from the State Archives of Udine and Venice, as well as on specialist publications from Udine Civic Library "V. Joppi", Isontina State Library of Gorizia and, above all, Ersa Library "L. Chiozza" in Pozzuolo del Friuli. I also benefited from my previous work, updated for the occasion, and to which I refer the reader to for any relevant literature. I refer in particular to the monographs Cafarelli (2009, 2010). I have also used some considerations published in my previous work: Cafarelli (1993–1994, 1997, 1998a, 2011, 2012, 2017).

A. Cafarelli (✉)
Department of Economics and Statistics, University of Udine, Udine, Italy
e-mail: andrea.cafarelli@uniud.it

S. A. Conca Messina et al. (eds.), *A History of Wine in Europe, 19th to 20th Centuries, Volume I*, Palgrave Studies in Economic History,
https://doi.org/10.1007/978-3-030-27772-7_6

21,500 hectares, 70% of which is in controlled designation of origin areas. There are over 6600 producers, that is about one-third of active agricultural enterprises. The sector covers almost 15% of the gross saleable regional agricultural production (Regione autonoma Friuli Venezia Giulia 2013, pp. 27–29).

In order to understand the historical importance of this crop, one just needs to consider the extension of the vined areas in the mid-nineteenth century. In Lower Friuli, for example, despite the widespread hydraulic instability, out of 58,850 hectares surveyed when the Austrian Land Registry was implemented,[2] nearly 16,000, or 72% of the cultivable fields[3] were occupied more or less extensively by grapevines.[4] In some municipalities, the percentage was so high that they were present in each arable field. This obviously had repercussions on the agricultural landscape, which was noticed by Johann Burger, a Carinthian agronomist and an adviser to the Habsburg government, who wrote in his 1828 travel diary:

> There is nothing that can amaze the northern traveller more than those parallel rows of trees of every kind, which rise amid the wheat fields, and from the foot of which the grapevines are raised, they climb to the origin of the branches and are then guided from tree to tree like garlands hanging in the air full of fruits. (Burger 1843, p. 27)

The extraordinary spread of grapevines in the Friulian cropping system represented also paradoxically one of the main limitations of the vine growing and winemaking sector.[5] The tendency to plant grapevines

[2]Archivio di Stato, Udine (hereafter ASU), *Demanio*, b. 22, fasc. 12: *Notificazione dell'I.R. Giunta del censimento del Regno Lombardo-Veneto*, 4 marzo 1851, n. 44631; ASU, *Demanio*, b. 22, fasc. 12: *Attuazione del nuovo Censimento. Regolamento ed istruzioni per l'attuazione del nuovo Censimento Prediale nel Regno Lombardo-Veneto*. There is a detailed analysis in Cafarelli (2009, pp. 7–48).

[3]ASU, *Sezione catasto fondiario*, registri Catasto.

[4]For details on these matters, Cafarelli (1998b, pp. 73–85). Some interesting reflections on this point are to be found in Scarpa (1972, pp. 35–53), Zalin (1978, pp. 44–56), and Berengo (1963, pp. 227–232).

[5]For an analysis of the whole question, see Dandolo (1989, pp. 35–56).

to obtain, not only a beverage with a high-energy value, but also an important component of agricultural profits, was rather widespread. Grapevines were planted everywhere, but good wine was produced only in certain limited areas, which were especially suited to its cultivation (Dorta 1914, p. 330). The first consequence of this widespread presence was that a large share of the operations to transform the grapes happened in farmhouses and a large part of the wine never made it to the marketplace. In addition, the increasing diffusion of grapevines in areas which were little suited to its cultivation led surely to greater production volumes, but also to noticeable consequences for the quality of the wines produced.[6]

In Friuli there were several areas where vine growing should have been abandoned, if one had followed the fundamental agronomic concept according to which each area should grow only those crops suited to its climate and its soil. In actual facts, another concept prevailed at the time, which was also fundamental and so embedded in the minds of the peasants to constitute a serious obstacle to the spread of a rational cultivation: the notion that each farm was to provide what was necessary to the livelihood of the peasant's family.[7] The advice often given to a peasant was: grow many things so that you will not miss everything at once. Hence, it was not appreciated that a field planted with grapevines would have yielded much more, if wheat or maize had been cultivated. Peasants continued growing wine without caring too much about the success of the harvest (Coceani 1912, p. 138).

At least throughout the nineteenth century, vine and wine production in the region aimed more at product quantity than quality,[8] following a logic detached from the market, since its wines could survive foreign competition only in qualitative terms and not in terms of price (Dorta 1914, p. 330). The qualitative shortcomings of vines and wines originated primarily from the setup of the cultivation system,

---

[6]Cf., Montanari and Ceccarelli (1950, pp. 92–93) and Panjek (1992, pp. 37–43).

[7]"Precetti e massime agricole" (1843, p. 240).

[8]This topic is closely related to the protectionist policy: Pecorari (1989, pp. 297–307) and Zalin (1994, pp. 215–257).

the poor selection of grape varieties and the outdated winemaking techniques. It is revealing that wine evaluation in accounting records was made *ex ante* and based almost exclusively on product quantity and not quality. This resulted directly in the peasants' disregard for any cultivation improvements (Panjek 1998, p. 87). At the same time, consumer preferences had been forcibly directed towards full-bodied and robust wines, that is towards grapevines less easily affected by cryptogams.

The motto of Friulian vine growers had to be: produce a lot, well and cheap. But if it was enough to work to produce wine, in order to produce a lot, well and cheap, it was necessary to work sensibly and wisely. In order to develop the sector and, above all, to improve the quality of the wines, it was desirable to rationalize crops, suggesting the implantation of specialized vineyards, in order to overcome the limits which are implicit in a promiscuous system. There were serious obstacles to the achievement of this objective, since farmers had to be convinced of the cost-effectiveness of this solution, while taking into account their traditional practices.[9]

The difficulty in starting specialized grapevine cultivation was precisely to convince farmers of the need to abandon the traditional promiscuous cultivation system, and substitute it with those crops most suitable to local natural features and sun exposure. Beyond rationalizing crops, it was also necessary to select plants, choosing the best quality grapevine. The Friulian system had an impressive number of grapes. It is enough to consider that during the 1863 exhibition organized by the Friulian Agricultural Association and which saw the participation of 47 exhibitors, a vast variety of grapes was on display: more than 300 varieties out of about 700 samples.[10] But the most important aspect was not so much that there were so many varieties, but rather that so many were cultivated all at once and on the same farm. The great variety of grapes, combined with landownership fragmentation, the type of soil, sun exposure and winemaking and preservation methods, greatly affected

[9]"Dei mezzi per migliorare la vinicoltura nella provincia di Udine" (1876, p. 64).

[10]Zanelli (1869, p. 40). Cf. also "Rapporto della Commissione per la Mostra d'uve e d'altri prodotti agrari" (1863, p. 572) and Pecile (1863a, pp. 629–642).

the quality of the final product. In order to get fine wines a limited number of grapes should have been selected, which would have allowed the creation of easily identifiable table wines, replacing the multitude of locally produced wines that to be drunk needed three people: "one to drink it, one to hold it in and one to send it down!" (Dorta 1914, pp. 326–327).

The third major limitation was the backwardness of winemaking and preservation techniques.[11] The widespread presence of grapevines in the Friulian countryside meant that grape transformation operations tended to happen within farms and that wine rarely arrived at the real market, so that the required standard was extremely low.[12] Small and medium producers, who constituted the majority, combined the stubbornness of not embracing progress to poor methods and to the lack of winemaking tools. They did not use the most suitable means and techniques to properly carry out the processing operations and they did not take proper care even of the important phase of preservation, using any place in their farm, without worrying too much about the requirements for preserving such a precious drink properly (Coceani and Gaidoni 1912, p. 355).

Gherardo Freschi, one of the pioneers of Friulian agricultural associationism, maintained that, in order to face the terrible competition from foreign markets, it was necessary to increase production, improve quality and become more competitive in price terms (Freschi 1863, pp. 186–193). In other words, produce the maximum possible at the lowest cost possible. This objective was reachable through the use of knowledge, machinery, cattle, capitals, but especially instilling in the minds of farmers "the idea of improvement", which, as recalled by Gabriele Luigi Pecile, was far from being considered a general belief (Pecile 1863b, p. 4). The difficulty was not so much in demonstrating the advantages obtainable for farming through financial resources or

[11] "Vinificazione. Come si faceva. Come si deve fare" (1891, pp. 344–346).

[12] Coceani and Gaidoni (1912, p. 355). See also: Pletti (1845, pp. 8–9).

with the aid of scientific discoveries and economic principles, but rather to convince the rural population of their real usefulness.[13]

Throughout the nineteenth century, the gap between agriculture as theorized and as practised was undoubtedly significant, although the role played by specialized publications should not be underestimated. In a context, which was more and more open to knowledge acquisition and exchange, publications worked as a catalyst for the complex development process of the regional economy, leading farmers to become more and more market-oriented entrepreneurs and vine growers to become "viticulturist".

In this brief contribution, it is difficult to deal with one of the issues which are most debated in historiography: the role played by academies, "*cattedre ambulanti*" (itinerant agricultural schools), agricultural associations and their media outlets in the development of the primary sector. At the same time, it is not possible to draw a comprehensive picture of the people, often of great cultural and scientific level, who favoured the dissemination of technical and agricultural notions in the countryside. Moreover, it is difficult to develop such a topic in a context that is known to be so diverse in political, administrative and geomorphological terms. It is also not possible to offer an analytical review of all publications available on this topic, as they are many and they were published also in non-specialized outlets and local newspapers, but also because "ideas have no borders". Hence, it would be methodologically unfound to deal with this topic without taking into consideration the contribution, which was determinant in this case, provided by publications from the Veneto region, starting from the "Scuola di Conegliano". Therefore, we will highlight the main changes which occurred in Friulian vine growing and winemaking and the ways in which specialized media favoured such changes, without pretending to offer a complete picture of issues and publication outlets.

---

[13] *On the diffusion of new agricultural practices see Rapporto della Camera di commercio e d'industria della Provincia del Friuli* (1857, pp. 32–33) and Vianello (1861, p. 17). For an analysis of the whole question: Fanfani (1979, pp. 287–307), Morassi (1981, pp. 361–370), Gullino (1992, pp. 113–127), Zaninelli (1990, pp. 1–16; 1992, pp. 11–19), Brianta (1994), and Brunello 1996, pp. 70–87).

The Dilemma: Quality vs. Quantity?

With the 16th April 1839 imperial patent Emperor Ferdinand I gave up all uncultivated or arbitrarily usurped municipal assets in favour of the municipalities of the Kingdom of Lombardy–Venetia.[14] Although this was not the only policy to regulate collective ownership, it represented in a sense a turning point for municipal heritage and for the myriad of small landowners and labourers for whom such land was a source of livelihood. Under the imperial patent the saleable assets, through purchase contracts or long leases, in the Venetian Provinces were estimated to sum up to 1,367,062 "pertiche" (an old measurement unit), of which 900,534, that is 66%, were in Friuli.[15]

The scope of this policy becomes more clear if one takes into account that a few years later almost 16% of the fields in the Province of Friuli were placed on the "market". This issue was the subject of extensive discussion in the pages of "*L'Amico del contadino*" ("The Friend of the Farmer"), a weekly paper, published on April 1842 by Pascatti of San Vito al Tagliamento. Gherardo Freschi, who assumed the more modest title of compiler, although he had been the inspirer, edited the publication until 1848, when he was forced into exile. The title of the paper revealed itself the Freschi's intention, that was to eradicate from our countryside ignorance and disseminate the art of agriculture in its true principles. This was to be achieved by offering to parish priests and landowners topics to educate peasants and give them the correct notions on issues on which they held false beliefs, in order to enable them to come out of the dark. The magazine tried to embrace the farming world as a whole, using both accessible language and ways considered particularly effective such as dialogues, anecdotes, poems and moral tales.

"*L'Amico del contadino*", which undoubtedly played a pioneering role in this area, did not devote much attention to vine growing, but

[14]Archivio di Stato, Venezia (hereafter ASV), *Biblioteca legislativa*, fasc. 358, c-16/16: *Istruzione per le Regie Autorità provinciali e Distrettuali, e per le Amministrazioni, e pei Consigli e Convocati comunali, onde rettamente eseguire la venerata Sovrana Risoluzione 16 aprile 1839 che ha prescritto l'alienazione de' beni comunali in generale, ed in particolare degli incolti*, p. 2.

[15]ASV, *Presidio di governo, 1845–1848*, XII, fasc. 6/5.

this is understandable when one considers the more pressing problems of the Friulian countryside, well-illustrated in "*Atti preparatori*" ("Preparatory Acts") in the Austrian Land Registry[16] and, subsequently, in the Morpurgo report "*Inchiesta Jacini*" ("Investigation Jacini").[17] The first contribution about vine growing, dedicated to wine acidity, arrived only after the publication of 7 numbers. This first article was followed by other articles, which were almost always signed and which dealt with improving the trade of wines from Friuli, vine coupling techniques with mulberry, scientific notions in winemaking, wine preservation processes.

It is also true that Freschi knew that knowledge dissemination did not pass only through printed papers, which was the necessary complement of a larger educational project. It was not by chance that in March 1843 he launched the idea of setting up a Practical school of agriculture in Friuli: an idea that was implemented on 26 November, when in San Vito al Tagliamento the "*Lezioni festive*" ("Festive lessons") of agriculture were inaugurated. "*L'Amico del contadino*" systematically published those lessons, starting with the famous disquisitions on silkworm and mulberry cultivation. "*Scuola festiva*" (a type of Sunday School) was the first step towards the constitution of the Friulian Agricultural Association, as it is clear from a review of the magazine, which demonstrated the commitment in this direction since 1843 not only by Freschi, but also by Alvise Mocenigo, Ludovico Rota, Giovanni Paolo Zuccheri and many other collaborators.

[16]ASV, *Biblioteca legislativa*, b. 350, fasc. 11-108: *Relazione [di P. Romieri] ragionata storico cronologica dell'Estimo provvisorio del Dipartimento del Tagliamento preso secondo l'antica sua circoscrizione eretto in ordine al disposto del Governo Italico con decreto 4 febbraio 1808, corredata di tutti gli Atti, che servon a far conoscere in pratica la base, le massime e le discipline che ebbero luogo nella sua compilazione coll'indicazione infine dello stato in cui si trova nell'anno 1814 e dei lavori dei quali si occupa attualmente la Commissione censuaria del Dipartimento suddetto.*

[17]*Atti della Giunta per l'Inchiesta agraria e sulle condizioni della classe agricola. Relazione del Comm. Emilio Morpurgo sulla XI Circoscrizione. Province di Verona, Vicenza, Padova, Rovigo, Venezia, Treviso, Belluno e Udine*, IV, Roma 1883. See also Morpurgo, e., "Interrogatori dell'Inchiesta agraria preparati dal ministro dell'agricoltura, industria e commercio", in *Bull*, II, 4 (1876), pp. 150–164.

The Friulian Agricultural Association, which was formally established in November 1846 and lasted until 1927,[18] largely promoted the development of agriculture and transmitted that spirit of solidarity, enterprise and progress that would be the basis for the economic and social growth of the province. The Association, born from the initiative of a group of landowners and agronomists from Friuli, was pursuing its intended purpose, that is to favour the improvement of Friulian agriculture. This goal was to be achieved by promoting researches, studies and experiences, by collecting and disseminating through a "*Bullettino*" ("Bulletin") news and economic-agricultural statistics regarding the Province, by informing the members of the conditions and needs of agriculture, giving awards and other encouragements, setting up a mobile agricultural library. The Association attributed to education great importance, considering it the basis for agriculture, but soon realized that changing the agricultural course of a country would not be an easy task. Although membership was free, only a few young cultured landowners took part in the first meetings organized in Udine in 1857 to impart the knowledge necessary for the exercise of the noble art of agriculture. The aim was instead to disseminate those scientific and practical notions essential to run a farm among all the inhabitants of the countryside.

The first issue of the "*Bullettino dell'Associazione agraria friulana*" ("Bulletin of the Friulian Agricultural Association") was released on 22 November 1855. It remained for nearly seventy years one of the most influential voices among agricultural communities in Italy and for vine growing in Friuli, that in the middle of the nineteenth century was still characterized by excessive promiscuity and the lack of a production surplus to sell on the market, as well as by widespread hydraulic instability, difficulties in gaining access to credit, a lack of specialized intermediaries, a lack of product competitiveness, limited dissemination of agronomic knowledge, deficiencies in the infrastructural system.

---

[18]About the origins of the Friulian Agricoltural Association: Freschi (1847, p. 98), Associazione agraria friulana (1855, pp. 5–8), Pecile (1862, pp. 9–11), Beretta (1895, pp. 3–7), Associazione agraria friulana (1900, 1948), Panjek (1980, pp. 3–65), and Rossi (1996, pp. 29–32).

The general debate on Friulian vine growing, which Freschi had just launched in "*L'Amico del contadino*" and Valussi continued in a less organic and more elusive manner in "*Giunta domenicale*" ("Sunday insert") of "*Il Friuli*", a weekly published in 1851, became more intense in the '50s of the nineteenth century, when "oidium" (powdery mildew) arrived in Veneto and Friuli and decimated crops and harvests, prompting owners and settlers to intervene to counter the cryptogam. It was a turning point for our country, because on the one hand, the sulphidation and other defence techniques, which were well-documented in "*Bullettino*", further reduced agricultural profits and kept increasing the debts of the peasants, while on the other hand, the decline in production led to wine, and later vine, importation from abroad, which would also put under discussion vine growing and winemaking techniques. The magazine published in the late 50s and early 60s tight debates on the low vineyard and the effects resulting from a system centred on self-consumption and crop despecialization, which saw the best known Friulian agricultural business representatives, from Pecile to Chiozza, share their differing opinions (Chiozza 1862, p. 122).

After presenting the most bizarre remedies to counter oidium (lime, tar, glue, hemp plantations next to vine rows), "*Bullettino*" published the first essays on sulphidation with the "Bordeaux mixture", but had to face the resistance of vine growers, who complained about the excessive cost and complexity of treatments. Not all the evil came to harm. Soon it became evident, to quote Gallesio, that to make good wine, good grapes were needed and to produce good grapes one had to take more care of grapevines, selecting among the myriad of "native" vines those who most deserved to be cultivated and focusing on the introduction of new varieties. The Friulian Agricultural Association's magazine was among the first to shift its focus on quality, when people normally still looked at unit yield.

The fact that there was a specific focus on the quality of the wines is also shown by the attempts, not successful, to create a wine company of Friuli (1870), as well as numerous articles on the benefits of wine pasteurization, which demonstrate the technical and scientific awareness with regards to vines and wine. It was clear that there had been a turning point in the history of winemaking, which had turned from an empirical process, exposed to the whims of nature, to full scientific explanations, which created an unbreakable relationship between wine, chemistry and microbiology. This relationship would continue consolidating in the following decades, when once the cryptogram crisis with oidium and peronospora (downy mildew) was over, people had to face Philloxera, a terrible small animal to whose name was so aptly added the qualifier of devastating ("vastatrix").[19] It should be recognized that "*Bullettino*" had the merit of having favoured a stable link between Friulian agriculture, agricultural research and experimentation. This same stringent bond in 1876 led in Conegliano to the birth of the first School of Vine Growing and Oenology of Europe, an organization which was always in close contact with the Agricultural Association.

In the 1860s and '70s "*Bullettino*" witnessed the scientific revolution which was taking place and promoted technical and vocational training, which was functional to support agricultural development as part of the broader process of economic transformation in the whole Country. This is demonstrated by the regular correspondence not only with the School of Conegliano, but also with the Italian Wine Commission and with the Wine Society from Trentino. As numerous articles on this topic demonstrate, the magazine in this period gave a lot of space to "scientific chemistry in its relationship with the practicalities of agriculture".

In 1884, Federico Viglietto became the director of "*Bullettino*". The magazine, now in its fourth season, had a new look but confirmed its objectives. Viglietto dedicated a series of "*Lezioni*" ("Lessons") to vine growing, which started with articulated considerations on "*Clima e terreno adatti alla vite*" ("Climate and soil suitable to vines"). There was a strong conviction of the necessity to support the vine and wine production at a time when Italian agriculture, heavily affected by the economic crisis (in 1884 the results of "*Inchiesta agraria*", "Agrarian Inquiry", became public), saw a generalized drop in prices with the exception of wine, whose prices kept stable because of the significant drop in French production, due to the devastating effects of Phylloxera.

---

[19]Cf., Rossler (1874, pp. 119–126), Levi (1875, pp. 113–140), Viglietto (1880), and Ambrosio (1894, pp. 371–376).

There were two recurring themes at the time: crop protection from mildew and Phylloxera and the effectiveness of American vines.

In 1888, when in neighbouring Austria, vineyards affected by phylloxera were discovered, the prefect dissolved the provincial ampelographic commissions and constituted a Commission for Vine Growing and Oenology. Simultaneously, the Friulian Agricultural Association established at the request of the Ministry for Agriculture, Industry and Commerce an anti-Phylloxera consortium for Friuli, which had to monitor the status of the vineyards. At the same time, some experience fields were started, where the more resistant American vines were tested, starting with Jaquez, Herbemont, Yorck Madeira, Blanc-Defiance, Elsimburg, Huntingdon. They all had the same importance, but it was interesting to extend such experience on as many vines as possible. The results of these tests were not always encouraging and were systematically published by "*Bullettino*". In 1879, the first wine fair was held in Udine and in 1893 "*Bullettino*" published "*Atti della seconda fiera e concorso vini e Congresso enologico tenuti in Udine dal 20 al 23 aprile 1893*" ("Acts of the second fair, wine competition and wine Congress held in Udine from 20 to 23 April 1893"). The proceedings offered a detailed picture of Friulian vine growing and winemaking from which the main critical issues of this sector emerged. In addition to encouraging the study of the most effective ways to counteract the phylloxera invasion, speakers lingered on the effects of the mildew invasion in the countryside of Friuli. These were: the abandonment of vine growing in locations where the soil seemed ill-suited for wine cultivation; the rejection of many varieties which suffered more than others the attacks of the parasite; the introduction of a grapevine (Isabella), which was not very refined but was very productive and resistant to oidium; the tendency to import from abroad, especially from France, new varieties which were disease resistant and able to give fine products.

A turning point for regional vine growing coincided with the serious agricultural crisis caused since the early 80s by the invasion of American grains and by the decline in freight rates. If oidium, caused by the *Uncinula necator* cryptogam, was quickly eradicated with the practice of sulphidation,[20] the same did not happen for late blight, which

[20]On sulphidation: Campana (1861), Camuzzoni (1861), and Pollacci (1864).

appeared in Friuli in the 80s, when American species such as *Isabella, Vitis labrusca* and *Vitis rupestris vulpina* started speading. They offered good resistance to fungal diseases, primarily to phylloxera, with the advantage of easy cultivation and considerable productivity.[21] The first news of the damage caused by the fearsome phytophagous pest in the Transalpine countries arrived in the late 70s. The Friulian Agricultural Association decided to strengthen its monitoring work and implement a very active propaganda through the press in order to counter the serious danger and introduce the American vines as the only ones able to offer a safe way to maintain the levels of wine production even in countries invaded by phylloxera.[22] Friuli was initially spared from the voracious aphid—the infection reached the province of Friuli only in 1901—perhaps thanks also to a system that focused on subsistence agriculture and small properties, which did not require the use of labourers from the areas attacked by phylloxera, thus reducing the risks arising from the spread of the epidemic through clothing and work tools.[23]

The much-vaunted American vines presented the major drawback of producing poor quality wine. Hence, some farmers preferred the latter and were content with producing some wine, just to make wine at all, while others chose to plant American vines grafting on their root some homegrown variety. The understanding that the root immunity developed by some American species could be used to build a two-limbed plant with American foot and European vegetative and reproductive system, stimulated the research of American varieties which were best suited to grafting and most tolerant to limestone which European vines were rather resistant to. It was a brave and, for certain aspects, "revolutionary" choice, because it put producers in front

[21]Cf., Le viti americane (1881, pp. 140–141) and Pecile (1901, pp. 280–283).

[22]Berthod (1903, p. 225). See also: Provvedimenti governativi in favore dell'agricoltura attuati nell'anno 1874 (1875, pp. 82–83), Levi (1883, pp. 105–110), Bigozzi (1899, pp. 7–12), I pericoli di un'invasione filloserica e i mezzi per prevenirla e combatterla (1899, pp. 193–195), Contro la fillossera della vite (1901, pp. 142–143), Sannino (1902, pp. 114–121), Berthod (1904, pp. 17–33), and Cavazza (1904, pp. 590–592).

[23]See the discussion of this question in Cossa (1875) and Peglion (1902).

of a dilemma: were they going to bet on quantity or quality? (Panjek 1998, p. 91). Starting from the fact that the most productive vines offered poorer quality grapes, it was concluded that agricultural innovations to improve wine quality would inevitably affect production. The opportunity offered by the need to proceed with the reconstitution of the vineyards destroyed by phylloxera, led to a deep, rational and bold reorganization of the winemaking industry: implantation, growing and cultivation systems were improved, varieties were culled, new fertilization, and in some areas also irrigation, techniques were introduced, greater determination was pointed at crop specialization. Not only that, the hard struggle waged first against oidium, and later against phylloxera, encouraged the launching of studies on organic agricultural chemistry and its various applications. Experimentation led to a better understanding of the pedological characteristics of the vine, it favoured the application of new processes of acclimatization and selection, it improved vineyard implantation with new solutions; it finetuned winemaking techniques. This was the first big step towards a new "viticulture" (Marescalchi and Dalmasso 1937, pp. 573–604).

This excitement was well-documented not only in "*Bullettino*" (Associazione agraria friulana 1906) pages but also by "*La Rivista: periodico quindicinale di viticultura, enologia e agraria*" ("The Magazine: fortnightly vine growing, oenology and agricultural periodical"), published from 1894 to 1917 from the School of Vine Growing and Oenology in Conegliano, which had become a reference point for regional vine growing. At the same time, as the wine industry was preparing for a lengthy goodbye to silkworm cultivation, it experienced a vast and organic renewal and was the focus of a lively debate that found some space in new magazines. In 1902 the Agricultural Society of Gorizia began the publication of the fortnightly "*L'agricoltore goriziano*" ("The farmer from Gorizia"). The same provincial authority of the Princely County of Gorizia and Gradisca revitalized local agriculture through a series of policies, culminating in 1905 with the establishment of a provincial agricultural office. An even more decisive step in favour of the diffusion of agrarian techniques among the rural population was made immediately after the transformation of the Agricultural School and the constitution of a "*Cattedra ambulante*" of agriculture, following what had already been done in Udine. In November 1906 the first issue of "*L'Amministrazione autonoma*" ("The Autonomous Administration"), the provincial government press service for the Princely County of Gorizia and Gradisca, was published.[24] On 1 May 1908 "*Il contadinello*" ("The peasant"),[25] an agricultural bimonthly periodical, was published by the Provincial Agricultural Office in Gorizia (Comel 1950). Moreover, in 1908 the first issue of "*L'Istria agricola*" ("Agricultural Istria"), a fortnightly magazine by the Provincial Agricultural Institute, was published in Poreč.

Towards the New Vine Growing

The Great War marked a setback in the difficult process of modernization of regional vine growing: the vineyards in Collio and Carso were devastated by trenches and by the battles fought to conquer them. Similarly, vineyards in Friuli at best were badly affected by a prolonged lack of care (Poggi 1940, pp. 187–207). Once the hostilities were over and as soon as the situation allowed it, the publication of "*L'Amico del contadino*"[26] was resumed and in May 1920, "after three years of silence" also "*Bullettino*" was published and it soon became the mouthpiece of the socio-economic section of the Friulian Agricultural Association. Beyond well-illustrated agrarian history issues and the facts that characterized the so-called "*biennio rosso*" ("two-red years"), "*Bullettino*" dealt from the start with vine growing, launching a campaign for the reconstitution of the Friulian anti-Phylloxera Consortium, founded in 1908 and active until October 1917. Why was this a priority for winemaking in Friuli? For various reasons, not only related to monitoring the possible spread of phylloxera, but also to keep current members informed about all matters pertaining to modern winemaking. In September 1921, the anti-Phylloxera Consortium organized

[24]"Un po' di programma" (1906, pp. 1–2).

[25]"Al lettore" (1908, p. 1).

[26]The first issue was published in 1897.

an exhibition of grapes for ampelographic purposes and a conference of winemakers to discuss matters pertaining to Friulian winemaking. Producers in the provinces of Gorizia and Udine were also invited. The results of these initiatives, regularly documented on "*Bullettino*", showed a renewed interest for these issues: there were 87 exhibitors and 708 grape samples.

The need to convey information, to offer suggestions to overcome the post-war crisis and favour the development of agriculture was fully felt also by the "*Cattedra ambulante*" in Udine, which from 1919 to 1920 began to print its own biweekly "*Bollettino*" ("Bullettin"), which was distributed freely to farmers, municipal authorities and agricultural institutions. In January 1922, the first issue of "*L'Agricultura friulana*" ("The Friulian Agriculture") was published as the weekly bulletin of the "*Cattedra ambulante*" of the province of Udine. It was edited by Enrico Marchettano and, while going through difficult times, it would remain until 1980 one of the most authoritative voices for regional agriculture and a source of reference for anyone who wanted to study its winemaking.

The "March on Rome" marked a turning point in the country's economic and agricultural policies, which resulted, at least in the "Neomachesterian phase" by De Stefani, in the search for production on several fronts, not only industrial. In order to achieve a balanced budget, the Verona economist to whom Mussolini had entrusted the leadership of the Treasury, promoted a plan of "administrative demobilization", which led to the suppression of the province of Gorizia and, consequently, of its Provincial Agricultural Office (Istituto chimico agrario sperimentale di Gorizia 1932). The new geographical and administrative structures were also reflected on "*L'Agricoltura friulana*", a magazine that two years after its first publication had more than 10,000 subscribers and was distributed throughout the region. Many articles were about winemaking in Friuli, starting from the brief but exhaustive contribution by Morelli De Rossi "*La ricostruzione viticola in Friuli*" ("The vine-growing reconstruction in Friuli") in 1925.[27]

[27]Morelli De Rossi (1925, pp. 66–75). See also Dalmasso et al. (1932).

There was also renewed interest for oenology, as demonstrated by the frequent articles published between 1922 and 1925. Their publication was also encouraged by studies and an increasingly firm collaboration with the Experimental Station for Growing Grapevines in Conegliano which was constituted in 1923. In 1924 the first volume of "*Annuario*" ("Yearbook") was published (Paccanoni 1923–1924, pp. 3–4); it was an achievement of the personnel from the Experimental Station, with names which would become households in Italian winemaking, from Michele Giunti to Giovanni Dalmasso, from Italo Cosmo to Luigi Manzoni. In "*Annuario*", which remained a reference point for specialist publications in Friuli until 1968, important ampelographic studies were published as well as articles about winemaking techniques, physiology and pathology, or articles of an economic and commercial nature, which Guido Poggi also benefited from when drafting his famous "*Atlante ampelografico*" ("Ampelographic atlas", 1939).

1925 marked a break, not only from a political point of view, but also for the agricultural history in Friuli: on 15 November, greatly rundown in its content, "*Bullettino dell'Associazione agraria friulana*" was shut down after having published volume number 40 of its seventh series. This is not the place to dwell on the Fascistization of the media, which was well described precisely in 1925 by Luigi Albertini, director of "Corriere della Sera", nor is it the place to illustrate the work of institutional reorganization in order to face, first, the "*Battaglia del grano*" ("Battle for grain") and, later, to implement the idea of a corporate state. The plan to focus Italian agriculture on producing grains, while causing long-term damages to the productive fabric of the country, slowed down, but did not stop, the renewal process of winemaking in Friuli. "*L'Agricoltura friulana*" kept the interest on changing tastes of the people in Friuli, who became more demanding and required better wines, with less acidity, a good alcoholic content, amiable, more velvety, clear and with the right colour. Hence, the need to offer rational indications to winemaking, favouring general winemaking techniques and the start of *cantine sociali*, wine cooperatives (Minutello 1930, pp. 1–2). The "*Cattedre ambulanti*" played, especially in the second half of the 20s, a decisive role to illustrate "*L'utilità dell'istituzione delle cantine sociali in Friuli*" ("The usefulness of the constitution of wine cooperatives in Friuli") by Guido Poggi.[28]

The implementation of the idea of a wine cooperative developed in a crisis context, stemming both from the effects of the agricultural policies under the Fascist regime and the deflationary and recessive consequences of the "*Quota 90*" policy (a revaluation of lira against sterling and US dollar undertaken by Mussolini), which led consumers to cut consumption. The way out was indicated in the simultaneous improvement of the "agrarian-grapevine" issue (variety selection) and of winemaking, that is with modern grape processing techniques. This solution could be promoted through the development of cooperation forms, which were also in line with the objectives of Fascist agricultural policies.[29]

In 1935 the "*cattedre ambulanti*" were turned into Provincial Agriculture Inspectorates and the following year, "*L'Agricoltura friulana*" became part of the agricultural and economic authorities in Friuli. The size of the magazine was reduced and was now published every fortnight, in order to reduce paper consumption to adapt to the measures taken by the government against the sanctions approved by the League of Nations. Even with its new outlook, which was functional to the autarkic design, the magazine continued to be an influential voice in a context which saw deep normative transformations for the implantation and reconstruction of the vineyards, for keeping wine production stable and increasing alcohol from wine materials, for regulating the production and trade of fine wines. In this context, the new issue for the industry rested in a huge dilemma illustrated by Arturo Marescalchi on "*L'Agricoltura Fascista*" ("The Fascist Agriculture"): in order to restructure of Italian winemaking, did the production of wine have to be decreased?

During the Second World War, "*L'Agricoltura friulana*" continued, albeit with understandable difficulties, to fulfil its role, taking care of

---

[28]*Agricoltura Friulana*, May 11, 1929, pp. 1–2. See also L'attività della Cattedra Ambulante di agricoltura (1928, pp. 1–6).

[29]Rubini (1931, p. 1) and Fuschini (1934, pp. 1–2).

both "*La preparazione agricola alla guerra totale*" ("The agricultural preparation for total war")[30] and the information campaign for winegrowing and winemaking. In 1942 the magazine published no less than 32 articles on this subject. A similar number was published the following year together with an interesting article on Tocai, which, together with Merlot and Verduzzo, was assigned the task of improving the results of our winemaking industry and take it to unexpected fortunes.

Dignity and Identity

The wine congress, organized during the 10th wine fair in Buttrio (5–6 May 1947) and reported in detail by "*L'Agricoltura friulana*", offered the opportunity to Giovanni Dalmasso to draw a picture of the post-war situation and to discuss "*Orientamenti della viticoltura friulana e miglioramento della tecnica enologica*" ("Guidelines of the Friulian wine industry and improved winemaking techniques").[31] There were several critical aspects for the industry. Despite Friuli which did not lack fields that could produce wines with high alcohol content and good preservation, production levels in the province were still low: more than 700,000 hectolitres were consumed per year compared with an average annual production of 300,000. Cuttings were missing, although the Friulian plant nursery industry was, perhaps, one of the most productive and well-equipped in Italy.[32] It was necessary to improve the grapevine guidelines and conduct a rigorous check of grafts. The Consortium for winemaking in Udine should become active again, as it was obvious that, not only in Friuli, there were many more good vine growers than winemakers. According to Dalmasso, the solution to these problems was two-pronged: improving education and multiplying the wine cooperatives.

Dalmasso explained these ideas, translating his intentions into action, in January 1948 in the first issue of "*Rivista di viticoltura e di enologia*"

[30] *L'Agricoltura friulana,* May 18, 1940, p. 1.

[31] *L'Agricoltura friulana,* May 16, 1947, p. 3.

[32] Nussi (1960, p. 1). By the same author, *Vivaistica, viticoltura ed enologia in Friuli* (1964).

("Journal of vine growing and Oenology"), a monthly magazine issued by the School of Conegliano and the Experimental Station of Vine Growing and Oenology, edited by Italo Cosmo and Luigi Manzoni (Dalmasso 1948, pp. 5–6). It is no coincidence that the introductory note, entrusted to Arturo Marescalchi, ends with the following warning: "The need to educate the masses who are dedicated to vine growing and winemaking is always pressing." The magazine, which filled a 30-year gap as only 12 volumes of "*L'Annuario*" were published between 1923 and 1945, made use of the most qualified experts on the subject. Their aim was to ensure Italy a top place among the winemaking nations, in the wake of the 1876 work by Antonio Carpenè and Giovanni Battista Cerletti.

The influence of the School of Conegliano is clearly detectable in "*Terra friulana*" ("Friuli land"), a bimonthly magazine about economics and agricultural techniques, founded in 1956 and edited by Domenico Feruglio, Guido Poggi and Gino Rojatti. The magazine, of which unfortunately we do not have the complete series, featured articles ranging from agriculture to economics, from history to local traditions, never exceeding in technicalities and with a good iconographic impact, often entrusted to promising young artists. There are numerous contributions dedicated to wine and vine. Dalmasso himself dealt with "*Nobiltà dei vini friulani*" ("Friulian wines nobility"),[33] recording "a gradual shift of the whole wine production", which resulted in the reduction of the number "of elite types and brands" and in the simultaneous increased production of good mass-consumer wines. A significant contribution was also given by Italo Cosmo, director of the Conegliano Experimental Station, who discussed "*Luci e ombre della viticoltura e dell'enologia friulana*" ("Lights and shadows of vine growing and oenology of Friuli"), pointing out that production had focused mainly on two basic varieties: Tocai (or Friulian Tocai) among white grapes and Merlot among red grapes.[34]

[33] *Terra friulana*, II, 4 (1957), pp. 3–5.

[34] *Terra friulana*, II, 4 (1957), pp. 25–27. See also Costantini (2013).

Despite publications which continued to emphasize "the firm path towards vine growing and, also, winemaking improvements", it is also true that the "Vineyard Friuli" was still busy looking for its own identity in an extremely dynamic environment pitched against the "economic miracle". Poggi was sure about this and in 1952, while offering a "*Panorama della viticoltura friulana*" ("Panorama of Friulian winemaking") to the Meeting of the Vine and Wine Academy in Friuli Venezia Giulia, said: "The Friulian wine industry had never been included before in the national framework: old and new vines with their range of local mediocre, good or even excellent products, have never crossed the borders of the region, except for the notable exception of Piccolit" (Poggi 1952, p. 1). Cosmo himself a few years later in the pages of "*L'agricoltura friulana*" (1955) tried to answer the following question: What are the fine wines from Friuli? (Cosmo 1955, p. 6). An "embarrassing" question to which the Consortium for vine growing and oenology of Udine answered, drawing up a list of wines that included the white wine from the (eastern and western) hills of Friuli, Malvasia from Ronchi, Picolit, Pinot Bianco, Pinot grigio, Friulian Tocai, Verduzzo. Among the red they included Cabernet Franc, Merlot and the red wine from the (eastern and western) hills of Friuli.[35]

In 1955, while a new provincial Chair of Agriculture was established (Marchettano 1955, p. 1), publications began to put more effectively emphasis on issues that would become crucial in the following years. For example, the effects of the reform of land leases, the contribution given by the mechanization of the wine industry, the arrival of *barrique* techniques, the refinement through the use of glass, the industrialization of the wine industry, pricing policies and foreign competition, as well as taxation levels for wine and agricultural credit were all debated at length. "*L'Agricoltura friulana*" often hosted "*Lezioni*" ("Lessons") by Italo Cosmo, which doubtfully lingered on vineyard profitability, production levels which were still too low to influence the high prices of local wines, the activities of wine cooperatives and mechanization issues for the wine sector, hybrids, but also on the use of electricity, materials

---

[35]Dalmasso (1959, p. 1). Cf. also Montanari and Ceccarelli (1952, pp. 98–100).

(in particular, steel) and of technologies to monitor fermentation, on the importance of the figure of the oenologist.[36]

It is true that in the mid-60s, thanks to the work of the Friulian institutions, it could be said that the region had "the youngest vineyard in Italy." The consolidation of a plant nursery post-phylloxera system had produced long-term results and the old conception of the manor winery was now giving way to a modern technology with guided implantations monitored by a specialist, the winemaker technician, able to produce healthy wines, well-made and tasteful (Dalmasso 1958, p. 1). After the establishment of the EEC, in a broader market, with more demanding consumers who were free to choose between the best products from the most diverse wine regions in Europe, wine production and marketing began to suffer a new and intense regulatory process. The commitment of the Friulian agricultural world towards the creation of a strong and lasting system was constantly accompanied by high profile research in the wine sector. Next to a consolidated "autochthonous" basis, that the agronomist and oenologist were progressively refining, in the vineyards and wineries there was a growing interest for grapevines from other highly favourable regions, especially Austrian, German and French. An underlying problem was widely discussed in publications, "the two agricultures" (Bucco 1961, p. 1). This refers to the existing dualism in terms of land structure and management: on the one hand, there were hundreds of small fragmented companies, often microenterprises with a dimension of less than 5 ha (87%); on the other hand, there were companies "managed independently, often family-run, and which together formed 13% of the total and had a surface area greater than 5 ha". The former were usually characterized by farming activities which were marginal and supplementary to other activities, whose income was the main earning source for the family or for this type of pseudo rural communities. In this type of companies mostly non-commercial choices played a role. The other companies were "independent, family-run and the entire family put its energies and most valid efforts" into agricultural activities. In this case, there was no other income, all hopes were anchored

[36]Some interesting reflections on this point are to be found in Cosmo (1950, p. 9; 1959, p. 6).

on the performance of agriculture and every technical progress was carefully screened to be later possibly applied. The "Renaissance" of the '60s was accompanied not only by the approval of the special Statute for the Region Friuli Venezia Giulia and the establishment of the first Regional Council in Trieste, but also by the DOC Law ("Denominazione di Origine Controllata", controlled designation of origin) of which the Collio (Eastern Hills) was the first area to benefit from, by the great plans for agricultural development led by the European Community, and in 1968 by the constitution of Ersa, the regional agency for rural development (Nussi 1961, p. 1). In that context, while with the retirement of Dalmasso (1962) and Poggi (1963) there was the sense that a very important season for Friulian, and more generally Italian, wine had come to an end, a new and effective way to instil that "idea of improvement" dear to Gabrile Luigi Pecile emerged.

In 1964 "*Vita nei campi*" ("Life in the fields") started as a Sunday radio programme and in over half a century it has continued to pass on the ancient values of Friulian agriculture through a serious and informative activity, always attentive to the problems and prospects of development for regional vine growing. After a pioneering phase in which Claudio Cojutti was on air for a few minutes in a national broadcast, in 1968 an editorial board was created in Udine, which was led by Isi Benini and by Cojutti, and a weekly edition of "*Vita nei campi*" started been broadcast for farmers in Friuli Venezia Giulia. Since then, the programme has always been broadcast, even during the critical moments when Friuli was devastated by an earthquake (1976). That there was a connection between the core group behind "Vita nei campi" and specialized publications was demonstrated by the fact that shortly afterwards Isi Benini launched a quarterly magazine about "wine and schnapps, beer and cuisine from the Friuli Venezia Giulia Region". The first issue of "*Il vino*" ("Wine"), the result of an editorial initiative in the making for a few years, was published in December 1971, with the aim of relaunching Friulian wine, "too unjustly considered the Cinderella among the Italian wine Gotha" (Benini 1971, pp. 10–12). The magazine, which was published for just over a decade, although enriched by a valuable iconographic outlook and a well-cared publishing plan, did not include articles of great depth, but has undoubtedly the merit of having helped enhance an all-round image of Friulian wine and vine growing, promoting it with strength and authority in the wider and more competitive international market.

Between Tradition and Innovation

In the early 70s, while "*L'Agricoltura friulana*" continued to question "*Le prospettive di sviluppo della viticoltura regionale*" ("The prospects for development of regional winemaking")[37] and the issue of the controlled designation of origin was debated by many, forcing growers to deal with an even more pervasive legislation, the Region made an important step forward in support of the wine sector: in 1973 the Regional Centre for the strengthening vine growing and oenology came into operation in Udine in order to promote the development of winemaking in the regional areas with this vocation through surveys for the identification and dissemination of the most suitable grape varieties as well as the best cultivation, pest management and bad-weather-defence systems. Simultaneously, the newly formed structure was given the important task of researching and disseminating rational winemaking, preservation and handling methods for oenological products. In 1983, ten years after its establishment, the Centre, chaired by Pietro Pittaro, started the publication of "*Un vigneto chiamato Friuli*" ("A vineyard called Friuli"), a periodical distributed to around 15,000 companies in Friuli Venezia Giulia which produced grapes or which traded wine without making it (Pittaro 1983, p. 3). The magazine was part of a larger extraordinary programme to enhance winemaking which the Region had entrusted the Centre with in 1981. Its objective was to disseminate information about new legislation, regional and national wine policies and regulations concerning vine growing and winemaking, as well as compliance deadlines. The magazine published also studies about vine growing and winemaking led by the most qualified institutes such as the Agricultural Experimentation Centre in Pozzuolo, the Institute for Vine Growing in

[37] *L'Agricoltura friulana*, August 15, 1970. Cf. also. Fabbro (1977).

Conegliano and, not least of all, the University of Udine, which by the 1979–1980 academic year had established a degree course in agricultural sciences (Salvador 1970).

In the same period, also the Regional Department for agriculture, forests and mountain economy, became active in these areas. In June 1978, it launched the first issue of "*Regione agricoltura*" ("Region agriculture"), a monthly bulletin with socio-economic information, edited by Giuseppe Pascolini. The periodical, founded with the aim of "fulfilling the needs for information and guidance on fundamental problems for the regional agriculture", had to report the progress of the regional development plan, in which agriculture "had been guaranteed a central role" (Pascolini 1978, p. 3). Little attention, however, was given to vine growing, leaving more space to themes that in that context had greater importance. We are referring to problems relating to land reclamation, irrigation and consolidation, as well as issues related to the improvement of company and inter-company structures, agricultural credit, the development of animal husbandry, as well as the enhancement of quality crops, the reconstruction of earthquake-stricken areas, the improvement of income levels and living conditions in the countryside.

In 1988, twenty years after the establishment of the Regional Agency for the development of agriculture in Friuli Venezia Giulia, the first issue of "*Notiziario Ersa*" ("Ersa News") was published (Del Gobbo 1988, p. 3). Once the realization of structural works and the reconstruction of animal farms destroyed or damaged by the earthquake of 1976, was over, the Regional Agency began a thorough reconsideration of its activities and aims in order to better adapt them to technological development and to changes in agricultural markets. The dissemination of information became not only functional to make Ersa accountable for its own work, but also to increase awareness among agricultural workers so that they would promote at different levels agricultural policies based on an efficient food farming system, on renewed cooperation, on a more effective promotional activity, thus achieving two other aims for Ersa, that is promoting a decrease in production costs and implementing technical assistance to farms. The issues addressed by the "*Notiziario*" were essentially those Ersa focused its activities on: from the development of rural properties to the professional training of farmers, from the commercial promotion of food farming products to the research and development of technologies against atmospheric adversities. It should also be noted that in the first years, little attention was given to vine growing. The first article about "*L'impegno dell'Ersa nella selezione clonale e nel miglioramento genetico*" ("Ersa's commitment to clonal selection and breeding improvements")[38] was published in 1990, but it was not until 1992 with "*Il ruolo dei microrganismi nella produzione dei vini destinati all'invecchiamento*" ("The role of microorganisms in the production of aging wines")[39] that an article about oenology was published. The focus of "*Notiziario*" with respect to vines and wines grew significantly in the mid-90s, in the wake of a general revival of interest for winemaking, which led, among other things, the University of Udine to establish a bachelor's degree on vine growing and winemaking in the academic year 1992–1993 (Del Zan 2009).

The beginning of the '90s saw an acceleration in the European integration project. Moving from a common to a single market, it became more and more important to understand—and here publications played a crucial role—that wine should not only be produced, but, above all, sold. The precious drink had to respond to a specific oenological and market plan, that would lead to satisfy consumers' tastes in terms of both quality and price. A complex process had brought wine to transform from an energetic drink to a vehicle of culture and enjoyment, not only in terms of sensory pleasures, such as smell and taste, but also in terms of emotions, imagination, socio-recreational associations and well-being (Fabbro 2005).

In spite of the recognition of its DOC and DOCG ("Denominazione di Origine Controllata e Garantita", controlled and guaranteed designation of origin) productions and the presence of numerous autochthonous grape varieties, the wine industry was confronted with more competitive and unstable markets, with lower growth rates than in the past, with a qualitatively more advanced demand and with rising production costs, related to the reduced size of many companies, the

[38] *Notiziario Ersa*, 3 (1990), pp. 23–24.

[39] *Notiziario Ersa*, 2 (1992), pp. 6–11.

increase in labour costs and labour shortages. It also had to deal with the diffusion of environmentally friendly farming practices, with the growing demand to integrate vineyards in the landscape, with the difficulty of working steep fields, and with the low mechanization level the countryside. Not to mention the significant proportion of vineyards which needed renovation and the proliferation of small wineries, together with an increase in wine culture, the growth of wine tourism, the presence of regional high-quality food farming products and other co-factors, such as the interest in biological products and the opening of non-traditional markets (Cisilino and Pozzi 2012, pp. 11–14).

Agricultural publications have undoubtedly brought the Friulian winemaking to look confidently to the future, seeking solutions based on efficiency, promoting the recovery of the industry from the distortions created by the rapid process of industrialization, encouraging research and development on all fronts, aiming at the improvement of cultivation techniques. But it is also true that, as in Emily Dickinson's words, "the past is not a package that you can put aside". In this spirit in 2009 the magazine "*Tiere Furlane*" was first edited by Umberto Alberini with support from Enos Costantini.[40] It is meticulous in its content and visually appealing, not technical, but about the "culture of the land", where in addition to current events, the reader can find history, art, literature of what the poet and writer Ippolito Nievo called a "small compendium of the universe" (Nievo 1867, p. 33). The constant reference to the history of Friulian agriculture and, in particular, of its vines and wines, does not only satisfy a curiosity, but helps strengthen and substantiate the image of products that are the result not only of secular transformations, but also of conquests and sacrifices by "unique people" (as stated in one of the Region's slogans): the actual confirmation that theorized agriculture could also be practise.[41]

[40]Violino (2009, pp. 2–3). Cf. also, Costantini et al. (2007a).

[41]Some interesting reflections on this point are to be found in Calò and Costacurta (1991), Costantini et al. (2007b), and Fabbro (2008).

References

Books

Associazione agraria friulana. (1900). *L'opera dell'Associazione agraria friulana*, I, *Dal 1846 al 1900*, Udine: Associazione agraria friulana.

Associazione agraria friulana. (1906). *L'opera dell'associazione agraria friulana dal 1900 al 1906*, II, Udine: Seitz.

Associazione agraria friulana. (1948). *Atti del Congresso tenutosi in Udine nei giorni 26 e 27 agosto 1948 a celebrazione del Centenario dell'Associazione agraria friulana*, Udine: Associazione agraria friulana.

Atti del Convegno nazionale di studi sul rilancio dell'agricoltura italiana nel III centenario della nascita di Sallustio Bandini. (1979). I, Siena: Monte dei Paschi di Siena.

Atti del Convegno Venezia e la Terraferma attraverso le relazioni dei Rettori (Trieste, 23–24 ottobre 1980). (1981). Milano: A. Giuffré.

Berengo, M. (1963). *L'agricoltura veneta dalla caduta della Repubblica all'unità*, Milano: Banca commerciale italiana.

Breschi, M., & Pecorari, P. (Eds.). (1998). *Economia e popolazione in Friuli dalla caduta della Repubblica di Venezia alla fine della dominazione austriaca*, Udine: Forum.

Brianta, D. (1994). *Agricoltura, credito e istruzione. La società agraria di Lombardia dal 1862 al 1914*, Milano: Cisalpino.

Brunello, P. (1996). *Acquasanta e verderame. Parroci agronomi in Veneto e in Friuli nel periodo austriaco (1814–1866)*, Verona: Cierre.

Burger, J. (1843). *Agricoltura del Regno lombardo-veneto*, Milano: Motta.

Cafarelli, A. (2009). *La terra avara. Assetti fondiari e forme di conduzione agraria nella Bassa Friulana (1866–1914)*, Venezia: Istituto veneto di scienze, lettere ed arti.

Cafarelli, A. (2010). *Il padrone non va per l'acqua. Assetti colturali e rapporti di produzione in un'azienda agraria della Bassa friulana (1875–1914)*, Udine: Forum.

Calò, A., & Costacurta, A. (1991). *Delle viti in Friuli*, Udine: Arti Grafiche Friulane.

Campana, B. (1861). *Sul metodo di insolfare le viti a secco ed a liquido*, Venezia: P. Naratovich.

Camuzzoni, G. (1861). *Rapporto sopra la insolfazione delle viti eseguita per la prima volta su grande scala in provincia dalla Società toscana nel 1860*, Verona: Vicentini e Franchini.

Comel, A. (1950). *L'Istituto chimico agrario sperimentale di Gorizia. 80 anni di sperimentazione agraria*, Gorizia: Peternolli.

Cossa, A. (1875). *Sopra alcuni mezzi proposti per distruggere la fillossera della vite: riassunto di una lezione data nel reale Museo industriale italiano in Torino nella sera del 5 maggio 1875*, Udine: Seitz.

Costantini, E. (Ed.). (2013). *Tocai e Friulano. Un racconto di civiltà del vino*, Udine: Forum.

Costantini, E. (Ed.). (2017). *Storia della vite e del vino in Friuli e a Trieste*, Udine: Forum – Accademia italiana della vite e del vino.

Costantini, E., Mattaloni, C., & Petrussi, C. (2007a). *La vite nella storia e nella cultura del Friuli*, I-II, Udine: Forum.

Costantini, E., Mattaloni, C., & Petrussi, C. (2007b). *Bevi une bote che no spandi une gote: vigneti storici e viticoltura tradizionale, aspetti colturali e culturali, frammenti di ottocento, parassiti dal Nuovo Mondo, vivaismo, ampelotoponomastica ed enotoponomastica, glossario illustrato, cantina e strumenti di vinificazione*, Udine: Forum.

Dalmasso, G., Cosmo, I., & Dell'Olio, G. (1932). *L'indirizzo viticolo da dare alla Provincia di Udine*, Treviso: Longo e Zoppelli.

Del Zan, F. (Ed.). (2009). *La terra indagata. I pionieri della ricerca in Friuli*, Gorizia: Ersa.

Fabbro, C. (1977). *Viti e vini del Friuli*, Gorizia: ed. Ducato Vini friulani.

Fabbro, C. (2005). *Il vigneto Friuli dall'arrivo dei romani alla partenza del Tocai*, Udine: Ducato dei vini friulani.

Fabbro, C. (Ed.). (2008). *Il vino in Friuli Venezia giulia, Storia terre e vitigni*, Udine: Editoriale FVG.

Fanfani, T. (Ed.). (1998). *Saggi di Storia economica. Studi in onore di Amelio Tagliaferri*, Pisa: Pacini.

Istituto chimico agrario sperimentale di Gorizia (1932). *La viti-vinicoltura nella Venezia Giulia con speciale riguardo alle Provincie di Gorizia, Trieste ed al Mandamento di Cervignano*, Gorizia: Iucchi.

Marescalchi, A., & Dalmasso, G. (1937). *Storia della vite e del vino in Italia*, Milano: Gualdoni.

Montanari, V., & Ceccarelli, G. (1950). *La viticoltura e l'enologia nelle Tre Venezie: memoria statistica,* tecnica, storica, descrittiva, Treviso: Longo & Zoppelli.

Montanari, V., & Ceccarelli, G. (1952). *La Viticoltura e la Enologia nelle Tre Venezie*, Treviso: Longo e Zoppelli.

Nievo, I. (1867). *Le confessioni di un ottuagenario*, I, Firenze: Le Monnier.

Nussi, E. (1964). *Vivaistica, viticoltura ed enologia in Friuli*, Udine: Consorzio provinciale per la viticoltura e l'enologia.

Panjek, G. (1980). *Contributo alla storia dell'agricoltura friulana (L'Associazione agraria dagli inizi al regime commissariale)*, Udine: Del Bianco.

Panjek, G. (1992). *La vite e il vino nell'economia friulana: un rinnovamento frenato, secoli 17–19*, Torino: Giappichelli.

Pecorari, P. (1989). *Il protezionismo imperfetto. Luigi Luzzatti e la tariffa doganale del 1878*, Venezia: Istituto veneto di scienze, lettere ed arti.

Pecorari, P. (Ed.). (2011). *Il Friuli economico. 150 anni di storia*, Udine: Forum - CCIAA di Udine.

Pecorari, P., & Ballini, P.L. (Eds.). (1994). *Luigi Luzzatti e il suo tempo. Atti del Convegno internazionale di studio. Venezia, 7–9 novembre 1991*, Venezia: Istituto veneto di scienze, lettere ed arti.

Peglion, V. (1902). *La fillossera e le principali malattie crittogamiche della vite con speciale riguardo ai mezzi di difesa*, Milano: Hoepli.

Pletti, D. (1845). *Dei vini del Friuli*, Udine: Trombetti-Murero.

Poggi, G. (1940). *La viticoltura in Friuli nel dopo guerra, in Il Friuli nel dopoguerra*, Udine: Arti Grafiche friulane.

Pollacci, E. (1864). *Del modo d'agire dello solfo sulla crittogama della vite e di un nuovo rimedio più dello solfo economico e meglio atto a combatterla: memoria letta al 10° Congresso degli scienziati italiani nella tornata del 20 settembre della classe d'agronomia e veterinaria*, Siena.

Rapporto della Camera di commercio e d'industria della Provincia del Friuli all'eccelso imp. reg. ministero del Commercio, dell'Industria e delle Pubbliche costruzioni sullo stato dell'industria e del commercio negli anni 1853, 1854, 1855 e 1856. (1857). Udine.

Regione autonoma Friuli Venezia Giulia. (2013). *6° Censimento generale dell'Agricoltura in Friuli Venezia Giulia. Dati definitivi*, Trieste.

Salvador, O. (1970). *La vitivicoltura della Regione Friuli Venezia Giulia negli anni '80*, Palmanova: Cartografia Visentin.

Scarpa, G. (1972). *L'economia dell'agricoltura veneziana nell'800*, Padova: Cedam.

Scienze e tecniche agrarie nel Veneto dell'Ottocento. Atti del secondo seminario di Storia delle scienze e delle tecniche nell'Ottocento Veneto. (1992). Venezia: Istituto Veneto di scienze, lettere ed arti.

Viglietto, F. (1880). *La fillossera: istruzione popolare*, Udine: Seitz.

Zalin, G. (1978). *La società agraria veneta del secondo Ottocento. Possedenti e contadini nel sottosviluppo regionale*, Padova: Cedam.

Zaninelli, S. (Ed.). (1990). *Le conoscenze agrarie e la loro diffusione in Italia nell'Ottocento*, Torino: Giappichelli.

Papers in Journals

Al lettore. (1908). *Il contadinello*, I, 1, p. 1.

Ambrosio, D. (1894). Conferenze agrarie tenute nella R. scuola pratica d'agricoltura in Pozzuolo del Friuli (Conferenza IV, s. II). *Bullettino dell'Associazione agraria friulana*, IV, 11, pp. 371–376.

Associazione agraria friulana. (1855). Riassunto brevemente l'operato della Presidenza anteriormente alla fine di novembre pp. riferiamo le proposte fatte e le risoluzioni prese ultimamente con cui si dà alla piena azione della Società il vero iniziamento. *Bullettino dell'Associazione agraria friulana*, I, 1, pp. 5–8.

Benini, I. (1971). I tanti perché. *Il Vino*, I, 1, pp. 10–12.

Beretta, F. (1895). I precursori dell'Associazione agraria friulana. *Bullettino dell'Associazione agraria friulana*, IV, 12, pp. 3–7.

Berthod, F. (1903). Commissione per la difesa del Friuli dalla filossera. Seduta del 3 marzo 1903, *Bullettino dell'Associazione agraria friulana*, IV, 20, p. 225.

Berthod, F. (1904). Verbale della seduta consigliare del 24 dicembre 1904. *Bullettino dell'Associazione agraria friulana*, IV, 21, pp. 17–33.

Bigozzi, G. (1899). Condizioni presenti del Friuli riguardo all'infezione fillosserica, *Bullettino dell'Associazione agraria friulana*, IV, 16, pp. 7–12.

Bucco, F. (1961). Le due agricolture. *L'Agricoltura friulana*, February 28, p. 1.

Cafarelli, A. (1993–1994). Un'azienda agraria friulana tra Ottocento e Novecento. *Atti dell'Istituto veneto di scienze, lettere ed arti, Classe di scienze morali, lettere ed arti, 152*, 223–277.

Cafarelli, A. (1997). Sull'indebitamento contadino in un'azienda agraria della Bassa Friulana (1875–1919). *Alsa, 10*, pp. 36–44.

Cafarelli, A. (2012). Riflessioni sull'evoluzione dell'agricoltura friulana negli ultimi 150 anni. *Atti dell'Accademia udinese di scienze, lettere ed arti, 105*, pp. 107–120.

Cavazza, D. (1904). Per la difesa del Friuli contro la fillossera. *Bullettino dell'Associazione agraria friulana*, IV, 21, pp. 590–592.

Chiozza, L. (1862). L'abolizione dell'attuale più comune sistema di coltura delle viti in Friuli porterebbe un considerevole aumento nella produzione dei grani e del bestiame. *Bullettino dell'Associazione agraria friulana*, I, 7, p. 122.

Cisilino, F., & Pozzi, E. (2012). Il settore vitivinicolo della regione Friuli Venezia Giulia: struttura, produzione, mercato (parte prima). *Notiziario Ersa*, 2, pp. 11–14.

Coceani, F. (1912). La questione viticola in Friuli e gli ibridi produttori diretti. *Bullettino dell'Associazione agraria friulana*, IV, 29, p. 138.
Coceani, F., & Gaidoni, A. (1912). La cantina. *Bullettino dell'Associazione agraria friulana*, IV, 29, p. 355.
Contro la fillossera della vite. (1901). *Bullettino dell'Associazione agraria friulana*, IV, 18, pp. 142–143.
Cosmo, I. (1950). Per una maggiore affermazione della produzione vitivinicola friulana. *L'Agricoltura friulana*, March 15, p. 9.
Cosmo, I. (1955). Quali sono i vini di pregio friulani? *L'Agricoltura friulana*, February 15, p. 6.
Cosmo, I. (1959). Il riassetto del settore vitivinicolo nazionale (con particolare riguardo al Friuli). *L'Agricoltura friulana*, May 15, p. 6.
Dalmasso, G. (1948). Trent'anni dopo. Riprendendo il cammino. *Rivista di viticoltura e di enologia*, I, 1, pp. 5–6.
Dalmasso, G. (1958). La vocazione viticola del Friuli. *L'Agricoltura friulana*, December 31, p. 1.
Dalmasso, G. (1959). Viticoltura collinare. *L'Agricoltura friulana*, May 31, p. 1.
Dandolo, F. (1989). Alcune indicazioni bibliografiche per la storia della viticoltura in Italia (1880–1910). *Bollettino bibliografico*, Centro studi per la storia comparata delle società rurali in età contemporanea (Ed.), 35–56.
Dei mezzi per migliorare la vinicoltura nella provincia di Udine. Relazione della Commissione nominata dell'Associazione agraria friulana, e composta dei soci signori dott. Niccolò Brandis, Niccolò Mantica e Piero Marcotti. (1876). *Bullettino dell'Associazione agraria friulana*, II, 4, p. 64.
Del Gobbo, E. (1988). Perché questo periodico? *Notiziario Ersa*, I, 1, p. 3.
Dorta, J. (1914). Per un razionale indirizzo della nostra viticoltura ed enologia. *Bullettino dell'Associazione agraria friulana*, IV, 31, 330.
Freschi G. (1847). Associazione agraria del Friuli. Adunanza generale del 20 maggio 1847. *L'Amico del contadino*, 6, p. 98.
Freschi, G. (1863). Di alcune cause che hanno osteggiato il progresso della viticoltura in Friuli. *Bullettino dell'Associazione agraria friulana*, I, 8, pp. 186–193.
Fuschini, A. (1934). La organizzazione commerciale delle cantine cooperative friulane. *L'Agricoltura friulana*, March 3, pp. 1–2.
I pericoli di un'invasione filloserica e i mezzi per prevenirla e combatterla (Sunto della conferenza tenuta in Cividale il 9 settembre 1899, agli agricoltori friulani dal dottor Cavazza, direttore dell'ufficio provinciale di agricoltura di Bologna). 1899. *Bullettino dell'Associazione agraria friulana*, IV, 16, pp. 193–195.

L'attività della Cattedra Ambulante di agricoltura dalla sua istituzione ad oggi. (1928). *L'Agricoltura friulana*, April 7, pp. 1–6.
Levi, A. (1875). Istruzione popolare sulla phylloxera vastatrix. *Bullettino dell'Associazione agraria friulana*, II, 3, pp. 113–140.
Levi, A. (1883). Appunti sul nuovo progetto di legge per i provvedimenti contro la fillossera. *Bullettino dell'Associazione agraria friulana*, III, 6, pp. 105–110.
Le viti americane. (1881). *Bullettino dell'Associazione agraria friulana*, III, 4, pp. 140–141.
Marchettano, E. (1955). La nuova cattedra provinciale per l'agricoltura. Si guarda all'avvenire ma si ricorda il passato. *L'Agricoltura friulana*, August 15, p. 1.
Minutello, E. (1930). La prima cantina sociale cooperativa del Friuli. *L'Agricoltura friulana*, September 20, pp. 1–2.
Morelli De Rossi, G. (1925). La viticoltura e i problemi della ricostituzione viticola. *L'Italia agricola*, 62, 2, pp. 66–75.
Nussi, E. (1960). Barbatelle, viti e vino. *L'Agricoltura friulana*, September 15, p. 1.
Nussi, E. (1961). Tutela dei vini d'origine. *L'Agricoltura friulana*, April 30, p. 1.
Paccanoni, F. (1923–24). Prefazione. *Annuario della Stazione sperimentale di Viticoltura di Conegliano*, I, pp. 3–4.
Pascolini, G. (1978). Si consolida un rango di tutto rispetto per le attività agricole. *Regione agricoltura*, I, 1, p. 3.
Pecile, D. (1901). Le viti americane e le recenti decisioni della Commissione consultiva per la fillossera. *Bullettino dell'Associazione agraria friulana*, IV, 18, pp. 280–283.
Pecile, G.L. (1882). A proposito di alcune franche parole sull'Associazione agraria friulana. *Bullettino dell'Associazione agraria friulana*, I, 7, pp. 9–11.
Pecile, G.L. (1863a). Iniziamento d'uno studio sulle vigne in Friuli. *Bullettino dell'Associazione agraria friulana*, I, 8, pp. 629–642.
Pecile, G.L. (1863b). La fede nel miglioramento agrario e la nostra educazione rispetto all'agricoltura. *Bullettino dell'Associazione agraria friulana*, I, 8, p. 4.
Pittaro, P. (1983). Perché un nuovo giornale? *Un vigneto chiamato Friuli*, I, 1, p. 3.
Poggi, G. (1952). Panorama della viticoltura friulana. *L'Agricoltura friulana*, July 15, p. 1.
Precetti e massime agricole. (1843). *L'Amico del contadino*, 1, p. 240.
Provvedimenti governativi in favore dell'agricoltura attuati nell'anno 1874. (1875). *Bullettino dell'Associazione agraria friulana*, II, 3, pp. 82–83.

Rapporto della Commissione per la Mostra d'uve e d'altri prodotti agrari ch'ebbe luogo presso lo stabilimento agro-orticolo della Associazione agraria friulana nel settembre del 1863. (1863). *Bullettino dell'Associazione agraria friulana*, I, 8, p. 572.

Rossi, F.R. (1996). L'Associazione agraria friulana e il suo Bullettino. *Sot la nape*, 48, 4, pp. 29–32.

Rossler, L. (1874). Della phylloxera vastatrix. *Bullettino dell'Associazione agraria friulana*, II, 2, pp. 119–126.

Rubini, D. (1931). Un sano orientamento dei viticoltori italiani verso le cantine sociali. *L'Agricoltura friulana*, January 31, 1931, p. 1.

Sannino, A.F. (1902). Che cosa si deve fare di fronte alle presenti condizioni dell'infezione filloserica in Provincia. *Bullettino dell'Associazione agraria friulana*, IV, 19, pp. 114–121.

Un po' di programma. (1906). *L'Amministrazione autonoma*, I, 1, pp. 1–2.

Vianello, A. (1861). Sul progetto di una Scuola d'agricoltura da attuarsi dall'Associazione agraria friulana. *Bullettino dell'Associazione agraria friulana*, I, 6, p. 17.

Vinificazione. Come si faceva. Come si deve fare. (1891). *Bullettino dell'Associazione agraria friulana*, IV, 8, pp. 344–346.

Violino, C. (2009). Da 'Terra fiulana' a Tiere furlane. *Tiere furlane*, I, 1, pp. 2–3.

Zanelli, A. (1869). Alcune osservazioni intorno ai vitigni ed ai vini del Friuli. *Bullettino dell'Associazione agraria friulana*, I, 14, p. 40.

Papers in Books

Cafarelli, A. (1998a). *Rapporti contrattuali e indebitamento colonico in un'azienda agraria della Bassa Friulana*, Fanfani (Ed.), pp. 361–378).

Cafarelli, A. (1998b), *Paesaggio agrario e forme di utilizzazione del suolo nella Bassa Friulana a metà Ottocento*, Breschi & Pecorari (Eds.), pp. 73–85.

Cafarelli, A. (2011). *C'era una volta un contadino*, Pecorari (Ed.), pp. 22–99.

Cafarelli, A. (2017). *Infondere l'idea del miglioramento. Vite e vino nella pubblicistica friulana tra Ottocento e Novecento*, Costantini (Ed.), pp. 225–261.

Fanfani, T. (1979). *Le società agrarie di Udine e Gorizia nel contesto politico economico di Venezia e di Vienna nel settecento* (Atti del Convegno nazionale di studi sul rilancio dell'agricoltura italiana nel III centenario della nascita di Sallustio Bandini), pp. 287–307.

Gullino, G. (1992). *L'apporto delle istituzioni: dove si accenna ai provvedimenti legislativi, all'università, a talune accademie* (Scienze e tecniche agrarie nel Veneto dell'Ottocento. Atti del secondo seminario di Storia delle scienze e delle tecniche nell'Ottocento Veneto), pp. 113–127.

Morassi, L. (1981). *La società di agricoltura pratica di Udine (1762–1797)*, (Atti del Convegno Venezia e la Terraferma attraverso le relazioni dei Rettori), pp. 361–370.

Panjek, G. (1998). *Coltura della vite e produzione del vino in Friuli nel periodo napoleonico e austriaco*, Breschi & Pecorari (Eds.), pp. 87–105.

Zalin, G. (1994). *Crescita economica, protezionismo industriale e politica dei trattati commerciali in Luigi Luzzatti, 1866–1911*, Pecorari & Ballini (Eds.), pp. 215–257.

Zaninelli, S. (1990). *Evoluzione agricola italiana ed evoluzione delle conoscenze agrarie nell'Italia dell'Ottocento*, Zaninelli (Ed.), pp. 1–16.

Zaninelli, S. (1992). *L'evoluzione dell'agronomia italiana tra Sette e Ottocento: alcune linee d'indagine* (Scienze e tecniche agrarie nel Veneto dell'Ottocento. Atti del secondo seminario di Storia delle scienze e delle tecniche nell'Ottocento Veneto), pp. 11–19.

The Development of Winegrowing and Oenology in Southern Piedmont and Oltrepò Pavese

Luciano Maffi

Introduction

This article aims to highlight the changes in winegrowing and wine production in the nineteenth–twentieth centuries, in southern Piedmont and Oltrepò Pavese (Fig. 1). The article analyses the factors underlying the changes and how operators addressed the various problems caused both by socio-economic development and by the environment.

This development embraced both permanence and discontinuity that, over the long term, led to improvement of production techniques based on knowledge of the *terroir*, the quality and character of the wines, as well as on communication targeting market needs (Loubere 1978; Berta and Mainardi 1997, 2015; Mainardi 2004; Gaddo 2013; Maffi 2010, 2012).

This article makes comparison possible, by looking at the evolution of the wine sector, between the various geographical areas of

L. Maffi (✉)
University of Genoa, Genoa, Italy
e-mail: luciano.maffi@economia.unige.it

S. A. Conca Messina et al. (eds.), *A History of Wine in Europe, 19th to 20th Centuries, Volume I*, Palgrave Studies in Economic History,
https://doi.org/10.1007/978-3-030-27772-7_7

Fig. 1 Southern Piedmont and Oltrepò Pavese winegrowing area (*Source* Author)

production, and also reveals, in the nineteenth century, notable social, economic and legislative differences in the various governments of the peninsula before the Unification of Italy. In Piedmont, which at the time included Oltrepò (1743–1859), for example, already by 1785 the Agricultural Society of Turin had been founded and, in 1798, training began on winegrowing and the best method of producing and conserving wines. Piedmont's ancient tradition of winegrowing coexisted, from the mid-nineteenth century, alongside an entrepreneurial activity set up by enthusiastic, capable men who embarked on practical projects, based on research and comparison with neighbouring France. These were the men who began large-scale production of special wines, that is, wines obtained with particular oenological techniques, such as Moscato Spumante and Vermouth, already being exported in the last decades of the nineteenth century. With their ability to adapt to technological innovations, to market requirements and to communication, some of these companies are still today of international importance.

The producers of the Langhe region promoted their territory, with its history, art, landscape, traditions and, naturally, its wine. They were among the first internationally to have unity of purpose and to attract tourists from all over the world. In the development of winegrowing, scientific research and publications were important. In nineteenth-century Piedmont there were already publishers of agricultural texts, such as Ottavi of Casale Monferrato. In the twentieth century, the Faculty of Agriculture of Turin University and the Institute of Oenology in Asti were responsible for many publications of significance in the field.

The data gathered enable the analysis of the evolution, through socio-economic changes, including the various crises in the sector, the structure of property, and rural exodus. This period also saw the influx of vine parasites in rapid succession, which led to the enforced evolution of the sector. First came the cryptogams: Oidium and Peronosperas, then Phylloxera, an insect that brought colossal change to the sector, leading to the introduction of *barbatella* (European grafts on American rootstock) and the abandonment of some native varieties.

There were numerous responses to problematic situations, one of the most important, between the nineteenth and twentieth centuries, being the introduction of winegrowers' cooperatives. Their arrival made it easier to control the production of the grapes and the relative volumes of wines. After the First World War, under the Fascist regime, agricultural produce in general underwent stricter inspections, while the national press supplied reliable data on production, as did the ISTAT statistics, published annually.

The Wine Production System—Permanence and Discontinuity

The eighteenth and nineteenth centuries were fundamental for the development of winegrowing in Piedmont, favoured by the region's annexation to Napoleonic France, enabling useful comparison with the various winegrowing regions of France, which led to significant progress for the sector. During the first half of the nineteenth century, alongside the vineyards already established in the hills, winegrowing also took place in the plains where the vines were usually "*married*" with trees such as ash, elm and maple (Gaddo 2013, p. 61; Novello 2004, pp. 83–86).

From the second half of the century, the link between winegrowing and the hillside was consolidated and vines definitively became the principal traditional element for agricultural progress in the hills (Rapetti 1984, pp. 14–15; Baltieri 2004, p. 143).

At the same time, there was an increase in expanse of land given over to vines. In the period under consideration, this phenomenon was caused by several factors: the selection of more resistant plants by the growers, the evolution of consumer tastes, exchanges with neighbouring vineyard areas and addressing the problem of vine diseases (Maffi 2010, pp. 116–121).

From the mid-nineteenth century until the first decade of the twentieth century, in the hills the woods and pastures gave way to increasingly specialized winegrowing. In the Alba area, the vineyards were significantly extended, partly owing to abundant manpower and to the need for increased productivity. The combination of the factors mentioned above represented an important turning point for winegrowing in the province of Cuneo and, for vineyards in the Langhe in particular, a new phase began that led this area to become extremely famous for its clarity and coherence. In general, however, when discussing agriculture in Piedmont, historians normally place the beginning of a significant new phase around the end of the 1870s. This phase is known as the "end of century decline" and appears to have a variety of characteristic elements: changes in economic policy, the birth of the "social question", variation in price levels, problems in world agricultural trade and growth of industrialization (Rapetti 1984, pp. 86, 115–130).

In the first decade of the twentieth century, the amount of land given over to vineyards in southern Piedmont and Oltrepò Pavese reached its maximum. Underlying this were various factors, such as the definitive consolidation of small landholdings and the reaction to damage caused by phylloxera, first recorded in the province of Alessandria at Valmadonna in 1898.

This indiscriminate expansion of winegrowing led to an enormous increase in grape production, with a consequent fall in prices, which reached minimum levels from 1906 onwards. In the province of Alessandria, which also includes the Asti area, land given over to vines reached a historic high in 1907 of 181,000 hectares. This led to a notable increase in productivity, which reached its maximum level between 1907 and 1914. Meanwhile, both in southern Piedmont and in Oltrepò, large numbers of wine cooperatives were being opened, to achieve freedom from the control of middlemen, to encourage better quality wine and to organize marketing (Rapetti 2009b, pp. 157–160).

Overproduction brought crisis to the sector, encouraging emigration and, together with the onset of the First World War, provoked great changes in the territory. After the war, in the hills of Piedmont and Oltrepò Pavese, it was necessary to make a fresh start with big investments in repairs and new planting and, with the coming of *barbatella* (European grafts on American rootstock), the foundations were laid for the reconstruction of the vineyards (Berta and Mainardi 1997, pp. 363–370; Maffi 2015, pp. 73–101).

All through the 1920s, however, experimentation and innovation were hindered by lack of dissemination among the winegrowers, while from the 1920s to the 1960s an evolution began that from 1966 continues to the present day (Rapetti 1984, pp. 228–236; Martinelli et al. 2009, p. 71).

One response to the ongoing crisis was a law of 1930, which enabled voluntary consortiums of producers to be set up to promote local wines, identifiable under a common brand. And it was in Piedmont that, in 1932, the first winegrowing consortium in Italy was founded—the Consortium for the Protection of local Moscato d'Asti and Asti Spumante Wines. Meanwhile, however, plummeting prices and phylloxera resulted in vines being pulled up and the area given over to vines being greatly reduced. This phenomenon was particularly found in the areas of Monferrato and Alessandria (Berta and Mainardi 1997, pp. 363–367).

Nonetheless, a fair number of winegrowers were able to keep the sector intact. And, bearing witness to a certain amount of turmoil, in 1909 the enterprising producers of the municipality of Barolo charged the Agricultural Society of Alba with defining the geographical area in which "Barolo" wine, based on Nebbiolo grapes and named after the village promoting the project, could be produced. Owing to the war, the Society completed its task only in the early 1920s, so in 1934, in the municipality of Barolo, the Consortium was founded to produce that wine (Vacchetto 2004, pp. 25–28).

All the territory analysed was still characterized by small family landholdings, which overcame difficulties through the strength of union and involvement of all available physical resources.

Devaluation at the end of the 1940s was followed by rapid growth from the mid-1950s onwards. This, together with an excess of Barbera vines whose wine was popular only in the northwest, brought sudden and profound changes to the sector: grape prices plummeted, while production costs continued to grow. In addition to the above factors, the majority of small landholdings were unable to sustain the costs of replanting and adapting buildings to the new requirements of work processes and of the market. It is worth noting that in 1950 Piedmont, with 852,168 tonnes (20.40% of the national total), was the Italian region producing the most grapes from single-crop vineyards Berta and Mainardi 1997, pp. 371–374).

Table 1 shows trends in the amount of land under vines (in hectares), whether single crop or intercropping, in three areas (plain, hill and mountain) of Oltrepò Pavese, for 1928, 1935 and 1953.

The table shows that the area of land under vines in Oltrepò Pavese from the period of phylloxera until the early 1950s remained fairly constant, with the majority of vineyards in the hilly zones, steadily increasing from 67.95% in 1928 to 71.93% in 1953. It is worth noting that, in the hills, on average over the three years shown, single-crop vineyards represent 86.14%.

Table 1 Trends in the amount of land under vines in Oltrepò (in hectares)

	Winegrowing	Giuseppe Medici 1928	Davide Zanardi 1935	Davide Zanardi 1953
Plain	Single crop	1195.00	1278.00	433.00
	Intercropping	3361.00	3561.00	3900.00
Hill	Single crop	13,935.00	10,770.00	13,677.00
	Intercropping	1929.00	1986.00	2264.00
Mountain	Single crop	1471.00	2896.00	723.00
	Intercropping	1456.00	317.00	1164.00
Total		23,347.00	20,808.00	22,161.00

Source Luciano Maffi, *Storia di un territorio rurale*, op. cit., p. 147

Table 2 Area of land under vines and grape production in the province of Alessandria

Year	Land given over to single-crop vines (ha)	Grapes produced (tonnes)	Average yield (tonnes/ha)
1935–1940	57,900	1643.00	28.40
1946–1950	55,800	2193.00	39.30
1951–1955	54,700	3238.00	53.30

Source Luciano Maffi, *Storia di un territorio rurale*, op. cit., p. 147

Table 2 shows comprehensive data for the same time period for the province of Alessandria which in 1935 was separated from Asti, thus modifying the geography of winegrowing.

The table shows that the province of Alessandria saw a constant fall in land under vines, from 57,900 to 54,700 hectares (−5.53%); by contrast, there was a significant increase in yield, rising from 28.40 up to 59.30 tonnes/hectare (Rapetti 2009c, pp. 202–205).

The mid-1950s saw the beginning of a phase of uprooting, renewal, consolidation and replanting that substantially changed the area under vines in southern Piedmont. In about thirty years, there was a fall of 57.86% from 142,247 hectares (census data 1961) to 59,936 hectares (census data 1991). The 1991 figures divided by province show: Asti 20,683 hectares, Alessandria 19,154, Cuneo 16,784 and Turin 3314 (Berta and Mainardi 1997, p. 466).

In neighbouring Oltrepò, too, over a longer period, there was a reduction in vineyard area of 34.57%, falling from 22,161 hectares in

Table 3 Change in average landholding size from 1970 to 2000 in Oltrepò

Year	Number of landholdings	Total area Oltrepò	Average size of landholding in hectares
1970	10,075	13,326	1.32
1982	8250	13,818	1.67
1990	6709	14,327	2.13
2000	4147	13,418	3.23

Luciano Maffi, *Storia di un territorio rurale*, op. cit., pp. 302–303

1953 to about 14,500 in 1995, 83.50% of this latter amount representing DOC-registered vineyards. The percentage of vines uprooted was 5% higher than the national average.

From the 50s onwards, the uncertainty of a reasonable income provoked an exodus—especially of young people—from the countryside. This phenomenon involved considerable numbers: in Piedmont in 1951 those employed in agriculture in the region numbered 572,000, which had fallen by 1986 to 154,000. In Oltrepò, too, young people preferred other occupations; however, the reduction of land under vines tended to slow down from the late 70s. Meanwhile, technical and mechanical developments and experimentation in winegrowing encouraged the merging of land (Maffi 2010, pp. 208–212; Berta and Mainardi 1997, p. 466).

Table 3, for Oltrepò Pavese, highlights changes in the territory for area under vines, as against the number of landholdings, from 1970 to 2000.

During the years under consideration, with a total area that was relatively stable, there was a great drop (58.84%) in those employed in the sector, from 10,075 to 4147; by contrast, there was a significant increase in the average landholding size which, in the same period, went from 1.32 to 3.23 hectares, an increase of 244.70%.

Evolution of Vines Cultivated, Their Terroirs and Their Markets

In the first national study of ampelography by Giuseppe Acerbi in 1825, for southern Piedmont there is an important description of vineyards found on the land of Count Lorenzo De Cardenas near Valenza.

Among the most common white grapes: Passeretta bianca, Passeretta grossa, Tokai, Barbsin bianco, Courteis bianco, Terbiau, Malvasia di Spagna, Vernassa, Malvasia bianca rara, Malvasia bianca agglomerata, Mouscatela, Muscatell bianco, Uva greca and Mouscatell di Spagna; black grapes: Lambrusca nera, Fresia, Doulsin raro, Nebbiol nero, Bounarda, Doulsin, Pignou, Belmestia, Barbera nera a Peduncolo rosso, Barbera nera a peduncolo verde, Uva Mora, Mouscatell nero agglomerato, Malvasia nera agglomerata, Malvasia nera piccola, Montepulciano and Malvasia nera oblunga. Of these vines, still in existence are: Cortese, Moscato Bianco and Freisa, Dolcetto, Nebbiolo, Bonarda, Barbera and Malvasia nera (Acerbi 1999, pp. 53–62, 291; Forni 2001, pp. 269–298).

We are indebted to the same author for the first information regarding the vines found in Oltrepò on the farms of Don Giacomo Pecorara and Count Carlo Vistarino in the municipality of Pietra de' Giorgi. Among the most common were, for white grapes: Sgorbera, Malvasia, Mostarino, Trebbiano and Durella; for black grapes: Moradella piccola, Moradella grossa, Nibiolo, Pignolo, Ughetta di Canneto, Uva d'Oro, Sgorbera or Croà, Bersegano, Bonarda, Coda di vacca, Bersmestica, Rossera. Of these vines, still in existence are: Moradella, Nebbiolo, Ughetta di Canneto and Bonarda (Acerbi 1999, pp. 53–62, 291).

At the beginning of the nineteenth century, some businessmen from Piedmont began to take an interest in a vine whose grapes were used as a basis for champagne: Pinot noir. On the arrival of this vine in southern Piedmont and Oltrepò, Giusi Mainardi aptly writes (author's translation): "In the climate of serious rethinking that pervaded nineteenth-century wine growing, the possibility of introducing foreign vines into the local vineyards was also considered. These experiments were mainly carried out by wealthier, more educated people, who were able to read specialist publications and make contact with other enthusiasts, agronomists expert in vines, international growers" (Mainardi 2009, pp. 99–100).

The first attempts to introduce Pinot into Piedmont date from 1820–1840, coinciding with the onset of a dynamism in agriculture that was favoured by constant dealings with winegrowers in nearby France. King Carlo Alberto himself tried to initiate production of Pinot Noir in emulation of French champagne, but the results were unsatisfactory.

But there was one place where the experiment of growing Pinot Noir was successful: "at the end of the investigation it was clear that the only lands in Italy that seemed to have some resemblance to those in France were to be found in Oltrepò Pavese" (author's translation). So the French vine found, in this territory, a suitable *terroir*, along with the most innovative growing structures (Maffi 2012, pp. 41–44).

A new phase began for the wine sector after the Unification of Italy, with a generation of agriculturalists, businessmen and scholars that, together with the means of dissemination, brought improved competences, enabling the winegrowing and oenology of Piedmont to lead the field, in Italy and abroad (Gaddo 2013, pp. 23–26).

There was an increase, in that period, of mentions of the principal vines in Piedmont and Oltrepò. At that time the Barbera vine was common, both black and white; the latter, local and native to the territory of Alessandria was later abandoned for its excessive susceptibility to oidium. Moscato, already found in the province of Cuneo, was greatly increasing in the zones of Strevi and Canelli (Rapetti 2009a, pp. 55–58).

Meanwhile, in the Langhe, Nebbiolo and Dolcetto were becoming increasingly common. There was also the Barbera vine, introduced from areas nearby. Considering the province of Cuneo as a whole, the most significant vines at the end of the nineteenth century were—for white grapes: Moscato bianco, Favorita, Arneis and Cortese; for black grapes: Barbera, Dolcetto, Freisa and Nebbiolo (Dalmasso et al. 1974, pp. 21–29).

In Oltrepò in March 1872, in an article published in the *Bollettino del Comizio Agrario Vogherese*, Angelo Guffanti mentions that the most common vines in Oltrepò Pavese were, in descending order: Croatina, Ughetta, Barbera, Moradella, Uva rara, Malvasia, Moscato, Artrugo, Cortese and Trebbiano (Maffi 2010, p. 117).

The choice of vines developed, influenced by two cryptogams, in particular oidium, and phylloxera, which favoured the growth of *barbatella*, promoted at the Wine Congress in Casale in 1890 and the variables created by rootstock of American origin (Novello 2004, p. 92).

In the zone of Gavi, province of Alessandria, in 1869 Demaria and Leardi described Cortese as "a native vine, hardy and vigorous in nature, long known and cultivated in the zone" (Gily 2009, pp. 137–139).

Table 4 List of Piedmont vines with black grapes, in 1995

Vines	Area in hectares	%
Barbera	19,313	65.30
Brachetto	424	1.43
Dolcetto	5595	18.92
Freisa	711	2.40
Grignolino	1092	3.69
Malvasia rossa	142	0.48
Nebbiolo	2228	7.53
Other vines—black grapes	69	0.25
Total area—black grapes	29,574	100.00

Source Pierstefano Berta—Giusi Mainardi, *Storia regionale della vite e del vino. Piemonte*, op. cit., p. XXIV

Table 5 List of Piedmont vines with white grapes, found in the territory in 1995

Vines	Area in hectares	%
Arneis	400	3.23
Chardonnay	598	4.83
Cortese	2115	17.08
Favorita	93	0.75
Moscato	9176	74.11
Total area—white grapes	12,382	100.00

Source Pierstefano Berta—Giusi Mainardi, *Storia regionale della vite e del vino. Piemonte*, Milan, Unione italiana vini, 1997, p. XXIV

In southern Piedmont, the ampelographic base of the late nineteenth century and most of the twentieth century remained practically unchanged, for the most important vines, at least. This analysis is based on the provincial registers of DOC and DOCG vineyards for 1995 (see Tables 4 and 5).

The data given show the importance, for southern Piedmont, of black grape vines, which cover 70.49% of the entire area under vines and listed in the DOC and DOCG Registers, while vines of white grapes or for white wine account for the remaining 29.51%. Of significance for the black grape vines was the huge presence (65.30%) of Barbera and the presence of Barbaresco and Barolo among wines based on Nebbiolo. Most important for the white grape vines was Moscato, with 74.11%, and Cortese, with 17.08% of the area analysed; worthy of mention, too, the undisputed growth of the native Arneis (3.23%), and Chardonnay, the first foreign vine popular with Piedmont winegrowers.

In Oltrepò Pavese, too, the wine situation was also static from the 1920s to the 1960s. In the mid-1950s the average production of grapes was about 1,720,000 tonnes, of which 1,600,000 tonnes were black grapes and only 120,000 tonnes white. Barbera, with 860,000 tonnes, accounted for 50% of total production and 53.75% of black grape production. Next came Croatina with 420,000 tonnes, Uva Rara with 110,000 tonnes and other less important grapes. Among the white grapes or grapes for white wine were recorded 50,000 tonnes of Moscato, 25,000 of Pinot noir, 16,000 of Riesling, 10,000 of Cortese and other less important varieties (Zanardi 1958, pp. 68–150).

In a few years, Oltrepò Pavese began reconverting the ampelography of its territory. If we compare Zanardi's information for the 1950s with the 1981 table, it is clear that within 25 years, in Oltrepò Pavese, a phase of evolution had begun that favoured more new vineyards with white grapes or grapes for white wine. For 1955 production in hectolitres can be quantified as 93% of black grapes and only 7% of white. By 1981 the situation has changed and can be quantified in hectares, with 84.34% of the area under black grapes and 19.66% under white grapes. The greatest fall in investments was seen by Barbera, which, from 50% of total production previously, fell to 39.98% of land area; by contrast, Pinot Noir saw considerable growth, from 25,000 hectolitres in 1955 to 1,534 hectares in 1981, for an estimated 100,000 hectolitres of wine (Failla 1988, p. 177).

Table 6 shows that the most important vines accounted for no less than 92.11% of all vines registered. The process of evolution begun in the 70s continues at a good pace and shows Barbera continuing to fall, while Pinot Noir takes over. Croatina also declined considerably, but this should be considered as temporary, for a Bonarda DOC was becoming popular on the market, a sparkling wine made from Croatina grapes, prompting in a few years new plantings of this vine, which is currently in first place in the territory.

Another factor of the development of winegrowing was that of the information transfer that facilitated the evolution of systems of training and pruning. In fact, an important turning point in ways of training

Table 6 List of the most important vines found in Oltrepò Pavese in 1981

Vines	Area in hectares	%
Barbera	2677,71	26.65
Pinot Nero	2127,30	21.17
Croatina	2006,71	19.97
Riesling	1776,84	17.58
Moscato	676,98	6.74
Other Vines	782,22	7.89
Total area	10,047,76	100.00

Source Maffi, *Storia di un territorio rurale*, op. cit

and pruning occurred in 1861 when Giovanni Boschiero, an oenologist from Asti, introduced the French "*Guyot*" system, named after its founder. This method was first adopted in La Galleria, near Asti, in a model vineyard, and then spread more widely, both in its original French form and with variations and improvements aimed at adapting it to the habits and attitudes of the winegrowers (Ghisleni 1961, p. 147).

At first, experimentation of the new system found few supporters and, in the reports of the jury at the International Exposition of Vienna in 1873, it is clear how little the importance of the *terroir* was understood by the majority of Piedmont's winegrowers. The jurists also refer to the irrationality of vineyard cultivation, but devote space to signs of improvement seen in recent years with the new technologies. In Giovanni Boschiero's report we also read considerations about the potential of winegrowing that reveal numerous problems and tend to incentivize winegrowing in the hills (Balbo Bertone di Sambuy 1873, pp. 22–23; Boschiero 1873, pp. 123–126).

Boschiero himself insists on the *terroir*, favouring the vines better suited to the terrain and the climate, and concludes his report with a series of facts about the latest systems of vineyard organization, choice of vines for planting and training methods (Boschiero 1879, pp. 61–64; Gay Eynard and Bovio 2004, pp. 345–346).

It was in the last twenty years of the nineteenth century that some positive results began to be seen of technical progress in winegrowing, especially from a theoretical and experimental perspective, less so, regarding widespread diffusion of the innovations. The Guyot training method, also-called "*alla francese*", which trained the vines along steel wires, began to spread and at the end of the nineteenth century this system was adopted almost unanimously in the Langhe (Maffi 2010, pp. 34–37).

In the 1830s winegrowing almost entirely converted to the training and pruning system of Guyot which today remains the most widespread. In the 1960s and 1970s, in some areas, other ways of training were used, such as: "*Casarsa*" a curtain of freely trailing shoots, with considerable savings in management of the growing plant and "*Cordone Speronato Basso*" a permanent low branch, taken to a height of 80–100 cm, on which four or five spurs are left. This form of training and pruning was well suited to vines such as Barbera, Merlot, Pinot Noir and Riesling (Donna and Villa 1988, pp. 219–227).

Technology Transfer in Winemaking: The French Model—"Champagne" and "Spumante"

In the first half of the nineteenth century in Piedmont it became evident that sparkling wines, also more difficult to make, were easily sold at high prices. The origins of spumante in Piedmont may be traced to 1839, when Professor Milano declared that "*the grapes with which are made sparkling wines are Gris Doré, Pinnau and they can be made also with other grapes. It is essential that they be well ripened. The above species greatly resemble Piedmont Nebbiolo: the Italians could imitate the wines of Champagne, and with a little practice equal them. With a friend of mine we have made and drunk them in one of the main hotels of Turin, and they were found to be rather good. They had all the exterior of the wines of Champagne, but I believe they might have been a little more delicate. But the first tastings are never perfect*" (author's translation). In the period immediately following the Unification of Italy, the new, national market pushed wine companies, too, towards commercial development. Although the wine industry of Piedmont had good potential, it still had difficulty in finding a secure path towards export markets.

The early international Expositions were an important point of encounter and encouragement for the world of sparkling wines, too, which had not yet reached the desired quality levels.

During the great fair in Vienna in 1873, oenologist Giovanni Boschiero expressly declared that "*the few Italian sparkling wines were found to be inferior to those of France, Germany and Austria, although it is recognised that the raw materials is not inferior in Italy*" (Berta 2004, pp. 364–367) (author's translation).

Following the Paris International Exposition of 1878, Marquis Sambuy noted in his report that at the event a clear improvement had been found in the quality of Piedmont wine production saying, however, that for the sparkling wines, the technique of second fermentation was still lacking (Ubigli and Borsa 2004, pp. 290–291).

Among the founders of the Italian Sparkling Wine Industry may be cited: Giovanni Boschiero, Tommaso Arrigo, Arnaldo Strucchi and Carlo Gancia, Alberto Contratto, Carlo Mensio and the directors of the Royal Wine Research Institute of Asti, Francesco Koenig, Mario Zicchini and Federico Martinotti. One of the undisputed fathers of Piedmont spumante was Giovanni Boschiero (Berta 2004, pp. 369–373).

Meanwhile, encouraged by Carlo Gancia, in the 1850s the estate of counts Giorgi di Vistarino planted the Pinot Noir vine, in Scurapasso valley in the province of Pavia, with the aim of producing Italian champagne. At Rocca de' Giorgi, the real Italian story of classic, French-style spumante began. A few years later, Domenico Mazza di Codevilla followed the same path; to him, we also owe the introduction of a personalized bottle, especially pressurized for spumante (Maffi 2012, pp. 44–46).

At the beginning of the twentieth century, in Casteggio, S.V.I.C. (Italian winemaking company of Casteggio) was founded by Agostino Guardamagna, Pietro Riccadonna di Broni, Angelo Ballabio, Mario Odero and Raffaello Sernagiotto known as Ello di Casteggio. Unfortunately, their adventure was short-lived owing to the events of the war. In Oltrepò Pavese, between the 70s and 80s, thanks also to some great businessmen from Piedmont, Bosca, Cinzano, Contratto, Fontanafredda, Gancia, Martini e Rossi and Riccadonna (known as the "Seven Sisters of Spumante"), the classic spumante of Oltrepò Pavese was finally affirmed, under the description of Oltrepò Pavese Pinot Noir Spumante, both classic method and Martinotti method (Maffi and Nosvelli 2006, pp. 74–75; Bolfo and Bozzini 1983, pp. 70–71, 125–145).

An analysis of the world of spumante in Piedmont cannot fail to give special mention to Moscato d'Asti for its character and uniqueness. This wine acquired considerable importance, both qualitative and economic, for the area under consideration. Initially the wine was named Moscato di Canelli, later becoming Moscato d'Asti, a denomination that was recognized and consecrated by law. Production of re-fermented spumante in bottles began from Moscato around 1870. Carlo Gancia, after brief experiences in the local winemaking sector, having spent from 1848 to 1850 in Reims, on his return to Piedmont settled in Chivasso where he began his business. In 1865 he rented a winery in Canelli that in 1889 became his company headquarters. In that period, with his business partner, oenologist Arnaldo Strucchi, he began producing sparkling sweet red wines and a spumante "*uso Champagne*". Around 1880 his company began making Moscato di Canelli with the method of secondary fermentation in the bottle. For that reason it was called "*Moscato—Champagne*" and required technical skill and great attention. To make the process easier, to the Moscato must was often added 10–20% of dry white wines such as Cortese or Pinot (Berta 2004, pp. 369–373; Bolfo and Bozzini 1983, pp. 88–93; Ratti 1895, p. 18).

Asti Spumante was mostly dominated by large companies from Turin that had set up business in the Asti area. Its commercial rise, between the end of the nineteenth century and the first fifteen years of the twentieth, encountered few obstacles (Lozato-Giotart 1988, pp. 246–249).

Selling Wine and the Development of the Wine Industry

Evolution and development had to follow market requirements. At the beginning of the nineteenth century, Giovanni Secondo De Canis, a historian from Asti, in his *Corografia astigiana* described the excellent grape varieties of Moscatella, Passeretta and Malvasia Bianca, remarking upon the good wines obtained from them, which were judged to be delicious by all the well-to-do inhabitants of Piedmont. He also adds "the people of Asti who derive great advantage from them are very careful to supply them to all the towns of Piedmont, not only, but foreign towns too, despatching them through the great centres of Pavia and Milan" (Gaddo 2013, p. 44; Massi 1967, pp. 21–23) (author's translation).

Later, Lombardy and Venice curtailed trade relations and duties were excessive, particularly after 1818. Most of the wine production in Piedmont and Oltrepò was seriously affected (Maffi 2012, pp. 55–56).

With Carlo Alberto of Savoy (1831), institutional activity directly influenced the area of economics and in the 1830s free trade was much debated, and steps were taken to liberalize imports and exports (Baltieri 2004, pp. 137–138). In 1833, this trade policy favoured much of Piedmont's production going to Milan, ruled by the Austrians. In fact, the Austrian government had lowered customs duties on Piedmont wines imported in territories under Austrian control, in Lombardy-Venice and in Emilia (Johnson 2012, pp. 630–635).

In Piedmont until the early 1840s there was much economic activism and development; the new Civil Code (1837) and the Code of Trade (1842) were passed.

Subsequently, however, in the mid-1840s, the markets contracted to regional dimensions and customs barriers became more severe. The low volume of sales, especially abroad, led to a fall in agricultural prices and the prices of wine were particularly hard hit. The duty on wines sent from Piedmont to Lombardy-Venice went from 9.10 to 21.45 Milan liras per hectolitre. The wine crisis had serious repercussions on wine production in Piedmont, about two-thirds of which was directed to markets in Lombardy. This led the average price of wine to drop by about one-third on the domestic market.

Despite the 1846–1847 crisis, savings banks and other credit institutions were being founded, which facilitated notable investments in agriculture. Under the Cavour administration, wine exports acquired a certain importance, with an average annual growth of about 18.60% between 1852 and 1858.

It should be noted that, at that time, railways and roads had been built in the territory, which assisted in trading with Lombardy-Venice and with a wider market. In the 1850s, for example, in Oltrepò Pavese, most wine was produced in the hills (75.53%), with only 21.47% being grown in the plain. The latter was destined almost entirely for local consumption while the former, more highly prized, was grown for the markets of the plain, but also for export (Massi 1967, pp. 27–31).

The fiscal policy of the first post-Unification governments had further negative effects on the organization of wine businesses. Considered as one of the most serious consequences was "having removed from many the will to unite to improve production and thereby address foreign competition" (author's translation). This focus on cooperation as an important support for developing the wine industry was the occasion of debate at all the wine congresses, which were convinced that this was the road to follow (Trova 2000, pp. 805–806).

In Canelli, in the province of Alessandria, special *Moscati* were produced which, under the denomination of *Moscati uso Canelli*, were chiefly exported to France. *Moscato appassito*, meanwhile, was mainly produced in the areas of Acqui and Asti, in the province of Alessandria, and was quite a successful export product, especially to the Americas.

Salvatore Mondini writes of a special sparkling wine, local to the region, Moscato, whose average annual production was calculated at about 100,000 hectolitres, divided among the provinces of Alessandria and Cuneo, and exported to the Americas, France, Switzerland and Belgium (Mondini 1899, pp. 31–42).

Before 1895 about 148,00 tonnes (about 109,000 hectolitres) of Moscato were produced. Of this, about 30,000 hectolitres were destined for sparkling wine. By 1895 almost the entire production was chiefly made into spumante and there was talk of the considerable request "*from foreign countries for the sweet, perfumed and sparkling white wine, by now known in the trade under the names of Moscato d'Asti or Moscato di Canelli*" (author's translation).

In the last decade of the nineteenth century, wine consumption in the towns was greatly reduced. There was significant consumption in Turin, which maintained about 168 litres of wine per year per inhabitant; Genoa consumed 141 litres; while Milan showed a certain fall, dropping to 98 litres (Mondini 1899, pp. 269–270).

A fall in domestic consumption and the difficulty of creating new markets should be seen in connection with the process of division of landholdings in the hills. This was a negative factor for farming, owing to

Table 7 Production of grapes and wine in Piedmont from 1870 to 1905

Year	Piedmont		Alessandria		% Alessandria over Piedmont
	Tonnes of grapes	Tonnes of wine	Tonnes of grapes	Tonnes of wine	grapes
1870–1874	4,191,000	2,766,000	1,440,000	994,000	34.30
1876–1881	0	0	934,000	624,000	0.00
1890–1894	5,741,000	3,789,000	3,826,000	2,551,000	66.60
1901–1905	6,874,000	4,537,000	3,820,000	2,522,000	55.60

Source Vittorio Rapetti, *Uomini, Collina e Vigneto in Piemonte*, op. cit., p. 92

structural problems connected with productivity, to the efficient use of resources, to farm organization, to the economics of management, and to the possibility of investing in land improvements or cultural transformations. It was these conditions that tended to push the small hill farm into a state of auto-consumption, from which the hill farmers were not yet detached, either in material or cultural terms (Rapetti 1984, pp. 79–81).

Table 7 shows the production of grapes and wine in Piedmont and in the province of Alessandria from 1870 to 1905 (five-yearly averages in 100 kg and hectolitres).

The table highlights the constant increase in production of grapes and wines, deriving from the great expansion of areas under vines in the region that can be identified across almost all of the area analysed.

The wine crisis lasted until the 1830s and the average price of red wine fell by 40–45%, worsening with the onset of the First World War and phylloxera (see Tables 8 and 9).

The situation deteriorated further after 1932, owing to a continuing fall in domestic consumption and to protective measures by many of the importing countries. After 1936 the prices of grapes and wines fell to a historic low. In Monferrato, for example, wines were bought at an average price of 75 liras per hectolitre, against the 190 liras of 1928. Even the more valuable grapes like Moscato did not avoid this serious crisis of wine in Piedmont and Oltrepò, as their market price in Canelli fell from 148.42 liras/100 kg in 1928 to 78.58 in 1934 (Berta and Mainardi 1997, pp. 355–367; Martinelli et al. 2009, p. 71).

Table 8 Average prices of grapes per 100 kg on the markets of Asti and Casale between 1880 and 1920 (index numbers of average prices, in liras fixed 1913)

YEAR	CASALE Common grapes	ASTI Common grapes	ASTI Barbera
1880–1885 average	121	122	125
1886–1890 average	171	121	123
1891–1895 average	84	82	84
1896–1900 average	103	101	98
1901–1905 average	96	91	93
1906–1910 average	79	84	75
1911–1915 average	108	0	0
1916–1920 average	113	0	0

Source Vittorio Rapetti, *Uomini, Collina e Vigneto in Piemonte*, op. cit., p. 128

Table 9 Prices of some grapes on the market of Asti between 1881 and 1910 (five-yearly averages in cash liras, per 100 kg)

Products	1881–1885	1886–1890	1891–1895	1896–1900	1901–1905	1906–1910
Common grapes	29.20	28.90	19.60	24.10	21.80	20.00
Barbera grapes	38.40	37.90	25.80	30.00	28.60	23.40

Source Vittorio Rapetti, *Uomini, Collina e Vigneto in Piemonte*, op. cit., p. 89

After the war, only the wines of Asti continued to grow, particularly Moscato, encouraged by large firms that had set up in the area: Fratelli Cora in Costigliole, Francesco Cinzano in S.Stefano Belbo and S.Vittoria d'Alba, Martini e Rossi in Montechiaro d'Asti and, later, in Pessione, Fratelli Beccaro in Acqui, Contratto and Alessandro Zoppa in Canelli, Baldi in Strevi, Pistone, Soria and Taricco in Asti, Calissano in Alba and Bosca and Riccadonna in Canelli (Lozato-Giotart 1988, pp. 262–264; Ratti 1895, pp. 57–59).

In 1982 the area under white Moscato grew to 5530 hectares; the rise of Asti Spumante was constant, reaching in that decade 50 million bottles (Bolfo and Bozzini 1983, p. 93; Lozato-Giotart 1988, p. 258).

Despite the trend, in the 1980s, of reducing the amount of land under vines in Piedmont, white Moscato continued to grow, by 1988 covering 9000 hectares in single-crop cultivation. This meant a production of about 70 million bottles which, for the period, represented 50% of DOC Piedmont wine sold in bottles (Cirio 1988, pp. 22–23).

A few years later, in 1994, there were 9040 hectares producing Moscato grapes. In the same year, about 2,500,000 bottles of Moscato d'Asti were sold while sales of Asti Spumante were about 85,000,000 bottles, 76% of which were exported. These sales were influenced by the introduction of the DOC denominations, proposed by Senator Paolo Desana of Casale Monferrato, which were made law in 1963. Between 1966 and 1970, the wines of Piedmont and Oltrepò were awarded this denomination (Berta and Mainardi 1997, pp. 388–390; Maffi 2010, pp. 158–160, 177–207).

From the 70s onwards, southern Piedmont brought its wine industries to the attention of the world, which played a major part in disseminating the region's image and became fundamental for export. Turnover of Piedmont wines sold for export, in quantitative terms, was about 4.4% of the national total. The purely commercial focus of the large groups and the above-mentioned figures include both wines made from local grapes, with particular reference to Asti and Asti Spumante, and also products derived from grapes, must and wines purchased outside the territory.

It should be noted that, at the same time, in southern Piedmont, excellent winegrowing was being carried on by farm businesses, which undertook their own marketing both in Italy and abroad through channels specializing in the sale of quality wines. Barolo and Barbaresco, without doubt, were the leaders, together with Asti Spumante, and other regional wines such as: of the red wines, Barbera, Dolcetto, Freisa and Nebbiolo; of the white, Arneis and Cortese.

In Oltrepò Pavese, wine sales remained tied to a market chiefly spread across the regions of northwest Italy, with a sales network that often targeted the end consumer. This territory was hindered by various factors, including excessive subdivision of holdings, resulting in many grapes being sent to the cooperative wineries from where, apart from La Versa, wine was sold in bulk to the big Piedmont industries or to wine dealers in the north-west.

Conclusion

This study reveals how winegrowers, affected by agricultural, cultural and social events, and supported by illuminated local players, were able to adapt to the various requirements of the market. From the mid-nineteenth century, the winegrowers became the protagonists, including in contacts with neighbouring France, and they introduced more vine breeding and pruning systems, aimed at holding down costs and at improving the quantity and quality of their production.

Those involved in the development of winegrowing and winemaking in Piedmont became more aware of the productive possibilities of the hills and of the importance of *terroir* in identifying for each habitat its predisposition for hosting the best-suited vines.

Undoubtedly worthy of note was the formation of human capital, in fact, the foundation in 1881 of the School of Wine Growing and Oenology in Alba was an important moment for the sector. A few years later in Voghera in 1895 the Royal Agricultural Technical School was inaugurated. Culture and experimentation were also at the service of new requirements, such as: the codification of local wines; the fight against cryptogams and phylloxera; the solving of market problems caused by overproduction; the opening of cooperative wineries.

Notwithstanding the difficulties arising in the twentieth century, connected to problems of market and of wars, the sector revealed signs of development, thanks to competent local producers, trade associations and regional and national agricultural policies. The distinct character of products such as Barolo, Barbaresco, Cortese di Gavi, Arneis, Bonarda, Asti Spumante and Spumanti of Oltrepò Pavese was recognized at home and abroad in trade journals, and alongside the wines, wine tourism and wine-and-food products acquired great importance.

References

Acerbi, G. (1999). *Delle Viti Italiane.* Lodi: Giampiero Zazzera.
Balbo Bertone di Sambuy, E. (1873). Vini italiani. *Relazioni dei giurati italiani sulla Esposizione universale di Vienna del 1873.* Milano: Regia Stamperia. V. 5, 22–23.

Baltieri, M. (2004). *La vita economica nel Piemonte preunitario: uno sguardo d'insieme* (Mainardi, Ed.).

Berta, P. (2004). *L'apparecchio Martinotti e la storia dello spumante piemontese* (Mainardi, Ed.).

Berta, P., & Mainardi, G. (1997). *Storia regionale della vite e del vino. Piemonte.* Milano: Unione italiana vini.

Berta, P., & Mainardi, G. (Eds.). (2015). *Enologia Italiana dell'Ottocento.* Canelli: Edizioni OICCE.

Bolfo, P., & Bozzini, G. (1983). *Cin Cin Italia: Guida agli spumanti italiani.* Milano: Mursia editore.

Boschiero, G. (1873). Industria dei vini in Italia. *Relazioni dei giurati italiani sulla Esposizione universale di Vienna del 1873.* Milano: Regia Stamperia. V. 5, 123–126.

Boschiero, G. (1879). Bevande fermentate (Classe 75). *Esposizione universale del 1878 in Parigi: relazioni dei giurati italiani.* Roma: Tipografia eredi Botta, 61–64.

Cirio, F. (1988). *Piemonte: Professione vino, rassegna di vitivinicoltura piemontese.* Castelnuovo Scrivia: DIEFFE.

Dalmasso, G. et al. (Eds.). (1974). *La vite ed il vino nella provincia Granda.* Cuneo: Amministrazione Provinciale di Cuneo.

Donna, P., & Villa, P. (1988). *Potatura e forma di allevamento* (Scienza, Ed., pp. 219–227).

Failla, O. (1988). *L'evoluzione della viticoltura oltrepadana: vecchi e nuovi vitigni* (Scienza, Ed., pp. 177).

Forni, G. (2001). *Le radici storiche della viticoltura nell'Oltrepò Pavese* (Failla & Forni, Eds., pp. 269–298).

Gaddo, I. (2013). *La vite e il vino nell'astigiano: Storia e cultura. Repertorio di fonti e strumenti di studio.* Torino: Accademia University Press.

Gay Eynard, G., & Bovio, M. (2004). *Le trasformazioni della viticoltura piemontese a seguito dell'arrivo, nel XIX secolo, di tre nemici della vite europea: dopo oidio e fillossera, la peronospora* (Mainardi, Ed., pp. 345–346).

Ghisleni, P.L. (1961). *Le coltivazioni e la tecnica agricola in Piemonte dal 1831 al 1861.* Torino: Museo Nazionale del Risorgimento.

Gily, M. (2009). Gavi e il cortese (Gily, Desana, & Rapetti, Eds., pp. 137–139).

Johnson, H. (2012). *Il vino, Storia, tradizioni, cultura.* Roma: Orme editori.

Loubere, L. (1978). *The red and the white. A history of wine in France and Italy in the XIX century.* Albany: New York University Press.

Lozato-Giotart, J.P. (1988). *Il vigneto di Asti*. Asti: Camera di Commercio di Asti.
Maffi, L. (2010). *Storia di un territorio rurale, vigne e vini nell'Oltrepò pavese*. Milano: Angeli.
Maffi, L. (2012). *Natura docens. Vignaioli e sviluppo economico dell'Oltrepò Pavese nel XIX secolo*. Milano: Angeli.
Maffi, L. (2015). «La resistenza del Paese sarà tanto più forte quanto più floride saranno le condizioni dell'agricoltura». Il settore primario in Provincia di Pavia negli anni della Grande Guerra. *Bollettino della Società Pavese di Storia Patria*, pp. 73–101.
Maffi, M., & Nosvelli, L. (2006). *Storie e vini d'Oltrepò*. Voghera: Edizioni Oltrepò.
Mainardi, G. (Ed.). (2004). *Il vino piemontese nell'Ottocento*. Alessandria: Editore dell'Orso.
Mainardi, G. (2009). *Vigneti e cantine. Scienze, tecnica e sperimentazione enologica tra '800 e '900* (Gily, Desana, & Rapetti, Eds., p. 97–119).
Martinelli, M. et al. (2009). *Appunti per una storia del Consorzio di Tutela Barolo, Barbaresco, Alba, Langhe e Roero e del suo territorio*. Alba: Consorzio di Tutela Barolo Barbaresco Alba Langhe e Roero.
Massi, E. (1967). *Momenti dello sviluppo dell'Oltrepò Pavese*. Milano: Giuffrè Editore.
Mondini, S. (1899). *Produzione e commercio del vino in Italia*. Milano: Hoepli.
Novello, V. (2004). *Problemi e prospettive della viticoltura del XIX secolo* (Mainardi, Ed., pp. 83–86).
Rapetti, V. (1984). *Uomini, Collina e Vigneto in Piemonte, dalla metà Ottocento agli anni Trenta*. Alessandria: Edizioni dell'Orso, Alessandria.
Rapetti, V. (2009a). *Uomini e colline: il paesaggio della vite* (Gily, Desana, & Rapetti, Eds., pp. 53–72).
Rapetti, V. (2009b). *Specializzazione e mercato. Sviluppo e crisi della produzione enologica fra fine '800 e primi '900* (Gily, Desana, & Rapetti, Eds., pp. 153–177).
Rapetti, V. (2009c). *Impresa e cooperazione, qualità e tutela* (Gily, Desana, & Rapetti, Eds., pp. 201–229).
Ratti, R. (1895). *L'Asti, Consorzio per la tutela dell'Asti spumante*. Vicenza: A.G.V.-Gruppo Mondadori.
Trova, A. (2000). *I congressi enologici italiani nell'Ottocento* (Da Passano et al., Eds., pp. 805–806).

Ubigli, M., & Borsa, D. (2004). *La regia stazione enologica di Asti tra il 1800 e il 1900* (Mainardi, Ed., pp. 290–291).

Vacchetto, P. (2004). *Le viti per il barolo.* Guarene: Arti e sapori.

Zanardi, D. (1958). *Monografia vitivinicola nell'Oltrepò Pavese.* Milano: Arti grafiche Setti e figlio.

The Improvement of the Production and Quality: The Case of Wine Production in the Eastern Lombardy During the Nineteenth and Twentieth Centuries (Provinces of Bergamo and Brescia)

Paolo Tedeschi

Introduction: Aims, Relevance of the Topic and Limits of the Paper

The aim of this paper is to illustrate the most relevant changes regarding production and retailing systems in the winemaking industry in the provinces of Bergamo and Brescia (Eastern Lombardy) during the nineteenth and twentieth centuries. The paper in particular describes how viticulturists and winemakers, who in most cases were the same person, improved the quality of their wine and transformed the economic role of viticulture: vines progressively became the only cultivated crop to be planted in the best terroirs of the Morainique hill areas and greatly increased the market for wine thanks to a greater emphasis on the quality of their products.

P. Tedeschi (✉)
DEMS, University of Milano-Bicocca, Milan, Italy
e-mail: paolo.tedeschi@unimib.it

S. A. Conca Messina et al. (eds.), *A History of Wine in Europe, 19th to 20th Centuries, Volume I*, Palgrave Studies in Economic History,
https://doi.org/10.1007/978-3-030-27772-7_8

The paper draws on various sources[1] to point out that, despite the large number of factors that influenced these changes, it is possible to discern the decisive role played by certain external events which forced viticulturists and winemakers to modify their approach and to improve their working methods both among the vines and in the cellars. Viticulturists, winemakers and vineyards in fact suffered a severe reduction in numbers due to these external events. This selection, together with the improvement of the technology and of the ampelographic knowledge, progressively raised the quality of vines and wine. During the last decades of the twentieth century, the increase of investments allowed to sell the wine in the main international markets and to rising profits. This strongly modified the economic importance of the wine which was until then considered a secondary product within the agricultural landscape of Eastern Lombardy.

The paper presents some limits concerning quantitative data, particularly with regard to the true figures for grapes and wine production and prices, which vary according to which sources are used. Besides, after the last decade of the nineteenth century when transport and conservation of grapes became more efficient, winemakers were able to produce wine using grapes from other regions and this got impossible to estimate the true volume of local grapes and wine production.

Data for the nineteenth century are approximate and incomplete and varies from one source to another. Besides, these data do not record production figures for all years and the data which are recorded have been questioned by other sources (e.g. in reports published by the Chambers of Commerce in Bergamo and Brescia). Real production volumes have been greatly underestimated in that they fail to account for increases in taxation imposed by the French and Austrian governments. In reality, the land tax burden was not as heavy as landowners made it

---

[1]Besides the articles and books quoted in the following notes, these archival sources were used: Archivio di Stato di Brescia, *IRDP*, bb. 3549, 4119; Archivio di Stato di Milano, *Agricoltura p.m.*, bb. 1–3, 112, *Catasto Lombardo-Veneto*, bb. 7275, 9353, 9537, 12141, 12142, 12190, 12191, 12194, 12197, 12202, 12203; *Commercio p.m.*, bb. 15; *Studi p.m.*, bb. 1139, 1142, 1144. These documents (and the related data) concern the first half of the nineteenth century only. They include: "Nozioni agrarie di dettaglio" and "Nozioni generali territoriali", that is detailed information about the conditions of the viticulture in the departments of Bergamo and Brescia.

seem since they were comparing it to the extremely low taxes applied by the Republic of Venice. Underestimating the true production figures in Eastern Lombardy created problems for wine producers when powdery mildew destroyed a large part of the grape harvest during the first half of the 1850s. Compensation payments allocated by the public authorities were, in fact, calculated according to official data, meaning that a substantial portion of producers' losses were not reimbursed.[2]

Since the newly created Kingdom of Italy kept taxes at their previous level, the true volume of wine production continued to be underestimated until the arrival of the phylloxera outbreak in the final years of the nineteenth century. Only then did producers partially modify their approach, although the production figures they provided were simply closer to the true figures rather than being fully accurate. The attitude of landowners in providing this type of data had become so endemic that wine production figures were not taken into account when calculating the value of land planted with vines in Austria's next property census. Similarly, no agricultural surveys carried out during the nineteenth century in Eastern Lombardy included wine production figures.[3] The 'Annuario Statistico Italiano' alone published data which included annual wine production for each province in Lombardy. However, these data were often compiled using figures the producers chose to declare: they were considered so unreliable that they were not used in the main volume describing rural manufacturing in the province of Brescia at the beginning of the twentieth century (Gnaga 1904, pp. 63–65).

During the first decades of the twentieth century, the situation changed because of the birth of cooperative wineries whose associates were obviously keen to have an idea of their actual volumes of wine production. Besides, the WWI and the government's consequent policy of tight controls on all agricultural products reduced the underestimation.

---

[2]For the production of wine in provinces of Bergamo and Brescia during the first half of the nineteenth century, see Tedeschi (2006a, pp. 338–344, 456), Marengoni (1996, pp. 10–15, 35–53), and Maironi da Ponte (1803).

[3]For the new land census, see Locatelli and Tedeschi (2012) and Locatelli (2003). For agricultural censuses during the nineteenth century, see Tedeschi (2013). For the constant underevaluation of farm production and earnings, see Tedeschi (2008a).

Furthermore, the advent of the fascist regime intensified State control of the production and profits of farms. Finally, new journals as the "Primo Annuario Generale Vinicolo illustrato" [First General Wine Yearbook illustrated] and in particular the documents edited by the national statistics body, Istat (born in 1926), provided more detailed information on the production of Italian grapes and wine. Even if some figures were sometimes overestimated by the fascist regime that wanted to show the good results of its agrarian policies, the data concerning the viticulture were closer to the true value than in the past. Only in the second half of the twentieth century, when Istat started to publish its "Annuario di Statistica Agraria" [Yearbook of Agrarian Statistics], the data about Italian wine sector became very accurate (Tedeschi and Vaquero Piñeiro 2018). All this explains why this paper shows few data concerning the production of grapes and wine in Eastern Lombardy.

The paper includes few data on wine prices too. For the nineteenth century, prices which were indicated in the public document draw for the land censuses depended on unconfirmed self-evaluations from respondents, who were usually the landowners themselves. Information is also sparse with regard to prices recorded in the local wine market, and there is often uncertainty on which currency was used. When official data concerning the wine market in a town are available (as in the case of Bergamo), it is not possible to know the quality of the wine traded: so the prices are useful only to observe the trend and to value the increase or decrease of wine producers' earnings, but it is important to note that there is no information about its origins (from the province or outside?). In the case of the twentieth century, the price of wine is clearly based on its quality, meaning that there can be a vast difference in value between the best and the worst wines. Recording the average price of these wines makes little sense, particularly where their quality varied so much, like in Eastern Lombardy. Another problem is that sources often fail to specify whether the prices they indicate were those of the producer or of the taverns, restaurants and supermarkets where they were sold. They also fail to mention whether they are referring to wine sold in a cask (the *fiasco*, that is the most common means of distribution of Italian wine until the 1950s) or in a bottle, or whether it is a new or aged wine. However, sources allow us to see that the difference in price between the best and worst wines increased during the period under investigation. In the 1830s the most expensive wine was three times the price of a poor quality wine.[4] At the end of the twentieth century, the highest quality wines can cost more than ten times more than one of medium quality.

The Viticulture in the Provinces of Bergamo and Brescia During the Nineteenth Century

Viticulturists and winemakers in the provinces of Bergamo and Brescia were already skilled practitioners in the Medieval and Renaissance periods: however the average quality of their wine was low at the beginning of the nineteenth century because they had no real incentive to make improvements. From the Napoleonic era to the mid-nineteenth century, the methods used for grape harvesting and for producing and conserving the must gave rise to a mellow, heavy-bodied wine. This product was mainly aimed at taverns, whose customers preferred cheap, low-quality wines. Most viticulturists and winemakers, then, had no interest in making investments to improve the quality of their product: they enjoyed the profits that were guaranteed by the local market. There were, nonetheless, some cases where higher quality wines were produced with closer attention to sensory attributes (like flavour and aroma), and more sophisticated production techniques, but the production of these wines was on a small scale, and limited to the areas of Franciacorta, Valtenesi and Lugana (province of Brescia) or in Scanzo (a small village

[4]For example, in 1837 on the wine market of Brescia one zerla of almost 50 litres was valued at 30.61 *lire austriache* in early May, with the price falling to 27.06 by the 8th of July. See Archivio di Stato di Brescia, IRDP, 4119, f. 1. Besides, the prices of the wine (in *lire milanesi* for one zerla) passed from 5 to 6.15 (in the plain and in the valleys), from 7 to 10 (in the hills), while the best wines of the Garda and Franciacorta arrived at 13 and 15. Wine priced below 6 *lire milanesi* was often considered of the lowest (infima) quality. The price of the wine in the market of Bergamo from 1859 to 1883 (that is from the entry in the Italian Kingdom to the start of the agrarian crisis) fluctuated among 30 and 40 Italian liras for one hl. until 1872 and after it reached prices among 50 and more than 60 Italian liras with wide variations. See Faccini (1986, pp. 263–409), Tedeschi (2006a, p. 482) (Table 94), and Della Valentina (1996, pp. 39–40).

in the province of Bergamo). The quality of terroirs of these areas was in fact superior in terms of quality. The highest quality grapes were in particular produced by vineyards where vines were the only cultivated crops on a piece of land. Winemakers separated red and black grapes during the harvest, enabling them to produce both white and red wine: they were also very attentive when preserving the must and carrying out successive winemaking stages in the cellars. This allowed them to obtain a good quality wine that could be sold to the wealthier families (or the higher clergy). However, this high-quality wine was produced in limited quantities because aristocrats, bishops and the wealthy bourgeois classes represented a relatively small market. The majority of consumers preferred less refined wines, and drank them mainly for their perceived effect of reducing the fatigue linked to work and, moreover, their price was very low and accessible to everyone. So most winemakers produced low-quality wines: they easily adapted to the customers' desires because this implied low-production costs and moreover no expenses for searching to improve the quality. Their confidence was also bolstered by the lack of competition and a sizeable local market, giving them little incentive to improve the quality of their wine.

At the beginning of the nineteenth century, producers in the department of Mella (the Napoleonic name of the province of Brescia) were unable to satisfy the local demand for wines and spirits, and "foreign" wines and liqueurs had to be imported at a cost of 250,000 *lire bresciane* even if the imported wine only amounted to 2000 hl., with a total value of 60,000 *lire bresciane* a year (Sabatti 1807, p. 284). For the department of Serio (the Napoleonic name of the province of Bergamo) the situation was worse because the local production of wine only covered a small part of the demand. Within this context, few producers made improvements to their harvesting and winemaking techniques: besides, they did not invest to plant new vines to produce more because they did not have money enough (small landowners) or they were simply rentiers (great landowners) who delegated winegrowers and winemaking to sharecroppers' families who rarely had capitals to invest in viticulture.

So, Eastern Lombardy imported wine arriving from the hills of the Mantua and the Oltrepo districts and the hills of Emilia; while the best wine came from France. With the exception of some bottles of Lugana, the local wine had a market in the provinces of Bergamo and Brescia only. Most winemakers' sales network was in fact very simple: their wine was transported from the cellars to the taverns on carts drawn by oxen. The short distances involved reduced the risk of accidental breakages of casks or of high temperatures which could cause a deterioration in the wine. A small number of bottles containing the best quality wine (as Lugana, produced in the Morainique hills of the Southern Riviera of lake Garda) were sent out of the two provinces, but sales wine were limited due to its low-production volumes and, moreover, strong competition from high-quality wines produced in other Italian and French terroirs.

During the *Restaurazione* (the period from 1814 to 1859 when the provinces of Bergamo and Brescia belonged to the Habsburg Empire), some innovators tried to improve their wine by implementing changes to their techniques and instruments for the cultivation of vines and for winemaking, but this happened on small plots of land and were therefore unable to provide enough profits to justify the necessary investments.[5] Furthermore, most new and innovative ideas regarding production were accessible only to the *élite* members of society like aristocrats and wealthy bourgeois. Everyone else continued to use older techniques because they were not able to afford the necessary investment. This was particularly true when the vineyards were worked by sharecroppers, who cultivated the vines in return for a share of the landowner's profits. Sharecroppers had few financial resources and could expect little benefit from efforts to improve the quality of vines and grapes. Sharecropping contracts, then, guaranteed the best returns for landowners (who in many cases simply acted as *rentiers*), but this also meant that there were no advances either in production volumes or in the quality of wines.[6] The quantity and quality of harvests fluctuated greatly under the influence of different weather conditions, and were

---

[5]About the innovators' suggestions concerning the winegrowing and wine making in Eastern Lombardy see, among others, Agosti (1814), Ferrini (1822), Bajoni (1823), Pagani (1826), and Gabba (1836). See also Tedeschi (2003, 2004) and Onger (2008).

[6]Landowners either employed paid workers on their farms, leased them out to tenants, or agreed contracts with sharecroppers. The choice depended on the landlord's discretion and on the quality of the land and its fruits: in the vineyards of Eastern Lombardy sharecropping contracts were the preferred option. Sharecroppers normally received either half or 9/20 of the grape harvest, while

especially vulnerable in the weeks leading up to the harvest. The risks related to harsh weather conditions diminished the returns on investments, which already took around 8–9 years to bear fruit (the time necessary for new vines to produce their first grapes). A rich grape harvest could be followed by very bad years and, although "normal" production was, in the province of Brescia, almost 400,000 hl., a far lower volume was recorded on many occasions.[7] However, true production levels were actually more than twice those of the official figures, since landowners declared only a fraction of their grape and wine production in order to avoid increasingly severe taxation.[8]

This situation progressively changed during the second half of the nineteenth century in response to external factors, like economic crises and diseases, which forced landowners to change their approach and invest more money in their vineyards. Various fungal diseases and insects (powdery mildew, peronospora and phylloxera) caused serious damage to the vines, forcing landowners to replant new ones and to begin protecting them with chemical products. In the early 1850s, powdery mildew practically wiped out the grape harvests. In some years the entire grape harvest was barely one-tenth of the worst recorded harvest in the first half of the century: for example, in 1854 the wine

some skilled peasants (like the fattore, or farm manager, and herdsmen) were paid in cash and in kind, with some receiving a barrel of grapes. On these choices and the social and economic position of sharecropping contracts in the rural economy of Eastern Lombardy, see Tedeschi (2006a, pp. 103–141) (for data showing that yields were higher in the presence of sharecropping contracts, see pp. 460–463). Please note that there are ongoing debates on this subject, and as yet there is no consensus either way on the value of sharecropping contracts: disagreements often hinge on the clauses in the contracts, which had a substantial effect on production and yields. All this obviously concerns other wine regions too. See, for example, Cohen and Galassi (1990), Galassi (1993, 1996), Luporini and Parigi (1996), Carmona and Simpson (1999), Garrett and Xu (2003), Câmara (2006), Carmona (2006), Federico (2006), Santos (2006), Finzi (2007), and Tedeschi (2017).

[7]All data concerning the production during the post-Napoleonic period clearly show the wide fluctuations linked to variations in the grape harvest. The wine production (in hl.) in the province of Brescia was: 155,000 (1815); 80,650 (1817); 267,150 (1823); 110,700 (1828); 220,800 (1833); 98,450 (1836); 198,000 (1841); 76,100 (1843). See Tedeschi (2006a, p. 456).

[8]For viticulture in Eastern Lombardy during the Restaurazione see Tedeschi (2006a, pp. 186–190, 313–320). For the production and trade of wine in Lombardy see also Romani (1977a). Concerning the Eastern Lombard agriculture during nineteenth century see Moioli (1978), Cova (1977), Tedeschi (2008b), and Della Valentina (1996, pp. 3–51).

production in the province of Brescia was 8500 hl. (Tedeschi 2006a, p. 486). It was only after the introduction of the *solforatura* (a system whereby vines were regularly sprayed with copper sulphate) in the early 1860s that average yields returned to their previous levels. This latest innovation, though, was followed by a further reduction in the volumes of grapes and wine production, along with a diminution of the land planted with vines. The *solforatura* increased production costs and was considered incompatible with the planting of cereals between rows of vines, meaning that landowners had to make a choice between the two types of crop. Vines, therefore, disappeared wherever they were not the principal crop, continuing to be cultivated in the hills. At the end of the 1850s, the total area of land planted with vines was merely a third of that recorded during the 1830s. Furthermore, in the hills the area of land planted with vines doubled during the second half of the century, surpassing the total area occupied by vines in the plains (which had gradually been reduced to make way for cereals and fodder crops). The change was relevant: in the first half of the century, vines were often considered a minor crop on the lands where they were planted, overshadowed by larger quantities of other plants like mulberry trees (whose valuable leaves were used for breeding silkworms), whereas by the early twentieth century most vines were cultivated as a dedicated crop.

The powdery mildew was just the first of a series of factors that reduced the value of land planted with vines, as well as the profits landowners earned from the sale of grapes or wine. A reduction in profits came with a growth in competition following the improvement of railway networks (1857) and the founding of the Kingdom of Italy (1861), reducing transport costs and eliminating the tariffs applied to other Italian wines (in particular those from the central and southern regions). These factors naturally made local wine market more competitive and led to a fall in prices which encouraged a minor improvement in quality. While the cost of investing in the improvement of vines and wine production rose, the increased competition meant that only the higher quality wines were able to remain profitable. The reduction of the price of all wines allowed consumers to drink better quality wines for the same amount of money, causing a substantial fall in the profits earned by winemakers. This resulted in a reduction in the number of these latter, while doing nothing to spread winemaking techniques and the production of good quality wine. It also led, during the 1880s, to an increase in yields in Eastern Lombardy from 10 to 36 hectolitres for each hectare (because vines disappeared in the less rentable land), and to a widening "quality gap" between wine from Lugana and Franciacorta and that produced in other districts.

The great agrarian crisis which arrived in the Eastern Lombardy at the end of the 1870s and another severe outbreak, the peronospora (or *plasmopara viticola* which destroyed grapes) created new great problems for viticulturists and winemakers. A solution to the outbreak was quickly found, consisting in the spraying of vines with the "Bordeaux mixture", a compound of cupric sulphate and slaked lime, leading to far less damage than had occurred during the 1850s. However, spraying with the Bordeaux mixture added further to production costs and resulted in another fall in the numbers of vineyards and of winemakers, who were also facing a reduction in consumption as a result of the negative economic trend which continued until the early 1890s. In such conditions, only the top vineyards run by the wealthiest landowners could afford to invest in the replacement of vines and in improving the quality of their wine, creating an ever-wider gap between high-quality wines and all the others. Yields were also higher for top wine producers, who could achieve more than three times that of the makers of low-quality wine. Higher yields, then, were directly connected to improved manufacturing techniques.[9]

The remaining wineries were able to survive thanks to an efficient retailing system and a solid local consumer base. They also benefited from a particularly fortunate turn of events which reduced foreign competition: the fall in prices and profit margins reduced the number of competitors from elsewhere in Italy; the "tariff wars" with France, and a general increase in trade tariffs resulting from the negative European economic trend, caused a reduction in high-quality wine imports. At the same time, as wine producers in Eastern Lombardy did not export their products, the tariffs introduced in foreign markets did

[9]Concerning changes in winemaking see, besides references quotes before, Monà (1875) and Bettoni Cazzago (1879a, b). Concerning the effects of the agrarian crisis in Eastern Lombardy see Trezzi (1974).

not influence their earnings. This also meant that those producers of low-quality wines who were still in business in the early 1890s could carry on as before without introducing improvements to their cultivation and winemaking methods. However, another serious crisis involving the viticulture was on the horizon, and was to have a definitive effect on the wine sector in Eastern Lombardy.

Production and Sale of Wine in Eastern Lombardy from the End of the Nineteenth Century to the Birth of the Common Agricultural Policy

At the half of the 1890s the new outbreak, the phylloxera (an insect which caused the death of vines), forced landowners to graft all their vines, the European *vitis vinifera* species, with American vines that were resistant to the insect. All vines in Eastern Lombardy had to be grafted, so the public authorities had to provide aid to the wine sector with the creation of *Consorzi Antifilloserici*, that is the anti-phylloxera consortia which financed and carried out the operations. While state support during the previous crisis had consisted in financial aid or tax reductions, the spread of phylloxera lead institutions to establish a wide-reaching series of interventions involving the distribution of American vines and the provision of training programmes to teach new grafting methods. The overwhelming invasion of the insect began in 1895 and was only fully eradicated in 1905.[10]

This crisis also highlighted the fact that viticulturists and winemakers of Eastern Lombardy had a lot of interests in common, and that they could defend these interests by uniting under a common cause.

---

[10]In the province of Brescia the anti-phylloxera consortia promoted the grafting of 144,000 new imported scions (talee), while the nursery of the main local agrarian school (Pastori) provided 513,000 scions and 195,000 small vines (barbatelle) grafted onto American vines. The nurseries of the Pastori agrarian school in Brescia and agrarian school in Grumello del Monte (and the related cooperative for the recreation of vines) supplied hundreds of thousands of new vine scions and hundreds of grafting courses were organized. See Statuto (1899), La lotta (1900), Consorzio (1922), Marengoni (1996, pp. 90–99), and Milesi (2001). About the general impact of the phylloxera on the Italian viticulture see Zaninelli (1977).

Nonetheless, in the early twentieth century they did not create an association and maintained their positions in existing landowners and tenants' associations (*Associazione dei Proprietari di Fondi* and *Associazione dei Conduttori di Fondi* which supported them during negotiations with sharecroppers and other peasants working in the wine sector, who were represented by Catholic or Socialist trade unions).[11]

Trade unions did not allow landowners to burden sharecroppers and other labourers with a significant portion of the increased manufacturing costs caused by the phylloxera outbreak. Besides, the growth of labour costs related to the increasing contractual strength of trade unions led to a further reduction in the amount of land planted with vines. As new sharecropping contracts established universal rules, demanding the same remuneration in fruit and cash in all oenological areas of the Eastern Lombardy, landowners and winemakers were forced to recognize a change of context. Labour costs were the same for all producers, while their income varied according to transport costs and the quality of their wine. Competitiveness, then, depended on the producers' ability to improve the quality of their wine and to reduce their operating costs, enhancing the importance of a well organized sales structure and, in particular, of reducing distribution costs.

Winemakers also had to deal with other major changes in the market. Transport networks became faster and less expensive thanks to the use of new rail convoys, and small trucks were introduced instead of ox-drawn carts for local distribution. At the same time, the average quality of wines increased while prices remained the same and the best wine producers were achieving a wider market for their product. Low-quality winemakers were suffering from the increased competition represented by good quality wines that were being brought in from other Italian wine regions: the end of the nineteenth century and moreover the early twentieth one were in fact characterized by a great improvement of the methods of winemaking (Cova 1989). Many consumers quickly became accustomed to drinking better wine, particularly

[11]On landowners and tenants' associations in Eastern Lombardy and their relationship with trade unions in the first decades of the twentieth century and the contracts agreed between them, see Tedeschi (1999a, pp. 190–228, 283–315, 341–350; 2002).

since they were no more expensive than local wines. All winemakers of Eastern Lombardy, then, were forced to offer better value for money in order to maintain their position in the local market.

Local winemakers' resistance to new competitors found support in another major factor which, from the last decades of the nineteenth century, had contributed to a gradual change in production techniques employed in vineyards and cellars. Innovations in production were, in fact, spreading throughout Eastern Lombardy thanks to the growth of agronomical studies, particularly those dedicated to viticulture, which were promoted by the new agrarian school founded in the outskirts of Brescia in 1876 and in Grumello del Monte (province of Bergamo) in 1874. Other agrarian schools were set up in the countryside over the following decades; this further favoured the growth of the knowledge concerning the viticulture and winemaking.[12] Before the foundation of these schools, the agronomic knowledge was a prerogative of few aristocrats and wealthy bourgeoisie who had access to agrarian journals and books and who were usually members of the local *athenaeum*. The new agrarian schools made this knowledge available to the sons of small landowners, tenants and sharecroppers. Graduates from these schools brought the innovations they had learned about back to the vineyards when they returned there to work with their families, passing on their new ampelographic knowledge to the landowners and sharecroppers living in their village.

Changes in the outlook of landowners and winemakers also contributed to the spread of new ideas in viticulture and winemaking. When, in the early twentieth century, the replanting of vineyards had been completed after the phylloxera outbreak, and new vines began to produce grapes,[13] they were forced to improve the quality of their wine and

---

[12] On agrarian schools in Eastern Lombardy (Istituto Pastori in Brescia, Colonia Agricola in Remedello and Scuola pratica di agricoltura di Grumello del Monte) and the growth in the understanding of agronomics in Eastern Lombardy, see Tedeschi (1999b, 2004, 2006b), Onger (2008), Paris (2008), Marengoni (1996, pp. 16–24), and Colombo (1909).

[13] Data put in evidence the growth of the wine production (in hl.) in the Eastern Lombardy after the positive results against the diffusion of the phylloxera. Province of Bergamo: 60,000 (1896); 45,000 (1898); 54,000 (1899); 127,000 (1909); 71,000 (1910); 217,000 (1911); 138,000 (1912); 173,000 (1913). Province of Brescia: 100,000 (1896); 115,000 (1898); 180,000 (1899); 363,000 (1909); 229,000 (1910); 244,000 (1911); 232,000 (1912); 239,000 (1913). See Annuario Statistico Italiano (1900) and MAIC (1914, p. 24).

their production techniques in order to recuperate their investment. Therefore these new innovations received a great deal of attention from operators in the wine sector who realized that there was very little space in the market for those who lacked financial resources or were not prepared to make substantial investments. The positive attitude and large investments in the wine sector helped the best viticulturists and winemakers to increase both production and yields and, at the same time, to improve the average quality of their grapes and their wine. Although the improvement in quality was not enough to significantly increase sales in markets outside of Eastern Lombardy (the only exceptions were represented by some varieties of the best Lugana), it did help winemakers to face increasing competition on the local wine market. Farmers who invested little were only able to produce wine for private consumption or for limited sales to the worst taverns where most customers were addicted to alcohol and unlikely to refuse even adulterated wine. The number of farmers who refused to invest gradually fell as it became clear that the renewal of vines and the adoption of new cultivation techniques provided significant advantages. Furthermore, some producers decided to create cooperatives which allowed them to raise more funds for investment and to improve the production quality and volumes. The new cooperative wineries improved yields and produced better quality wine. Although the distribution of different types of vines continued to show that winemakers preferred vines that produced more grapes rather than those which gave a better quality of fruit (even though a lot of vines continued to be cultivated together with other crops), the outlook for local viticulture was surely better than it had been in the previous century. The new attitude of cooperation had ideological origins which were related to the growth of local catholic and socialist movements, and was connected to the landowners' experience of fighting together against the phylloxera outbreak, which also helped to create other consortia (that is the Consorzi Grandinifughi) to defend against damage caused by hail.[14]

[14]Since winemakers preferred to cultivate vines which produced more grapes, the schiava variety was more commonly used than marzemino, corva and groppello, which guaranteed better quality, of which the latter two were replaced by negrara. Besides, in the province of Brescia the plots planted only with vines occupied 14,650 ha., while the total surface area cultivated with vines

The number of winemakers wishing to improve their products grew during the period of the WWI, as did the amount of land planted with vineyards (also considering that the production was reduced in some terroirs of the province of Brescia because they were near the battlefront).[15] After the war and during the 1920s investments in new vines by top winemakers widened the quality gap between vineyards planted with varieties like Isabella and Clinton (as well as the best varieties from France, Piedmont, Veneto and Tuscany), and the others where no renewal was implemented. A substantial portion of the latter was gradually eliminated. Between 1909 and 1929 many vines that produced low-quality wine for private use or for the worst taverns disappeared, with reductions of more than a fifth in the plains, a quarter in the hills, and a tenth in the lower valleys. However, many landowners still considered vines a secondary crop, and some of them decided to go back to combined cultivation of cereals and vines. This choice was also dictated by the agrarian policy of the fascist regime, which promoted the cultivation of cereals like wheat, which was at the centre of the *battaglia del grano*. The agrarian institutes also showed less interest in viticulture than in the past. Local and low-quality wine also found little support from the fascist regime, which only sponsored high-quality wines and liquors that could be exported. Fascist propaganda encouraged producers of low-quality wine to use their vines to produce grapes for consumption as fresh fruit. The vineyards of Eastern Lombardy did, in fact, have a long tradition in this particular sector. Grapes produced

was 27,640 ha., meaning that a substantial portion of wines were made using low quality grapes. Furthermore, there were 56 Consorzi grandinifughi in 1903, but only 20 were actually operative and able to limit the effects of hailstones (Gnaga 1904, pp. 64–65). In the province of Bergamo the situation was better because the communities with these consortia were 30 and they were all operative (Marengoni 1996, pp. 99–102).

[15]In 1913 the total surface area dedicated exclusively to vines was for the province of Brescia 14,500 ha., and the 5-years average production was 295,000 q. of grapes, while another 15,700 ha. of plots of land planted with a combination of vines and other crops had a 5-years production of 124,000 q. of grapes. In 1917 the figures related to surface area were, respectively, 15,100 and 14,100 ha., while and they produced 224,000 and 77,000 q. The data concerning the province of Bergamo were, respectively: (1913) 4000 ha.; 143,000 q.; 6200 ha.; 82,000 (1917) 5000 ha., 200,000 q., 4000 ha., 109,000 q. See: MAIC (1914, p. 14) and Primo Annuario Generale Vinicolo illustrato (1919–1920, p. 12).

in the outskirts of Brescia were particularly appreciated. The quality of grapes cultivated in the hills close to the town (Ronchi produced 500 q. at the beginning of the twentieth century) was very high and they were sold throughout Northern Italy (in particular in Milan, Venice and Genoa).

At the same time the work of the best winemakers made it possible to raise the overall output of the cellars of Eastern Lombardy. They also used imported grapes and, during the 1920s, the annual production of wine varied between 400,000 and 600,000 hl., or twice that recorded before WWI. However, the quality of grapes and moreover the method of winemaking did not allow to improve the average quality of local wine, and in particular it prevented the creation of a "constant wine", that is a wine which maintained its quality and taste over long periods, and without great differences from year to year. So quality increased greatly only in the Lugana and Valtenesi, while minor results were obtained in Franciacorta and in the department of Bergamo. In any case new wines which were more resistant to climate variations were made by the best producers: a "special perfumed" wine was in particular created in the hills of Brescia, while it was improved the wine produced in Scanzo (department of Bergamo) by dried grapes which were obtained by the vineyards called "Moscato di Scanzo" (having a surface of only 31 ha.).

The 1930s also saw a gradual increase in the quality of wines and in sales figures. This encouraged landowners to invest in new vines and, before WWII, the total area of land occupied by vines registered a minor increase: more than 3.5% overall and 9% in the low valleys. Finally, even though high-quality white wine was only produced in Lugana and most sales were limited to the local market, the adoption of most of the latest production techniques made it possible to create better wines which were also easier to preserve thanks to the introduction of demijohns This improvement in quality was also a result of the agreement between winemakers, who wished to define the character of new wines based exclusively on local grapes, with the intention of reassuring consumers that their wine was of high quality, and of increasing their sales in other Italian provinces.

However, the agreement failed due to the onset of WWII and the consequent reductions in production and consumption. The negative trend continued during the post-war reconstruction years, causing the numbers of vineyards and winemakers to fall once again. The lack of funds for improving and renewing vines, which had suffered another outbreak of phylloxera, and a succession of poor harvests (in the winter of 1956 the temperature fell to −14.6°, destroying many of the vines) squeezed the sector even further. The reduction in the size of the winemaking industry did not have a negative effect on the quality of the remaining winemakers or on their entrepreneurship. They benefited from substantial institutional and technological changes designed to encourage the process of modernization in the sector. New agrarian reforms banned sharecropping contracts and encouraged former sharecroppers to purchase the vines they worked with. Grape yields were also greatly increased by improvements in viticulture technologies.

In order to definitively relaunch the wine sector in Eastern Lombardy, a number of large winemaker's cooperatives were set up with the aim of improving the quality of wine and reduce sales costs. The first "disciplines of wines" were drafted following the "statutes of *Bresciani* wines", created in 1942, that is during WWII. Using these guidelines, and with the help of new production methods, most wines boasted well-defined and stable characteristics. In this period the first cement barrels arrived in the cellars, providing better conservation conditions for the wine which, nonetheless, continued to be pasteurized meaning that it lost some of its flavour. At the same time the custom of combining vines with other plants was abandoned and spraying with cupric sulphate was reduced, leading to an improvement in the quality of grapes and the taste of wine. The value of the wine sector increased by 19% during the 1950s, reaching 3,990,000 Italian lire by 1961. Even though there were still a number of serious problems in the retailing sector (e.g. most Franciacorta wines were sold in unlabelled demijohns), the viticulture was ready to play a new role in the agricultural industry of Eastern Lombardy.

Beginning in the 1960s, when the Common Agrarian Policy (CAP) was introduced, leading to an increase in competition but also to a wider market, the "enotechno-revolution" greatly influenced the quality of wines and the way they were sold. In 1961 the first 3000 bottles of a new sparkling wine, the first Franciacorta *spumante* were produced by

Ziliani, the foremost winemaker of the Berlucchi company, following the "classic method" and using some white Pinot. This wine was named "Pinot di Franciacorta" and it was the first time that a geographical name appeared on the label of an Italian wine. The differentiation of wines according to quality began, and involved manufacturing processes, supply chain logistics, and market recognition based on the quality of wines through labelling. The reduction in the size of barrels, the *barriques* made of oak, an increase in the supply of oxygen during the fermentation process, and a recourse to new giant tanks (firstly in stainless steel, and then in fibreglass, which guaranteed a more constant taste and flavour) for the conservation of their wines allowed producers to introduce new types of wine with a higher average quality and more competitive prices. At the same time, a new fermentation process (malolactic fermentation) made it possible to reduce acidity and mellow the wine; and new stalk-removing machines were introduced for the production of white wine. Furthermore, new cultivation techniques allowed producers to increase their yields from 67.7 q./ha. (in 1960) to 99.4 (in 1970) while reducing the overall cultivated surface area (less than 5000 ha. during the 1980s) so that only the best quality land was used.

Finally, winemaker's associations established new guidelines for the creation of wines labelled with a certificate of origin that provided consumers with a guarantee that certain manufacturing standards had been followed: in 1962 the new consortium of winemakers of Eastern Lombardy was set up (the *Consorzio volontario dei vini tipici e pregiati della provincia di Brescia*) to protect local winemakers, after which the province was divided into seven new wine districts. Producers gradually came to understand the importance of demonstrating a connection with the terroir in order to market themselves effectively and develop strong customer relationships, particularly with regard to the profitable metropolitan markets. It was also necessary, especially during the economic crisis of the 1970s, to improve quality while at the same time reducing production levels and planting fewer rows of vines with more space between them. The competitive intensification of the low-quality wine market encouraged the foremost producers to create better wines which could achieve a more stable market. Wealthy consumers, in fact, guaranteed a more constant consumption during negative economic periods. Other customers were prepared to pay more if they believed the wine they were buying for a special occasion offered good value for money. During the same period, the first examples of "wine tourism" appeared in Franciacorta. Cellars were opened to the public who could buy wines in special boxes of six or twelve bottles. In the 1980s there were more than 6500 winemakers' cellars, selling over 500,000 hl. of wine each year, at least 10% of which was high-quality wine exported to the international markets.[16]

The "enotechno-revolution" of the 1960s was followed by relevant transformations in the production and sale of wine in Eastern Lombardy. These latter were mainly related to differentiation between the quality of products, and to the strategic role of food retailers in relation to the management of wine supply chains. The new CAP rules helped to improve the quality of wine thanks to an increased diversification in the origin of products. Moreover, retailers played an important role during negotiations due to their strategic position within the supply chain and their structural characteristics. While new technologies began to be adopted in vineyards and cellars, winegrowers' associations were establishing new guidelines aimed at the creation of wines displaying a certificate of origin. These guidelines indicated the country and province of production, and designated a product whose origins and characteristics were due exclusively or mainly to the geographical place of origin. These latter were "DOC" (Controlled Designation of the Origin), and DOCG (Controlled and Guaranteed Designation of the Origin), Among the distinctive features of these products were factors including human capital and natural resources, and consumers came to see it as a guarantee of the quality of the wine.

---

[16]The most common varieties were: tocai, riesling, trebbiano, pinot, vernaccia, moscato, erbamat, luglienga (for white wines); brugnera, besegana, maiolina, marzemino, groppello, barbera, nebbiolo, bordò e bordonsì (for red wines). The new wine regions were: Riviera del Garda bresciano (rosso, rosso superiore and chiaretto), San Martino della Battaglia, Lugana (bianco and spumante), Botticino, Cellatica, Capriano del Colle (bianco and rosso) e Terre Franciacorta (bianco, rosso, spumante brut and rosé); Valcalepio (bianco, rosso, rosso riserva and Moscato passito), Moscato Di Scanzo. For the 'enotechno-revolution' and its impact on the wine sector in Eastern Lombardy, see Carugati (2012), Berlucchi (1988), Milesi (1984), Camera di Commercio (1973), Compagnoni (2000), and Marengoni (1985; 1996, pp. 114–120).

Wine producers and retailers in Eastern Lombardy worked well together and favoured the distribution of the local wine products. The wines that were awarded with these quality labels were those which were already well known and sold before the "enotechno-revolution", like Lugana and Franciacorta, but they also included a number of wines produced in the vineyards of the hills around Brescia (in Capriano del Colle, Poncarale and Botticino), near the western Riviera of Lake Garda (e.g. the Valtenesi), or in the province of Bergamo (Valcalepio and Moscato di Scanzo). At the end of twentieth century, some of these, in particular, the sparkling wines (*Spumante*), continued to be exported, with very positive results, to the main international markets. Moreover, some wines, produced in Franciacorta cellars (e.g. Berlucchi), and using grapes from outside the province, also greatly increased their sales in international markets. In this case, quality and high sales performances depended on wine producers' advanced manufacturing systems.

Conclusions

The production and sale of good quality wine in Eastern Lombardy increased from the Napoleonic age to the new millennium, with particular improvements in the quality of wines. The surface area represented by vines gradually became smaller, as did the number of viticulturists. Winemakers, for their part, created consortiums for the protection and sale of local wines. This situation was the result of the diminished industry resulting from vine diseases in the second half of the nineteenth century. The surviving viticulturists and winemakers invested in the improvement of their manufacturing systems and the quality of their cellars, going on to create consortiums for the protection of their wines and the promotion of their identity and heritage. Finally, they dedicated a growing attention to retailing systems and consumer preferences.

Recently, the structural growth of retailers has led to their empowerment during negotiations, and their strategic position within the supply chain has given them a competitive advantage over winemakers. The growing power of retailers represents a new challenge for wine producers, who must strengthen the vertical relationships between different economic players in the supply chain and improve manufacturing processes through the rationalization of the transport of raw materials, the reduction of waste products, and a more sustainable management of production within the wine supply chain.

Appendix

See Fig. 1 and Tables 1, 2, and 3.

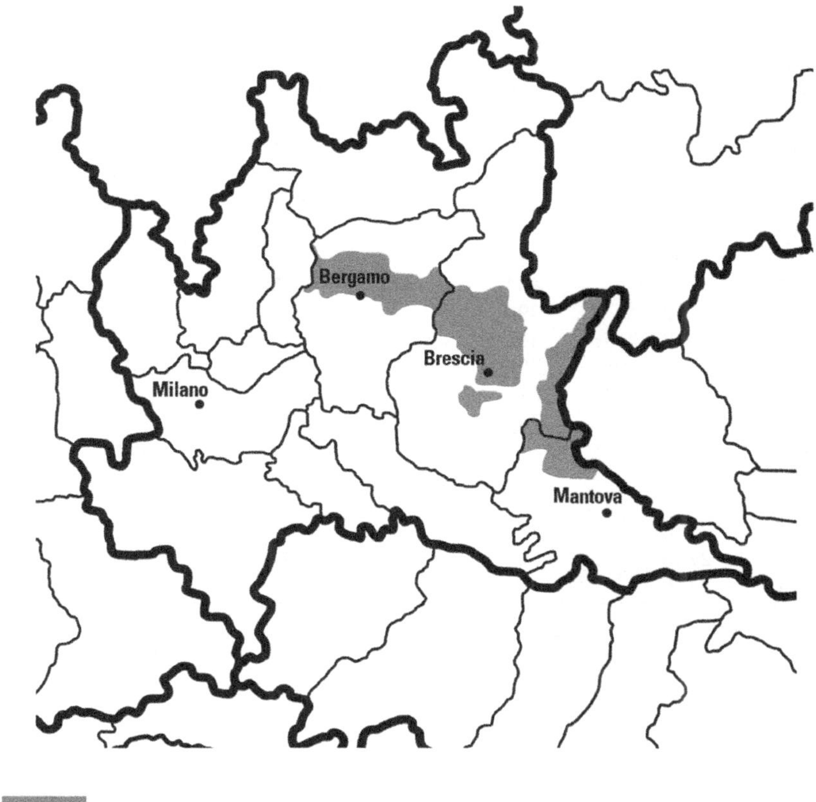

Fig. 1 Eastern Lombardy winegrowing area (*Source* Author)

Table 1 Vines (in ha.) in the provinces of Bergamo (BG) and Brescia (BS) (1952–1982)

Year	Only vines (BG)	Vines and other crops (BG)	Only vines (BS)	Vines and other crops (BS)
1952	6196	10,410	9344	38,540
1953	6196	10,410	9278	38,540
1954	6196	10,410	9278	38,546
1955	6196	7450	9278	38,546
1956	6196	7450	9278	38,546
1957	6196	7450	8271	35,959
1958	6196	7450	8271	35,959
1959	6196	7450	8271	35,959
1960	6196	7450	8271	35,959
1961	5692	6848	8191	35,959
1962	5712	6772	8191	35,959
1963	5713	6742	8128	35,803
1964	5122	5600	8149	33,098
1965	4883	5464	8217	30,890
1966	4536	4955	8191	28,608
1967	4334	4565	8417	25,288
1968	4245	3897	8417	24,000
1969	3310	1613	8270	12,739
1970	3190	422	7833	6619
1971	3027	404	7776	6597
1972	2912	390	7776	6597
1973	2898	382	8123	5911
1974	2834	356	8077	5793
1975	2919	271	8151	5676
1976	2920	245	8147	5571
1977	2914	245	8093	5546
1978	2849	207	8104	5523
1979	2812	138	8122	5509
1980	2768	78	8188	5459
1981	2758	52	8194	5408
1982	2756	42	8181	5372

Source Istat, *Annuario di Statistica Agraria* (1952–1982)

Table 2 Grape and wine production in the province of Bergamo (1952–1982)

Year	Grape production (q.)	Grape used for wine (q.)	Wine production (hl.)
1952	389,200	364,000	255,000
1953	391,500	367,300	286,100
1954	361,000	336,800	235,700
1955	349,600	326,400	228,500
1956	354,700	331,200	231,800
1957	207,700	189,500	132,600
1958	378,400	351,700	246,200
1959	359,300	318,000	222,600
1960	316,000	296,800	222,600
1961	165,800	157,500	118,100
1962	389,700	379,800	284,500
1963	191,700	180,300	98,000
1964	217,400	203,800	130,300
1965	293,800	284,700	191,100
1966	184,500	183,900	115,800
1967	240,000	239,200	155,500
1968	171,800	171,500	99,400
1969	155,200	154,700	92,800
1970	148,800	148,300	97,900
1971	138,800	138,800	91,700
1972	130,200	130,200	84,600
1973	167,200	165,000	112,300
1974	156,500	150,000	102,600
1975	91,200	90,000	61,200
1976	173,800	170,000	115,600
1977	156,400	154,000	104,700
1978	175,100	170,000	119,000
1979	240,300	240,000	175,000
1980	153,800	153,400	104,000
1981	116,200	116,000	76,000
1982	159,800	159,500	107,000

Source ibid.

Table 3 Grape and wine production in the province of Brescia (1952–1982)

Year	Grape production (q.)	Grape used for wine (q.)	Wine production (hl.)
1952	1,359,400	1,308,200	908,100
1953	1,263,700	1,211,900	850,700
1954	1,025,700	964,600	646,900
1955	1,264,700	1,199,400	839,600
1956	1,401,000	1,321,100	924,700
1957	742,700	685,100	479,600
1958	1,609,700	1,531,700	1,072,200
1959	1,002,500	927,000	648,900
1960	1,170,100	1,092,000	764,400
1961	732,700	663,300	418,500
1962	1,216,200	1,139,800	752,200
1963	752,300	752,300	744,300
1964	1,189,500	1,181,000	862,100
1965	1,179,400	1,165,600	815,900
1966	1,011,400	1,002,900	692,000
1967	1,113,000	1,104,500	828,400
1968	701,500	693,500	471,600
1969	802,800	794,800	572,300
1970	775,200	767,200	537,100
1971	527,300	520,800	359,300
1972	614,100	608,900	414,100
1973	716,500	751,500	533,000
1974	648,200	655,900	459,100
1975	562,500	562,500	382,500
1976	519,900	519,900	348,300
1977	600,300	600,100	432,100
1978	489,100	489,100	342,400
1979	604,600	604,600	417,700
1980	559,100	559,100	374,600
1981	464,600	464,600	325,200
1982	607,700	607,700	416,300

Source ibid.

References

Agosti G.C. (1814), *Regole per la coltivazione delle viti secondo la pratica e l'esperienza*, Bergamo, Duci.

Archetti G. (ed.) (2003), *La civiltà del vino: fonti, temi e produzioni vitivinicole dal Medioevo al Novecento*, Brescia, Centro culturale artistico di Franciacorta e del Sebino.

Archetti G. (ed.) (2006), 'Giovanni Bonsignori tra memoria e attualità', *Civiltà Bresciana*, pp. 3–4.

Bajoni C. (1823), *Metodo per fare, migliorare e conservare il vino che felicemente può riuscire nella collina e nel piano di Lombardia con note e aggiunte dell'autore per il vino forzato e vinetto economico*, Bergamo, Mazzoleni.

Belfanti C.M., Taccolini M. (eds.) (2008a), *Storia dell'agricoltura bresciana*, vol. I, *Dall'antichità al secondo Ottocento*, Brescia: Fondazione Civiltà Bresciana.

Belfanti C.M., Taccolini M. (eds.) (2008b), *Storia dell'agricoltura bresciana*, vol. II, *Dalla grande crisi agraria alla politica agricola comunitaria*, Brescia: Fondazione Civiltà Bresciana.

Berlucchi M. (1988), 'Il vino di ieri e oggi', *Commentari dell'Ateneo di Brescia*, pp. 237–247.

Bettoni Cazzago L. (1879a), 'Monografia sulla vite del lago di Garda', *Commentari dell'Ateneo di Brescia*, pp. 19–25.

Bettoni Cazzago L. (1879b), 'Il vino del lago di Garda', *Commentari dell'Ateneo di Brescia*, pp. 45–51.

Bourillon F., Vivier N. (eds.) (2012), *La mesure cadastrale. Réflexion sur la valeur des estimations cadastrales*, Rennes, PUR, pp. 17–39.

Câmara B. (2006), 'The Portuguese Civil Code and the Colonia Tenancy Contract in Madeira (1867–1967)', *Continuity and Change*, 2, pp. 213–233.

Camera di Commercio di Brescia (1973), *I vini bresciani*, Brescia, Sardini.

Carmona J. (2006), 'Sharecropping and Livestock Specialization in France, 1830–1930', *Continuity and Change*, 2, pp. 235–259.

Carmona J., Simpson J. (1999), 'The "Rabassa Morta" in Catalan Viticulture: The Rise and Decline of a Long Term Sharecropping Contract, 1670s–1920s', *The Journal of Economic History*, pp. 290–315.

Carugati D.G. (ed.) (2012), *Berlucchi 1961–2011. Sogno e realtà Franco Ziliani, pioniere in Franciacorta*, Milan, Electa.

Cohen J.S., Galassi F.L. (1990), 'Sharecropping and Productivity: "Feudal Residues" in Italian Agriculture', *The Economic History Review*, 4, pp. 646–656.

Colombo F. (1909), *Notizie storico-statistiche della scuola ed alunni che la frequentarono e che furono licenziati dal 1874 al 1908*, Bergamo, Cooperativa begamasca d'arti grafiche.

Compagnoni D. (2000), *Vitigni in provincia di Bergamo*, Bergamo, Provincia di Bergamo.

Consorzio antifillosserico bresciano (1922), *I 25 anni di attività del Consorzio antifillosserico bresciano (1897–1922)*, Brescia, Apollonio.

Cova A. (1977), *Aspetti dell'economia agricola lombarda dal 1796 al 1814. Il valore dei terreni, la produzione, il mercato*, Milan, Vita e Pensiero.

Cova A. (1989), 'Problemi tecnici ed economici della produzione di vino in Italia tra Otto e Novecento', *Il vino* (1989), pp. 319–337.

Della Valentina G.L. (1996), 'L'agricoltura (1870–1945)', in Zaninelli, Zamagni (1996), pp. 13–88.

Faccini L. (ed.) (1986), *Agricoltura e condizioni di vita dei lavoratori agricoli lombardi: 1835–1839. Inchiesta di Karl Czoernig*, Milan, Ed. Bibliografica.

Fatti e idee di storia economica nei secoli XIX–XX. Studi dedicati a Franco Borlandi (1977), Bologna, Il Mulino.

Federico G. (2006), 'The "Real" Puzzle of Sharecropping: Why Is It Disappearing?', *Continuity and Change*, 2, pp. 261–285.

Ferrini G. (1822), 'Nuovo metodo di fare il vino condensando i vapori che esalano nella fermentazione per trarne profitto', *Commentari dell'Ateneo di Brescia*, pp. 1–23.

Finzi R. (2007), *Mezzadria svelata? Un esempio storico e qualche riflessione fra teoria e storiografia*, Bologna, Clueb.

Gabba A. (1836), 'Due nuove macchine utili nella fabbricazione del vino di Giuseppe Torri falegname abitante in Cologne, provincia di Brescia', *Giornale Agrario Lombardo-Veneto*, 6, pp. 174–176.

Galassi F.L. (1993), 'Mezzadria e sviluppo tecnologico tra '800 e '900', *Rivista di Storia dell'Agricoltura*, 2, pp. 103–116.

Galassi F.L. (1996), 'Innovazioni tecniche e mezzadria alla fine dell'Ottocento: critica di un modello', *Innovazione* (1989), pp. 99–112.

Garrett M., Xu Z. (2003), 'The Efficiency of Sharecropping: Evidence from the Postbellum South', *Southern Economic Journal*, 69, pp. 578–595.

Gnaga A. (1904), *La provincia di Brescia e la sua Esposizione*, Brescia, Geroldi.

Il vino nell'economia e nella società italiana medioevale e moderna (1989), Florence, Accademia dei Georgofili.

Innovazione e sviluppo. Tecnologia e organizzazione fra teoria economica e ricerca storica (secoli XVI–XX) (1989), Bologna, Monduzzi, pp. 99–112.

Ismea (2007), *I vini Doc e Docg. Una mappatura della viticoltura regionale a denominazione d'origine*, Rome.

Istituzioni Agrarie in Provincia di Brescia. Storia e documenti (1999), Brescia, Squassina.

La lotta contro la fillossera nella provincia di Bergamo. Iniziative della R. Scuola d'Agricoltura di Grumello del Monte e del suo direttore prof. D. Tamaro (1900), Bergamo, Bolis.

Locatelli A.M. (2003), *Riforma fiscale e identità regionale: il catasto per il Lombardo-Veneto (1815–1853)*, Milan, Vita e Pensiero.

Locatelli A.M., Tedeschi P. (2012), 'Entre réforme fiscale et développement économique: les cadastres en Lombardie aux 18ème et 19ème siècles', in Bourillon, Vivier (2012), pp. 17–39.

Luporini A., Parigi B. (1996), 'Multi-task Sharecropping Contracts: the Italian Mezzadria', *Economica*, 251, pp. 445–457.

MAIC Ministero Agricoltura, Industria e Commercio (1914), *Il vino in Italia. Produzione – Comemrcio con l'estero – Prezzi*, Rome, Cecchini.

Maironi da Ponte G. (1803), *Osservazioni sul Dipartimento del Serio*, Bergamo, Natali.

Marache C., Vivier N. (eds.) (2013), 'L'Etat et les sociétés rurales: enquêtes agricoles, enquêteurs et enquêtés en Europe du Sud aux XIXe et XXe siècles', *Annales du Midi*, p. 284.

Marengoni M. (1985), 'Moscato di Scanzo: quando la tradizione del viticoltore incontra la nobiltà del vitigno', *Vignevini*, n. 6.

Marengoni M. (1996), *Vite e Vino in terra bergamasca dai tempi più antichi ai giorni nostri*, Bergamo, Provincia di Bergamo.

Milesi O. (1984), *Spumanti in Franciacorta*, Brescia, Grafo.

Milesi O. (2001), *Fillossera a Brescia. Dalla scoperta alla sconfitta*, Brescia, Graficadinamica.

Moioli A. (1978), 'I sistemi agricoli nella Lombardia orientale durante la prima metà dell'Ottocento. Il caso delle zone ex-venete (province di Bergamo, Brescia e Cremasco)', *Rivista di Storia dell'Agricoltura*, 3, pp. 15–70.

Monà A. (1875), 'Principali innovazioni tentate in questi ultimi tempi nella vinificazione', *Commentari dell'Ateneo di Brescia*, pp. 108–112.

Onger S. (ed.) (2004), *L'Ateneo di Brescia (1802–2002). Atti del Convegno Storico per il Bicentenario di fondazione dell'Ateneo di scienze, lettere e arti di Brescia*, Brescia, Ateneo di Brescia.

Onger S. (2008), *Istruzione agronomica e innovazione tecnica in agricoltura (1797–1859)*, in Belfanti, Taccolini (2008a), pp. 311–345.

Pagani G.B. (1826), 'Sul maritaggio delle viti coi gelsi', *Commentari dell'Ateneo di Brescia*, pp. 104–105.

Paris I. (2008), *La nascita del Comizio Agrario e la formazione delle scuole agrarie nella seconda metà del XIX secolo*, in Belfanti, Taccolini (2008b), pp. 1–40.

Romani M. (1977a), 'Produzione e commercio dei vini in Lombardia nei secoli XVIII e XIX', in Romani, pp. 514–539.

Romani M. (1977b), *Aspetti e problemi di storia economica lombarda nei secoli XVIII e XIX. Scritti riediti in memoria* (S. Zaninelli ed.), Milan, Vita e Pensiero.

Sabatti A. (1807), *Quadro statistico del dipartimento del Mella*, Brescia, Bettoni.

Santos R. (2006), 'Risk-Sharing and Social Differentiation of Demand in Land-Tenancy Markets in Southern Portugal, Seventeenth–Nineteenth Centuries', *Continuity and Change*, 2, pp. 287–312.

Statuto del Consorzio Cooperativo per la ricostituzione dei vigneti nel comune di Grumello del Monte (1899), Bergamo, Istituto italiano d'arti grafiche.

Strangio D. (ed.) (2018), *Istituzioni, disuguaglianze, economia in Italia. Una visione diacronica*, Milano, FrancoAngeli.

Tedeschi P. (1999a), *Economia e sindacato nel Bresciano tra primo dopoguerra e fascismo: le Unioni del lavoro (1918–1926)*, Milan, FrancoAngeli.

Tedeschi P. (1999b), 'La formazione delle Istituzioni Agrarie Raggruppate', *Istituzioni* (1999), pp. 13–53.

Tedeschi P. (2002), 'Contratti agrari e produttività del fattore lavoro nei primi decenni del '900 nelle province della Lombardia orientale', in Zaninelli, Taccolini (2002), pp. 555–572.

Tedeschi P. (2003), 'Il rinnovamento colturale. Aspetti della viticoltura bresciana fra Ottocento e Novecento', in Archetti (2003), pp. 789–816.

Tedeschi P. (2004), 'L'Ateneo e gli studi d'agricoltura nell'Ottocento', in Onger (2004), pp. 227–275.

Tedeschi P. (2006a), *I frutti negati: assetti fondiari, modelli organizzativi, produzioni e mercati agricoli nel Bresciano durante l'età della Restaurazione*, Brescia, Fondazione Civiltà Bresciana.

Tedeschi P. (2006b), *Padre Giovanni Bonsignori e l'agricoltura bresciana all'inizio del XX secolo: innovazioni nei processi produttivi e nell'istruzione agraria*, in Archetti (2006), pp. 49–84.

Tedeschi P. (2008a), 'Marché foncier et systèmes de production agricoles dans l'Italie du nord au XIXe siècle: le cas de la Lombardie orientale', *European Review of History*, 5, pp. 459–477.

Tedeschi P. (2008b), 'L'economia agricola bresciana dall'età napoleonica alla grande crisi agraria: assetti fondiari, contratti, tecniche colturali e produzioni', in Belfanti, Taccolini (2008a), pp. 231–310.

Tedeschi P. (2013), 'Les enquêtes agraires en Lombardie au XIXe siècle', in Marache, Vivier (2013), pp. 525–541.

Tedeschi P. (2017), 'Note sull'evoluzione dei contratti di compartecipazione nelle campagne lombarde', in Varini (2017), pp. 153–177.

Tedeschi P., Vaquero Piñeiro M. (2018), 'L'agricoltura italiana dagli anni '30 al nuovo millennio nelle statistiche dell'Istat: crescita produttiva e benessere', in Strangio (2018), pp. 141–169.

Trezzi L. (1974), 'La grande crisi agricola nella stampa cattolica bergamasca e bresciana (1879–1895)', *Bollettino dell'Archivio per la storia del movimento sociale* cattolico *in Italia*, 1, pp. 108–147.

Varini V. (ed.) (2017), *L'uomo al centro della storia. Studi in onore di Luigi Trezzi*, Milan, FrancoAngeli.

Zaninelli S. (1977), 'Un tema di storia dell'agricoltura italiana fra Otto e Novecento: la diffusione della fillossera ed il rinnovamento della viticoltura', *Fatti* (1977), pp. 861–878.

Zaninelli S., Taccolini M. (eds.) (2002), *Il lavoro come fattore produttivo e come risorsa nella storia economica italiana*, Milan, Vita e Pensiero.

Zaninelli S., Zamagni V. (eds.) (1996), *Storia economica e sociale di Bergamo*, vol. *Fra ottocento e novecento*, t. 1, *Tradizione e modernizzazione*, Bergamo, Fondazione per la storia economica e sociale di Bergamo.

Viniculture in the Italy of the Mezzadria (Tuscany, Umbria and Marche)

Luca Mocarelli and Manuel Vaquero Piñeiro

Between Past and Renewal

The spread of an agronomic culture in Italy during the second half of the eighteenth century, as clearly demonstrated by the founding of the Accademia dei Georgofili (Georgofili Academy) in Florence in 1753, contributed significantly to the multiplication of studies on viticulture and wine production in Italy (Pisani 2007). In 1772, the physician and botanist, and member of the Academy, Giovanni Cosimo Villifranchi wrote "Oenologia toscana, o sia memoria sopra i vini ed in specie toscani" (Tuscan oenology, an essay on wines and Tuscan species). In 1793 the Florentine agronomist Adamo Fabbroni published

L. Mocarelli (✉)
Department of Economics, University of Milano-Bicocca, Milan, Italy
e-mail: luca.mocarelli@unimib.it

M. Vaquero Piñeiro
Department of Political Science, University of Perugia, Perugia, Italy
e-mail: manuel.vaqueropineiro@unipg.it

S. A. Conca Messina et al. (eds.), *A History of Wine in Europe, 19th to 20th Centuries, Volume I*, Palgrave Studies in Economic History,
https://doi.org/10.1007/978-3-030-27772-7_9

his "Dissertazione sopra la maniera di perfezionare i vini nello Stato Pontificio" (Dissertation on how to perfect wines in the Papal States). In 1809 Giovanni Brignoli printed "Istruzione sul miglioramento de' vini nel dipartimento del Metauro" (Instructions on improving wines in the region of Metauro). Due to the influence of the French, writings on the manufacture and storage of wine increased in number during the first decades of the nineteenth century as concretely demonstrated by the volumes of Count Vincenzo Dandolo "Enologia ovvero l'arte di fare, conservare e far viaggiare i vini del Regno" (Oenology or the art of making, preserving and distributing the wines of the Kingdom), of the priest Jacopo Ricci "Del vino, delle sue malattie e de' suoi rimedi e dei mezzi per iscoprirne le falsificazioni dei vini artificiali e della fabbricazione dell'aceto" (On wine, its diseases and its remedies and ways to discover counterfeiting of artificial wines and the production of vinegar), of Adamo Fabbroni "Dell'arte di fare il vino per la Lombardia austriaca e metodi pratici per fare i migliori vini toscani" (The art of making wine for the Austrian Lombardy and the practical methods to make the best Tuscan wines) and of the Marquis Cosimo Ridolfi "Memoria sulla preparazione de' vini Toscani" (Essay on the preparation of Tuscan wines) (Berta 2016; Storchi 2016).

The titles and contributions that could be cited could be many more, as is quite evident by the numerous writings on viticulture and wine making published in the *Giornale Agrario Toscano*.

However, the above-mentioned authors have been chosen as an example of the step by step progression in Italy of the transition from the eighteenth to the nineteenth century of the theoretical-scientific basis of the problems regarding grapes and wine (Ciuffoletti 2000). Though there is quite a disparity of viewpoints and approaches, generally the authors, while intent on applying useful scientific reasoning, are also insistent on the necessity to render the production of wine a solid and productive economic sector (Simpson 2011). Their attention is not only focused on the various remedies for combatting plant diseases or how to harvest and produce wine according to the dictates of rational criteria, but also on the choices to be made for the production of luxury wine, such as the shape and seal of the bottles (Lomeni 1834, pp. 251–272).

During the nineteenth century, the Italian wine industry counted on a rich heritage of scientific publications, many of which focused on Tuscany, at the top of the fledgling national winemaking industry at the time. But the wines of the central regions that made their entry into the Kingdom of Italy had a poor reputation. The situation during the period of national unification was even more problematic, because of the consequences that arose from the spread of Oidium. The traditional remedies proved to be completely unfounded and useless and were unable to prevent the destruction of the vineyards (Ciuffoletti 2000, pp. 140–143). Only the new fungicidal substances containing sulphur gave concrete results, but in order to use them, it was necessary to overcome the consolidated opposition of the farmers, who were against the use of such techniques, not only because of the costs, but also because they required the acceptance of the scientific theories of the time.

After the birth of the Kingdom of Italy, in order to try to overcome this know-how, which was largely anchored to the past, there was a multiplication of measures aimed at modifying such a sluggish scenario. According to the model of the "Società enologica toscana" (Tuscan Society for Oenology), constituted at Leghorn in 1837, similar companies were created in Loreto, Perugia and Florence in 1870–1871 (Vaquero Piñeiro 2012, pp. 92–93). These were associations generally promoted by large merchants and landowners whose objective was the production of quality wines. The president of the association of Perugia, the Marquis Raffaele Antinori, professor of the University of Perugia, had a winery furnished with all the equipment necessary for the manufacturing of white wine (Bordeaux method, Cote d'Or method and Rhenish method) and red wine (Bordeaux method). Clearly, the intention was that of achieving a winemaking process similar to the far more prestigious winemaking of France and Germany, in an attempt to emulate these countries.

These oenological societies, although stilted by a chronic lack of capital and a vague business vision, represented the first important signal of change, to which undoubtedly the constitution of the Comitato Centrale Ampelografico Italiano (Italian Central Ampelographic Committee) in 1872 must be added. In the following years, similar organisms, at the regional level, also began to operate. They dealt with the vineyards in their respective provinces, and carried out analyses of musts and wine production made with the grapes of the established vineyards. For example, the Ancona commission arranged an ampelographic display where 273 grape samples were analysed and 27 varieties of vines identified (Silvestroni 2013; Vernelli 2003). This was an important step because it was evident that knowledge of the conditions of vine cultivation was essential in order to promote the inclusion of local wines in the circuits of important national and international trade (Federico and Martinelli 2018).

And though the mechanism for the investigation and transmission of information did not always work perfectly, it was the first time that such systematic research and collection of technical-scientific data on the cultivation of vines and the production of wine was conducted. The farmers were asked to send clusters of grapes with the branch and leaves, labelled with the common names of the vines used by the farmers. The question of the nomenclature is only apparently formal because, in order to teach and apply a modern style of agriculture, the first major obstacle to overcome was the multiplicity of names traditionally assigned to the various grape qualities (Kolleen 2003).

The 70s of the nineteenth century therefore appear to be characterized by numerous novelties. Alongside private and public initiatives, such as those highlighted above, which tried to break with tradition, at least in theory, exhibitions also gained increasing importance. Such exhibitions offered individual producers concrete opportunities to interact with an ever-growing complex and competitive national and international market (Teughels and Peter 2015). It is true that many of the exhibitors, attracted by the novelty, frequently participated in competitions for reasons of vanity and a desire to appear. Nevertheless, there were producers and merchants who had quite a different approach to wine production. Exhibitions in London, Vienna or Philadelphia offered opportunities to get in touch with the international market, and all observers, both national and foreign, shared the idea that Italian wines in general, and those of the central regions in particular, did not quite meet with the quality standard. Despite the presence of some positive notes, the panorama was dominated by the lack of oenological knowledge and the inability to break with a tradition accustomed to producing wines tied to the local taste. As a result, it was difficult to gain ground in the international market (Fumian 2016).

Moreover, the authors of the Jacini Agrarian Survey seem to agree that the three regions of Central Italy (Tuscany, Umbria and Marche) produced a poor quality wine. The main criticism was basically the system of cultivation used, the so-called "*maritate*" or "*alberate*" vines that is to say vines "married to trees". It was an old practice that involved the use of trees as living supports to allow the vines to grow in height, resulting in tall plants full of leaves which prevented the correct ripening of the grapes.

Another problem that plagued the viticulture and winemaking of these areas stemmed from the wide variety of grapes that were grown in bulk, a practice which effectively prevented the wines from obtaining a constant and typical quality. In addition, by following the dictates handed down by the old medieval statutes (Vernelli 2003, pp. 116–117), the different types of grapes present in the fields, though ripening at different times, were all harvested at the same time, mixed and pounded in the same containers. Furthermore, the antiquated systems in the fermentation of the grapes produced bitter wines, that easily turned into vinegar and were often characterized by unpleasant tastes, due to the use of mouldy vats.

When considering the social aspects, and not only the technical ones, it is immediately apparent that what put a break on the qualitative development of oenology of the three regions of central Italy, was without doubt the undisputed prevalence of the practice of *mezzadria* (sharecropping), an agrarian pact on which there is an ample bibliography available (Giorgetti 1974).[1] It is well known that this pact entailed a system of assignment of the land which provided for the halving of crops between farmers and the owners of the land. Thus, what tended to predominate was the purely quantitative aspect of the production, and predictably it was clear that among the peasants there was a habitual lack of incentive for making good wine with "the grapes of the master". As a result the wine, which did not enjoy the necessary care

[1]For a European comparison, Biagioli (2013).

and attention, consequently did not have the characteristics for exportation and was therefore intended for family consumption or, at most, for sale on the local market.

The most obvious consequence of this situation was that, as late as the 1880s, in Umbria, but also in Tuscany and Marche, there were still few farmers cultivating low vineyards, and specialized vineyards were still rare. In the province of Ancona, for example, there were 23,354 hectares of promiscuous vineyards, and only 432 hectares of specialized vineyards (Vernelli 2003, p. 127). This confirms how the overall picture would continue to be dominated by the weight of tradition, even in the presence of abundant yield and excellent quality grapes. In those years, these three regions produced over 5.6 million hectolitres of wine, about 15% of the national production[2] (see Tables 1 and 2). However, these data are rather approximate since the estimates available for that time are not completely reliable. No doubt, there was an enormous gap between the exports of Italian wine, which amounted to just 300 thousand hectolitres, and the French exports which were ten times higher, around three million hectolitres (Anderson and Pinilla 2018).

The Birth of the Wine Industry

Although the general picture seems to be largely dominated by the weight of a far too traditional agriculture and the impact of a long series of factors that slowed any effort towards decisive change, it should be noted that over the remaining decades of the nineteenth century in the regions of the centre of Italy, a small oenological revolution was beginning to take place. Its most striking result was the creation of the myth of Tuscan wine, in particular of Chianti (Nesto and Di Savino 2016, pp. 21–35). A successful operation carried out by the Baron Bettino Ricasoli, a prominent figure of a new class of enterprising rural owners (Biagioli 2000), who were quite attentive to agricultural modernization also in view of the realization of products, such as wine that was suitable

[2] For the evolution of Italian wine exports, Anderson and Pinilla (2018).

for export. It should be pointed out, however, that the fortunate history of Chianti is inextricably linked to the political season in which Florence was the capital of the Kingdom of Italy from 1864 to 1871, and in which the noble Tuscan occupied the position of Prime Minister from 12 June 1861 to 3 March 1862 and then again from 20 August 1866 to 10 April 1867.

For Bettino Ricasoli, already fully engaged from of the middle of the century in the promotion of an agriculture capable of raising the economic destiny of the country, political experience represented an occasion to fully realize that Italy lacked quality bottled wines that could be sold abroad or usable at official receptions. Good Italian wine was generally exported abroad in bulk, and at court banquets the French and German bottles of whites and reds dominated.[3] Not only for commercial reasons, but also because of political pride, in the newly united Italy, the owners of large companies were spurred on to engage in the creation of a modern oenological culture. Following in the footsteps of the French, and learning from them, they pursued a land management policy that finally led to the creation of a prestigious Italian viticulture (Harvey et al. 2014). A prime example is that of the Marquis Vittorio degli Albizi, who, after careful studies and prolonged stays in Burgundy, undertook an energetic wine experimentation and propaganda in the Pomino and Nipozzano farms, which then passed on to the Frescobaldi.

Guided by his belief in the technical and scientific renewal of agriculture, Baron Bettino Ricasoli transformed his Tuscan "Castle of Brolio" into an oenological laboratory to create Chianti, which he presented as the true "perfect Italian wine" (Ciuffoletti 2009). Thanks to the results achieved by Bettino Ricasoli, who had also succeeded in convincing the farmers to modify obsolete cultivation criteria, the luck of "Tuscan wine" began. Though not all wines met the standards of the Brolio Chianti, there was an increased interest in accredited meal wines and thus the custom of selling off wines because of a lack of demand was finally abandoned (Kovatz 2013; Vannuccini 1884, pp. 70–73). Soon after, the first commercial enterprises aimed at selling wine abroad

[3]The profound differences between French and Italian wines, Loubére (1978).

began to flourish in Tuscany, in the wake of the successes of Vittorio degli Albizi, Bettino Ricasoli, but also of other noble families, such as the Antinori, who had begun to see quality winegrowing as a promising vector of economic growth. In 1870, in Rufina (Bandinelli et al. 2012), Cesare Caselli established a company for the sale of wine and oil and in 1872, two other companies, Luigi Laborel & Melini and Ilario & Leopoldo Ruffino, started similar businesses in Pontassieve.

At the same time, producers began to look for solutions that favoured the marketing of these new wines: from the unique and fortunate shape of the Chianti bottle to the creation of restaurants where it was common practice to combine wines to dishes, an advertising strategy of great effectiveness; from connecting to shipping companies, as in the case of the Pisan wine company Salvadori which, through the shipping company Florio, exported Tuscan wine to England, India, Egypt and North America (Pinilla and Ayuda 2007); finally, to the choice of betting on selling wine in thermal resorts, at the time the most popular tourist structures, as in the case of the Counts Spalletti company from Pistoia (Ciuffoletti 2007, p. 99). At the beginning of the twentieth century, thanks to these transformations, Tuscany had already become a well-established wine-producing region, confirmed by the rapid appearance of the first publications specifically dedicated to wine, such as the *Tuscan Wine Guide: Illustrated with Road Maps*, published in 1902 by Edoardo Ottavi (1902)—true precursors to the modern guides for the practice of enogastronomic tourism.

Another important sign of the ongoing changes is the success, especially since the late nineteenth century, of Chianti on the international market. This success is confirmed by the significant exports to the United States and the growing commercial consolidation in Argentina (Chiaromonte 1906; Trentin 1895), which required learning to adapt to the conditions of the markets of other countries (Federico 1992). In addition to the negative consequences of prohibition propaganda that in some states began to impose limits on the consumption of alcoholic beverages (Hames 2012), wine sent to the United States had to conform to the rules imposed by Pure Food and Drugs Act (1906) in matter of substances harmful to human health and the marketing of foodstuffs (Rumbarger 1989). For example, it was mandatory to indicate on the bottle label that the wine contained sulphur dioxide, albeit in a smaller quantity than the ones provided for by the legislation to allow for the sale of the beverage, a requirement aimed at guaranteeing the quality of the food but which did not encourage the purchase of the wine and in particular of Chianti.

Though Tuscan wine was quite successful among the American elite, it still had to meet the required parameters (Vaquero Piñeiro and Maffi 2018). It had to lower the alcoholic content to 12% and also try to adapt to the tastes of the US clients, who preferred soft wines, that were not austere but soft and delicate to the palate (Ottavi 1911, p. 313). If, on one hand, these regulations did not make it easy to export Italian wines to the United States, on the other, they helped the Italian wine producers, to comply with the laws of other countries with regards to food hygiene and health, to learn to produce lighter wines and to control the quality of bottled products. In this way they started to develop a wine sector attentive to the tastes and habits that, with the help of more innovative publicity (Vaquero Piñeiro 2016) techniques, was soon differentiated from the traditional exportation of bulk wine (Chiapparino 1998).

The important novelties from Tuscany quickly spread to other regions. First to the neighbouring Umbria, where even before the end of the nineteenth century innovative producers had already begun to use the "Tuscan method" (Passerini 1916) of producing wine. This created the conditions for the emergence of an initial nucleus of wine-growing entrepreneurs, though it was a phenomenon that involved the agricultural structure of the region in a limited way. When in 1886 the Ministry of Industry, Commerce and Agriculture organized a prize competition reserved for the best agricultural companies in the province of Umbria, in the numerous memoirs written for this occasion, it became apparent that Umbria intended to follow in the footsteps of Tuscany, a source of continuous knowledge and stimuli and a model to imitate, especially in the production of the red wines of noble presence.

At the head of the new generation of the modern Umbrian wine growers, were the Counts Zeffirino and Eugenio Faina, who conferred on their companies of Collelungo and San Venanzo a land restructuring similar to that of Baron Bettino Ricasoli's farms. They replaced the grapevine-bearing trees with low specialized vineyards for the cultivation of Sangiovese, Malvasia and Canaiolo, the three grape varieties used to make Chianti (Faina 1899; Monaldi 1881, 1882). Another important example for the renewal of Umbrian oenology was the Piedmontese engineer Michelangelo Bonelli, who in 1894 took over the direction of the San

Valentino winery, at the gates of the town of Marsciano where, in addition to the safe Sangiovese and Trebbiano varieties, he introduced northern vines such as Malbech and Dolcetto for black grapes and Sauvignon and Riesling for white grapes (Vaquero Piñeiro 2012, pp. 135–136).

The Roman Prince Ugo Boncompagni Ludovisi also deserves to be remembered among the names mentioned so far. In the 1880s he acquired the property of Scacciadiavoli, near the town of Montefalco, to plant a winegrowing company with a production capacity between 2000 and 3500 hectolitres. It was a highly innovative enterprise. He began with the cellar, which was essentially unlike the traditional cave excavations of the time or those found in the basements of monumental buildings. It was built along French construction models and was highly innovative compared to the standards in Umbria at that time. Its interior was greatly admired. It was divided into four levels. The basement was underground and supported the top floor by means of an effective system of columns and cast-iron beams. The grapes were transported by trolleys that ran on tracks up to the weighbridge. The grapes were then sent to the winepress, which was placed over the mouths of the vats. After fermenting in the vats, the must was brought to the third floor, and poured into the barrels. The plant was furnished with decanting pumps, Krauss filters, numerous presses, and a boiler that steam cleaned the containers.[4] In short, the company of Prince Boncompagni was "equipped with all the finest machines and containers" and produced excellent red wine for fine dining, which, in addition to deserving many awards, was the subject of "progressive and widespread export on a large scale to America, Africa and Asia".

On the eve of the outbreak of World War I, wine production in the three central Italian regions had reached the eight million hectolitres mark (Tables 1 and 2; Graph 1). This growth trend still continued up to the early 1920s, when the production of wine in Tuscany, Umbria and Marche accounted for 21% of the national production, the highest value ever achieved. However, the production of specialized cultivated grapes continued to be less common—in 1919, Tuscany's specialized winegrowing company occupied an area of 2500 hectares, and produced 80,000 quintals of grapes (ISTAT 1925, p. 219).

[4]On the important role played by technological renewal in the development of modern viticulture, Tattersall and Desalle (2015, pp. 196–214).

The 30s: Towards the Delimitation of the Production Areas

After the 1891 Madrid Convention on Trademarks, the debate on the protection of typical wines also began in Italy. Once again it was the Chianti area that led the change (Meloni and Swinnen 2018). In 1902 an Association was formed to promote the commercialization of Chianti, and in 1903 the cooperative wine union of Chianti (*Sindacato Enologico Cooperativo del Chianti*) (Ciuffoletti 2007, p. 103). came to light. However, not until the bill of law of March 7, 1924, later converted into law on 18 March 1926, was the significant stride forward made because, among controversy and conflict of opinions, the principle was finally established that the typicality of the wines was to be defended by means of the formation of consortia (Di Gerardo 1929, p. 74), and one of the first to be founded was that of Chianti.[5] But a consortia served little purpose in the absence of a precise delimitation of the areas of production, which was finally achieved in 1932 (Mocarelli 2013), when the ministerial commission, which had the precise intention of eradicating counterfeiting and commercial scams, clearly defined the confines of the Chianti area and other typical Tuscan wines (Montalbano, Colli fiorentini, Rufina, Colli senesi, Colli aretini, Colline pisane, Nobile di Montepulciano, Elba) (*Per la tutela del Chianti* 1932). At the same time, the commission sought to address other delicate issues such as the choice between creating a single consortium or the formation of separate consortia, or defining the rules to be adopted for the name and brand of the consortia.

These regulations did not apply only to Tuscany but also to Umbria, in the case of Orvieto wine. And though the request made by six Orvieto producers to join a consortium for the protection of the original wine of that territory was not accepted, in 1931, the government stepped in to geographically delimit the territory of origin of the typical "Orvieto" (Vaquero Piñeiro 2012, pp. 186–187) wine. However, it must be acknowledged that, despite the experience of Chianti being a

[5]In France in 1935 he was born the "Comité National des Appellations d'Origine", Humbert (2011). For the previous law of 1919, see Trimaille (2011).

model to be applied to other geographic realities, the thorny issue of wine denominations has remained for a long time without a precise solution, not only because of the strong opposition from the producers of blended wine, but also because the regulatory framework has remained ambiguous and confusing due to the different, and often contradictory measures concerning typical wines.

Moreover, we can not ignore the fact that this first season of legislative measures went hand in hand with a substantial stagnation of the sector in central Italy, attested by the fact that between the crises of 1929 and the end of the 1930s, the hectares of vineyards specialized in Tuscany were between 25,000 and 26,000, in Marche between 8000 and 11,000, while in Umbria less than 3000 (ISTAT 1940, p. 274). Furthermore, the Fascist regime in Italy certainly did not favour the development of specialized viticulture, mainly because the pounding pressure of the regime to allocate efforts and resources to increase cereal production as a result of the "wheat battle" inevitably reduced the cultivation of vines, which were then further penalized by the fall in exports and prices (Fabiani 2015, pp. 139–140). In addition, such an autarchic policy led to a radical contraction in the access to chemicals needed to combat the phylloxera and other plant diseases. All these factors together finally resulted in a depletion of the winegrowing heritage that had made so many strides forward in the previous decades. This negative spiral was further compounded in Central Italy by the stiffening of the contractual terms of the *mezzadria* pacts that led farmers to abandon the good practices previously acquired. This profound change in the countryside and socio-political conditions was accompanied by a 40% collapse in production at the beginning of the 1930s, which was only partially recovered in the following years.

1945–2000: From Tradition to Typicality

In the aftermath of World War II, Italian viticulture, as well as that of the three central regions, appeared to be on its knees and yet within a few years, the production returned to very high levels, to the extent of producing a strong over-supply imbalance compared to consumption (Table 1;

Graph 1). As a result wines were sold without proper ageing and care, and prices dropped. The only product that continued to enjoy a good reputation was Chianti. In the absence of precise rules on production areas, Chianti, for it to continue to deserve this denomination, was simply sold in its typical straw-wrapped bottle or "fiasco". This was the result of the persistent absence, due to the continuous cross-fire presentations, of precise legislative directives and this certainly did not favour the emergence of modern business ventures. Producers continued to be too small and poorly equipped for trade and exports remained low, barely reaching a million hectolitres in 1951. Moreover, there was another peculiar factor in the central regions of Italy that threatened the winemaking sector—the farmers were abandoning their farms, attracted by the higher incomes and improved living conditions of the cities of the plains (Tappi 2013).

The phenomenon particularly affected the most important wine region, the Chianti, and as a consequence, the protection of hillside vineyards became increasingly necessary through measures aimed at the valorization of typical fine wines. However, the legislative efforts made in the 1950s to regulate the denomination and origin of wine on a national scale did not encounter a suitable political climate capable of transforming such regulations into law. So that by the end of the 1950s, the sector fluctuated annually, depending on the more or less favourable conditions of the climate and yield. Furthermore, precise rules and regulations with regards to the production levels of fine wines were still lacking. The only positive note in this "depressive qualitative picture" was the high growth of social wineries.

Despite this limited picture, the first general census on agriculture (1961) (ISTAT 1966, pp. 230–239) underscores the first signs of a consolidation of the specialized vineyard, particularly in Tuscany where there were 63,464 farms totalling 32,452 hectares. To a lesser extent, this also occurred in Marche, with 39,682 farms on 8953 hectares and in Umbria, with 7123 farms on 3711 hectares. It is important to note that these were generally small or very small farms. The average size was just over half a hectare in the case of Tuscany and Umbria, and as small as 0.2 hectares in Marche. Predictably, this transformation was reinforced by the promulgation of the law of 2 June 1961 concerning the five-year plan for the development of agriculture, which among other things was intended to promote the transition of the promiscuous or scattered cultivations to specialized ones (Desplanques 2006, p. 744).

These stimuli in the direction of renewal were then strengthened by Law No. 930 of 12 July 1963, which finally established and regulated in Italy the DOC—Denominazione di Origine Controllata (controlled designation of origin) label (Pazzagli 1998, p. 189). The confirmation of how the timing for such a measure was at that point abundantly mature is the DOC recognition in 1966 for the Vernaccia of San Gimignano, Brunello of Montalcino, the Nobile of Montepulciano and the white of Pitigliano, and in the following year for Chianti (Barzagli 2007). But the effects of the law on DOC wine can also be referred to Umbria, with the recognition of the Torgiano wine in 1968, the Orvieto wine in 1971 and Trasimeno wine in 1972; and to the Marche region, where in a few years, between 1967 and 1975, there was a marked multiplication of DOC wines (Verdicchio of Matelica, Rosso Piceno, Colli Maceratesi, Verdicchio of Colli di Jesi, Bianco of Metauro, Colli Pesaresi). These results were impossible just a few years earlier and they had quite a significant impact on the territorial development of those regions. Concurrently, this impact was also aided by a European Community agricultural policy conceived in terms of modernization shielded by strong protectionist policies (Marinelli 2002).

Of particular significance is what happened in Umbria and in Marche where there was a loss of lands of the purists of traditional wine making. Their production was traditionally made for relatives and friends and for personal consumption. They vigorously opposed the ongoing transformation and considered it a mere commodification. It was clear, however, that in contrast with the traditionalists, the modern winegrowers had gained certain technical skills and commercial and distributive capacities, essential in overcoming the local distrust and above all the fierce competition of other regions with consolidated traditions. Being the last to join the bandwagon could also have its advantages, provided that one was quick to learn, especially in gaining good communication strategies. Only in this way could the producers of Umbrian and Marche wines hope to gain in competitive capacity over the more renown Tuscan, Piedmontese or French products.

The consolidation of "fine-wine" viticulture produced a rapid disappearance of the typical *mezzadria* landscape (Bartolotti 1986, p. 806), but also a sharp contraction in the production levels that marked a 42% decrease between 1979 and 1994, with a downward trend that continued throughout the first two decades of the twenty-first century (see Table 1). Practically, within a few decades, even through numerous works of replanting of the vineyards, there was a shift from an extensive and family-grown viticulture to a new highly mechanized and income-based viticulture, organized according to market demand. The most obvious indicator in this regard is the increasing growth of the specialized vineyard. This growth took place with particular significance in Umbria, a region at the lowest level, where from 1970 to 1990 the viticulture hectares cultivated became 23,238 (an increase of 494%). But this growth is also evident in Tuscany, where over the course of the last 20 years, the hectares of specialized vineyards totalled 125,006 (an increase of 272%); and to a lesser extent, in Marche, with 28,557 hectares (an increase of 142%) (ISTAT 1981, p. 185). The figures clearly demonstrate that in the late twentieth century, in the context of a general socio-economic repositioning of agriculture and a gradual decline of the "agricultural question", the development of a quality viticulture in the Italian regions of the *mezzadria* tradition was a decisive factor of economic revival, even in terms of image and tourism (Harvey et al. 2014).

For these reasons, the multiplication of wines with a controlled and guaranteed denomination of origin continued into the new millennium (Planas 2016); especially in Tuscany where wine production accounted for 18% of all agricultural production, and quality DOC and DOCG wines amounted to 13% of those present in Italy (ISMEA 2007, p. 63). Marche and Umbria have a somewhat different situation, primarily because they contain less agricultural land. In both regions, the volumes of wine are in fact much smaller (from 3.5 to 2%, respectively, of the national wine production). Indeed, these small wine productions, have created important opportunities for the niche market—in some areas such as in Bevagna-Montefalco (Melelli and Fatichenti 2011) or on the hills of Jesino (ISMEA 2007, pp. 67, 70–71), these are particularly appealing from the point of view of tourism.

Today, thanks to these advances, in the three regions of Central Italy there are 87 of the 405 DOC and DOCG wines in Italy: 52 in Tuscany, 20 in Marche and 15 in Umbria. These last two regions have quite a number of "high-quality wine" labels when compared to their production. To the DOC and DOCG wines, 13 Typical Geographical Indication (*Indicazione geografica Tipica*—IGT) wines should also be added, out of a national total of 118. The IGT wines allow the producer greater flexibility in terms of production, since they are not subject to the same disciplinary framework, and thus they become a major player in winning the highly profitable international markets. This is clearly demonstrated by the "Super Tuscans", which have attracted fierce criticism by the cultists of Chianti wine, produced according to the directions of Bettino Ricasoli (Mocarelli 2013, pp. 337–340). The proliferation of "high quality wines, that are not subject to a specific disciplinary framework" (Barzagli 2007, p. 597) does not only regard Tuscany, but also the other important Italian wine areas, such as the Langhe, because it allows a freer hand in intercepting new customers in a market where the name of the producer is becoming much more important than the name of the winegrowing area.

Conclusions

At the time of political unification, the wine produced nationally did not have much of a reputation. It was hardly sold abroad, and essentially served the local market based on poor quality products (Kovatz 2002). After a century and a half, the situation has radically changed and today wine is the key to the success of some of the most dynamic territories of the country. A prime example are the hills of the Florentine-Sienese region (Intesa San Paolo 2016), where Chianti, as well as Brunello of Montalcino or Nobile of Montepulciano, have become the strong points of a reality that in the course of the twentieth century has gained great advantages from the fortuitous intuitions of the Marquis Bettino Ricasoli (Higgins 2018).

However, the enormous progress of Umbrian and Marche wine production also confirms that the sector has been enriched with significance and value that go far beyond the simple production of wine. Nowadays the production companies, in addition to having to adapt to the changes imposed by an ever-increasing demand for quality, are at the centre of a fruitful interplay between agriculture, the environment and tourism.[6] The proof of this is the construction of the contemporary image of the regions of central Italy, where rows of vineyards have become perfect icons of a harmonious rural landscape. The vineyards, arranged in terraces or following the contours of the hills, seem to be entrusted with the task of serving as symbols of the overall landscape, like set pieces of furniture. Thus they become a visual strong point for an emotional charged quality tourism which is the basis of a ramified economic input (Boatto and Gennari 2011).

The traditional image of the farmer who produced a very "genuine" wine that was hardly "drinkable" is now just a distant memory and, in the three regions of the sharecropping tradition, the wine sector is increasingly committed to offer a wide range of goods and services—such as the direct sale of products, the provision for accommodation, the organization of cultural events, the creation of precise business packages. In this regard, it is sufficient to mention the transformation of the cellar, that for centuries was only used for storing wine, and that has now taken on a new role. The new "cathedrals of wine", carefully designed to attract the tourist-customer, in fact, solicit admiration since they are real works of art, as demonstrated by the Antinori cellars or the "Carapace" set in the Bevagna hills, designed by the sculptor Arnaldo Pomodoro for the Lunelli Group (Colonetti 2012). Today, it is mainly the enchanting architectural design of the building, which elicits the tourist's interest and creates expectations, making the wine cellar the centre-point of the vineyard landscape.

When the wine sector became a cultural and social phenomenon as well, the three regions of the centre of Italy found themselves with an extraordinary asset. Indeed, the landscape built by the almost millenary presence of sharecropping contributed to the creation of a particularly suitable rural context for interpreting these epochal changes (Anselmi 1978). After the mid-twentieth century, when the *mezzadria* was considered an element of backwardness and a brake to agrarian economic

[6]A large bibliography is available on this topic. We limit ourselves to recalling, see Antonioli Corigliano (1999), Costantino and Artista (2003), and Hausmann (2005).

development, the rural areas in Central Italy have been able to create their own specificity by means of a balanced and harmonious dialogue with the past. If the grape vines no longer climb on trees, neither have they radically changed the landscape by creating extensive specialized vineyards. And so the plains and hills of Tuscany, Umbria and Marche continue to present a structure of small plots placed in an environment that still preserves the rural areas that originated through a *mezzadria* polyculture farming (Bellicini 1989).

If the traditional promiscuous agriculture has finally disappeared, the fields, where a little bit of everything was once cultivated, have been used for non-invasive specialized cultivations, that to some extent are respectful of the past. Thus, it is not uncommon to see rather small compact vineyards placed along side olive trees, fields of grain and small forests. The result is a colourful and varied landscape, the expression of the continuous play of the maturation and ripening of the fruits of nature, enriched further by the capillary presence of small villages, isolated houses, towers, and rows of cypresses. This is, as evidenced by the growing influx of domestic and foreign tourists, a unique territory, and a clear example of the economy of beauty built around a landscape where wine is an essential component. So, in the lands where during the Renaissance there were country villas as wonderful examples of human ability to harness and bring order to the surrounding wilderness, today's wineries take up that legacy and represent the best *testimonial* of the uniqueness of the territory that has been shaped by the *mezzadria*.

Appendix

See Tables 1 and 2 and Graph 1.

Table 1 Wine production in Tuscany, Umbria and Marche (1881–2015). Hectolitres

Years	Tuscany	Umbria	Marche	Total
1879–1883 (average)	3,068,426	2,490,934		5,559,360
1909–1913 (average)	4,136,000	1,269,000	2,383,000	7,788,000
1917–1921 (average)	4,990,000	1,192,000	1,866,000	8,048,000
1933	2,880,000	621,000	1,310,000	4,811,000
1936–1939 (average)	4,277,000	1,261,000	2,149,000	7,687,000
1947	3,232,930	732,730	1,694,760	5,660,420
1948	3,787,850	717,750	1,914,410	6,420,010
1952	4,196,300	898,400	2,068,500	7,163,200
1953	4,818,400	988,100	1,588,300	7,394,800
1964	4,584,000	761,000	2,474,000	7,819,000
1969	3,862,000	644,000	2,308,000	6,814,000
1974	4,840,000	854,000	2,562,000	8,256,000
1979	5,803,000	1,082,000	2,834,000	9,719,000
1984	3,527,000	1,089,000	3,202,000	7,818,000
1989	3,166,000	1,326,000	1,917,000	6,409,000
1994	2,681,000	1,003,000	1,980,000	5,664,000
2010	2,854,000	875,000	927,000	4,656,000
2015	3,282,000	754,000	1,042,000	5,078,000
Total	76,656,052	16,906,080	36,235,070	134,205,482

Source ISTAT (*Annuario statistico italiano*)

Table 2 Wine production in Tuscany, Umbria and Marche than Italy (1881–2015). Hectolitres

Years	Italy (hectolitres)	Centre of Italy (hectolitres)	%
1879–1883 (average)	36,760,035	5,559,360	15
1909–1913 (average)	46,017,000	7,788,000	17
1917–1921 (average)	38,865,000	8,048,000	21
1933	32,900,000	4,811,000	15
1936–1939 (average)	38,246,630	7,687,000	20
1947	31,881,460	5,660,420	18
1948	35,583,720	6,420,010	18
1952	44,853,700	7,163,200	16
1953	52,541,600	7,394,800	14
1964	66,124,000	7,819,000	12
1974	66,867,000	8,256,000	12
1979	84,337,000	9,719,000	11
1984	70,250,000	7,818,000	11
1989	60,327,000	6,409,000	11
1994	59,277,000	5,664,000	10
2010	46,745,000	4,656,000	10
2015	48,237,000	5,078,000	10

Source ISTAT (*Annuario statistico italiano*)

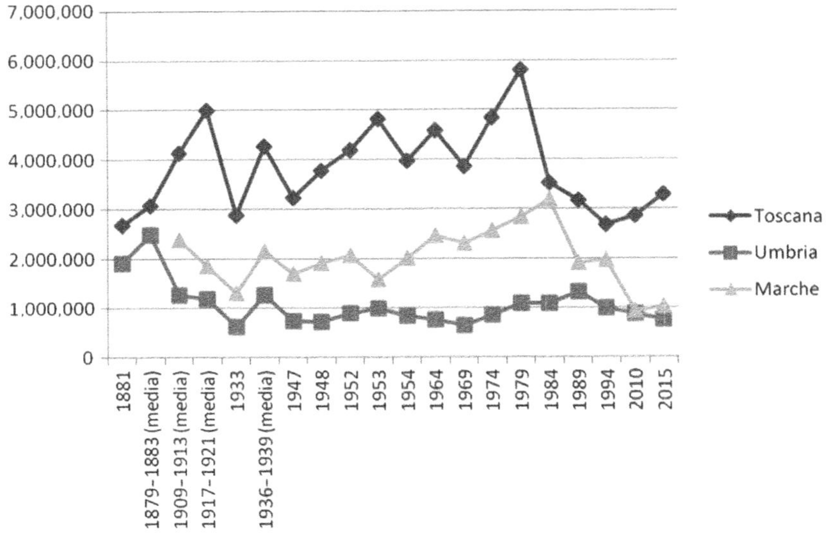

Graph 1 Wine production in Tuscany, Umbria and Marche (1879–2015). Hectolitres (Source *Annuario statistico italiano*)

References

Books

Anderson, K., & Pinilla, V. (Eds.). (2018). *Wine Globalization: A New Comparative History*. Cambridge: Cambridge University Press.

Anderson, K., Nelgen, S., & Pinilla, V. (Eds.). (2017). *Global Wine Markets, 1860 to 2016: A Statistical Compendium*. Adelaide: University Adelaide Press.

Anselmi, S. (1978). *Mezzadri e terre nelle Marche. Studi e ricerche di storia dell'agricoltura fra Quattrocento e Novecento*. Bologna: Il Mulino.

Antonioli Corigliano, M. (1999). *Strade del vino ed enoturismo. Distretti turistici e vie di comunicazione*. Milano: Franco Angeli.

Bandinelli, R., Ceseri, L., Pieragnoli, L., & Grati, G. (2012). *Storia e ampelografia del territorio del Chianti Rufina*. Firenze: All'Insegna del Giglio.

Berrino, A., & Buccaro, A. (Eds.). (2016). *Delli aspetti de paesi. Vecchi e nuovi media per l'immagine del paesaggio*. Parte II. *Descrivere, narrare e comunicare il paesaggio. L'età contemporanea*. Napoli: Cirice.

Bevilacqua, P. (Ed.). (1989). *Storia dell'agricoltura italiana in età contemporanea*, vol. I, *Spazi e paesaggi*. Venezia: Marsilio.

Bevilacqua, P. (Ed.). (1992). *Storia dell'agricoltura italiana in età contemporanea*, vol. III, *Mercati e istituzioni*. Venezia: Marsilio.

Biagioli, G. (2000). *Il modello del proprietario imprenditore nella Toscana dell'Ottocento: Bettino Ricasoli. Il patrimonio, le fattorie*. Firenze: Leo S. Olschki.

Boatto, V., & Gennari, A. J. (Eds.). (2011). *La roadmap del turismo enologico*. Milano: Franco Angeli.

Campbell, G., & Guibert, N. (2007). *Wine Society and Globalization: Multidisciplinary Perspectives on the Wine Industry*. New York: Palgrave Macmillan.

Ceccarelli, G., Grandi, A., & Magagnoli, S. (Eds.). (2013). *Typicality in History: Tradition, Innovation and Terroir*. Brussels: Peter Lang.

Chiaromonte, T. (1906). *Il commercio dei vini nella Repubblica Argentina nel decennio 1895–1904. Istruzioni e consigli agli esportatori italiani*. Roma: Tipografia Nazionale G. Bertero e C.

Ciuffoletti, Z. (2000). *Storia del vino in Toscana. Dagli Etruschi ai nostri giorni*. Firenze: Edizioni Polistampa.

Ciuffoletti, Z. (2009). *Alla ricerca del«vino perfetto». Il Chianti del barone di Brolio. Ricasoli e il Risorgimento vitivinicolo italiano*. Firenze: Leo S. Olschki.

Colonetti, A. (Ed.). (2012). *Arnaldo Pomodoro. La cantina della tenuta di Castelbuono*. Bologna: Compositori.

Costantino, S., & Artista, A. (Eds.). (2003). *Le strade del vino e le vie dello sviluppo*. Milano: Franco Angeli;

De Bernardi, A., & Varni, A. (Eds.). (1998). *Annali della Storia d'Italia. Storia dell'alimentazione*. Torino: Einaudi.

Desplanques, H. (2006). *Campagne umbre. Contributo allo studio di paesaggi rurali dell'Italia centrale*. Perugia: Quatroemme.

Di Gerardo, A. (1929). *I vini tipici d'Italia*. Catania: Francesco Battiato editore.

Fabiani, G. (2015). *Agricoltura-mondo. La storia contemporanea e gli scenari futuri*. Roma: Donzelli.

Faina, E. (1899). *La tenuta di S. Venanzio nell'Umbria. Venticinque anni di lavoro in un vasto possesso di montagna*. Roma: Tip. Camera dei Deputati.

Firpo, M., Tranfaglia, N., & Zunino, P. G. (Eds.). (1998). *Guida all'Italia contemporanea 1861–1997*, vol. I, *Risorse e strutture economiche*. Milano: Garzanti.

Giorgetti, G. (1974). *Contadini e proprietari nell'Italia moderna*. Torino: Einaudi.

Hames, G. (2012). *Alcohol in World: History*. London and New York: Routledge.

Harvey, M., Frost, W., & White, L. (Eds.). (2014). *Wine and Identity. Branding, Heritage, Terroir*. New York and London: Routledge.

Hausmann, C. (Ed.). (2005). *Marketing e strade del vino. In viaggio tra saperi e sapori*. Roma: A.G.R.A.

Higgins, D. M. (2018). *Brands, Geographical Origin, and the Global Economy: A History from the Nineteenth Century to the Present*. Cambridge: Cambridge University Press.

Lomeni, I. (1834). *Del vino, sua fabbricazione, conservazione, sue degenerazioni, ecc*. Milano: presso Antonio Fortunato Stella e figli.

Intesa San Paolo. (2016). *Economia e finanza dei distretti industriali*. Rapporto annuale, n°9, Intesa San Paolo-Direzione studi e ricerche, dicembre.

ISMEA (Istituto di Servizi per il Mercato Agricolo Alimentare). (2007). *I vini D.o.c. e D.o.c.g. Una mappatura della vitivinicoltura regionale a denominazione di origine*. Roma: Ismea.

ISTAT (Istituto Nazionale di Statistica). (1925). *Annuario statistico italiano. Anni 1919–1921*. Roma: Ministero dell'Economia Nazionale.

ISTAT (Istituto Nazionale di Statistica). (1940). *Annuario statistico dell'agricoltura italiana, 1936–1938*. Roma: ISTAT.

ISTAT (Istituto Nazionale di Statistica). (1966). *1° censimento generale dell'agricoltura. 15 aprile 1961*, vol. III, *Coltivazioni*. Roma: ISTAT.

ISTAT (Istituto Nazionale di Statistica). (1981). *Annuario di statistica agraria*, vol. XXVII. Roma: ISTAT.

Kolleen, M. G. (2003). *When Champagne Became French: Wine and the Making of National Identity*. Baltimore: Johns Hopkins University Press.

Loubére, L. A. (1978). *The Red and the White: The History of Wine in France and Italy in the Nineteenth Century*. Albany: State University of New York.

Mainardi, G., & Berta, P. (Eds.). (2013). *Ampelografia italiana del 1800*. Canelli: Edizioni OICCE.

Mainardi, G., & Berta, P. (Eds.). (2016). *Enologia italiana del 1800*. Canelli: Edizioni OICCE.

Maldonado Roso, J. (Ed.). (2002). *Actas del I simposio de la asociación internacional de historia y civilización de la vid y el vino*, vol. II. El Puerto de Santa María: Asociación internacional de historia y civilización de la vid y el vino.

Monaldi, L. (1881). *Il vino di Collelungo ossia il presente e l'avvenire dell'industria enologica dell'Umbria*. Forlì: Tipografia fratelli Cherardi.

Monaldi, L. (1882). *Le vigne ed i vini della fattoria di Collelungo (Perugia) del conte Zeffirino Faina al concorso agrario regionale di Arezzo nel settembre 1882*. Padova: Tip. Bartelli.

Mori, G. (Ed.). (1986). *Storia d'Italia. Le regioni dall'Unità a oggi. La Toscana.* Torino: Einaudi.

Nanni, P. (Ed.). (2007). *Storia regionale della vite e del vino in Italia. Toscana.* Firenze: Edizioni Polistampa.

Nesto, B., & Di Savino, F. (2016). *Chianti Classico: The Search for Tuscany's Noblest Wine.* Oakland: University of California Press.

Ottavi, E. (1902). *Guida vinicola della Toscana: illustrata con carte stradali.* Casale: C. Cassone.

Ottavi, E. (1911). *Vademecum del commerciante di uve e di vini italiani.* Casale: C. Cassone.

Passerini, N. (1916). *Il governo del vino: come si pratica in Toscana.* Casale: C. Cassone.

Per la tutela del Chianti. (1932). *Per la tutela del Chianti e degli altri vini tipici Toscani. Relazione della commissione interministeriale per la delimitazione del territorio del vino Chianti.* Roma: Tipografia Antonio Brunelli.

Rumbarger, J. J. (1989). *Profits, Power, and Prohibition: American Alcohol Reform and the Industrializing of America 1800–1930.* Albany: State University of New York Press.

Scaramuzzi, F., & Nanni, P. (Eds.). (2002). *Storia dell'agricoltura italiana*, vol. III, *L'età contemporanea*, t. II, *Sviluppo recente e prospettive.* Firenze: Edizioni Polistampa.

Simpson, J. (2011). *Creating Wine: The Emergence of a World Industry 1840–1914.* Princeton: Princeton University Press.

Tattersall, I., & Desalle, R. (2015). *A Natural History of Wine.* New Haven and London: Yale University Press.

Teughels, N., & Peter, S. (Eds.). (2015). *A Taste of Progress: Food at International and World Exhibitions in the Nineteenth and Twentieth Centuries.* London: Ashgate.

Trentin, P. (1895). *Manuale del negoziante di vini italiani nell'Argentina: esportare dall'Italia, importatore nell'Argentina, rivenditore all'ingrosso e al minuto.* Buenos Aires: Tipografia Elzeviriana di P. Tonini.

Vannuccini, E. (1884). *L'avvenire del vino italiano e del vino toscano. Metodo più atto e più pronto a creare il vino tipo uniforme e costante e mezzo di ridurre molti vini italiani a tipo di vino toscano.* Firenze: G. Pellas.

Vaquero Piñeiro, M. (2012). *Storia regionale della vite e del vino in Italia, Umbria.* Perugia: Volumnia.

Wolikow, S., & Jacquet, O. (2011). *Territoires et terroirs du vin du XVIIIe au XXIe siècles. Approche internazionale d'une construction historique.* Dijon: Editions Universitaires de Dijon.

Paper in Journals

Biagioli, G. (2013). Mezzadria, métayace, masoveria. Un contratto di colonia parziaria e le sue interpretazioni tra Italia, Francia e Catalogna. *Proposte e ricerche*, XXXVI, *71*, 5–30.

Fumian, C. (2016). L'Italia e la mondializzazione degli scambi di tardo Ottocento. *Storia contemporanea*, *282*, 18–44.

Meloni, G., & Swinnen, J. (2018). Trade and Terroir: The Political Economy of the World's First Geographical Indications. *Food Policy*, *81*, 1–20.

Planas, J. (2016). State Intervention in Wine Markets in the Early 20th Century: Why Was It So Different in France and Spain? *Revista de Historia Económica. Journal of Iberian and Latin American Economic History*, *35*(2), 175–206.

Tappi, A. (2013). La terra è troppo bassa. La fine della mezzadria nella provincia di Perugia. *Proposte e ricerche*, XXXVI, *71*, 104–121.

Vaquero Piñeiro, M., & Maffi, L. (2018). The Diffusion of Italian Wine in the United States (1861–1914). *Rivar. Revista Iberoamericana de viticulture, agroindustria y ruralidad*, *15*, 176–196.

Vernelli, C. (2003). Vite e vino nella provincia di Ancona fra tradizione e la DOC del Lacrima di Morro d'Alba. *Proposte e ricerche*, XXVI, *51*, 110–133.

Papers in Books

Bartolotti, L. (1986). *L'evoluzione del territorio* (Mori, Ed., pp. 773–820).

Barzagli, S. (2007). *La situazione produttiva* (Nanni, Ed., pp. 589–607).

Bellicini, L. (1989). *La campagna urbanizzata. Fattorie e case coloniche nell'Italia centrale e nordorientale* (Bevilacqua, Ed., pp. 77–130).

Berta, P. (2016). *La chimica e l'enologia all'inizio dell'Ottocento: il conte Dandolo, illustre Veneziano* (Mainardi & Berta, Eds., pp. 97–110).

Chiapparino, F. (1998). *Tra polverizzazione e concentrazione. L'industria alimentare tra l'Unità al periodo tra le due guerre* (De Bernardi & Varni, Eds., pp. 205–268).

Ciuffoletti, Z. (2007). *Dall'Unità d'Italia alla metà del Novecento* (Nanni, Ed., pp. 89–110).

Federico, G. (1992). *Oltre frontiera: l'agricoltura italiana e il mercato internazionale fra Otto e Novecento* (Bevilacqua, Ed., pp. 189–222).

Federico, G., & Martinelli, P. (2018). *Italy to 1938* (Anderson & Pinilla, Eds., pp. 130–153).

Harvey, M., Frost, W., & White, L. (2014). *Exploring Wine and Identity* (Harvey, Frost, & White, Eds.).

Humbert, M. F. (2011). *La naissance du système des AOC: étude sur la mise en place du Comité National des Appellations d'Origine (1935–1938)* (Wolikow & Jacquet, Eds., pp. 315–335).

Kovatz, S. (2002). *La ricerca di un vino di qualità in Italia nel secolo XIX: fonti e problemi storici e storiografici* (Maldonado Roso, Ed., pp. 1001–1011).

Kovatz, S. (2013). *The Geography of Quality Wine in United Italy Areas and Producers* (Ceccarelli, Grandi, & Magagnoli, Eds., pp. 305–321).

Marinelli, A. (2002). *Politica agricola nazionale, comunitaria e globale* (Scaramuzzi & Nanni, Eds., pp. 197–223).

Melelli, A., & Fatichenti, F. (2011). *Les constructions des territoires du vin dans l'Italie du Centre pendant ces cinquante dernières années avec une attention particulière pour l'Ombrie* (Wolikow & Jacquet, Eds., pp. 277–296).

Mocarelli, L. (2013). *The Long Struggle for the Chianti Denomination: Quality Versus Quantity* (Ceccarelli, Grandi, & Magagnoli, Eds., pp. 323–340).

Pazzagli, R. (1998). *Agricoltura* (Firpo, Tranfaglia, & Zunino, Eds., pp. 165–237).

Pinilla, V., & Ayuda, M. I. (2007). *The International Wine Market, 1850–1938: An Opportunity for Export Growth in Southern Europe* (Campbell & Guibert, Eds., pp. 179–200).

Pisani, P. L. (2007). *Scienza e tecnica nella storia della vitivinicoltura toscana. Il contributo dei Georgofili* (Nanni, Ed., pp. 111–146).

Silvestroni, O. (2013). *Ampelografia, vitigni e vigneti nella Marche del 1800* (Mainardi & Berta, Eds., pp. 129–146).

Storchi, P. (2016). *Progressi ed innovazioni nell'enologia toscana del XIX secolo* (Mainardi & Berta, Eds., pp. 111–121).

Trimaille, G. (2011). *La loi du 6 mai 1919 relative à la protection des appellations d'origine et la difficile définition des «usages locaux, loyaux et constants»* (Wolikow & Jacquet, Eds., pp. 135–144).

Vaquero Piñeiro, M. (2016). *La réclame enologica e l'immagine del paesaggio italiano tra XIX e XX secolo* [The Wine Réclame and the Image of the Italian Landscape Between the Nineteenth and Twentieth Century] (Berrino & Buccaro, Eds., pp. 1231–1241).

Viticulture and Winemaking in Abruzzo from the Unification of Italy to the Development of the Cooperation System

Dario Dell'Osa

Introduction

Nowadays, viticulture and winemaking are two of the most promising aspects of agriculture in Abruzzo, and three out of the eight most famous DOC labels of the region—Montepulciano, Trebbiano and Cerasuolo d'Abruzzo—are known and appreciated both in Italy and abroad. The history of local wine production, though, hasn't been always characterized by business and market success. Although wine history in Abruzzo may be traced as far back as the classical age, it is only in the mid-nineteenth century that a turning point started the modernization of the sector.[1] It was at that time that farmers first became

[1]For more on the history and the characteristics of wine growing in the South of Italy see De Rosa (1971). On the history of wine in Abruzzo until the eighteenth century see Giuliani (1975), Cercone (2000), and Cercone (2008).

D. Dell'Osa (✉)
University of Bari Aldo Moro, Bari, Italy
e-mail: dario.dellosa@uniba.it

S. A. Conca Messina et al. (eds.), *A History of Wine in Europe, 19th to 20th Centuries, Volume I*, Palgrave Studies in Economic History,
https://doi.org/10.1007/978-3-030-27772-7_10

aware of the problems related to the various phases of the wine production cycle and started a real process of production improvement.[2] Between the nineteenth and the twentieth century, viticulture moved from the hinterland—which presented a more difficult climate and soil conditions—to the more adequate areas of coastal hills.[3] Mixed crops gradually made room for special crops, which were characterized by a higher yield per hectare and by more rational cultivations (De Rosa 1971). At the same time, wine producers understood their territory's potential and, through local ampelographic committees, started a profitable selection of local vines for the production of wines able to meet market needs.[4] That's how the growth process of viticulture and winemaking in Abruzzo started which, after a phase of ups and downs, led to a more intensive development after the Second World War.

The aim of this essay is to trace the economic history of viticulture and winemaking in Abruzzo, from the Unification of Italy to the 1960s, with a focus on the events that affected production, on the description of the areas most widely involved in grapes and wine exports, and on the contribution of the wine sector cooperation for development.

The Viticulture and Winemaking in Abruzzo After the Unification of Italy

Studies on viticulture and winemaking in the South of Italy before the Unification pinpointed the many limits of wine production in Abruzzo which, although excellent in some areas, was in a state of absolute

[2]On the dynamics of wine production in Italy see, among others, Dalmasso (1961) and Cova (1988). On the role of viticulture in the agrarian crisis of the late nineteenth century see d'Angiolini (1969); about Italian viticulture in the first decades after the unification, see Dandolo (2010).

[3]On the characteristics of the Abruzzo economy see Bettoni and Grohmann (1989, p. 610); about the dynamics that have affected the Apennine agriculture in the nineteenth century see Cormio (1981).

[4]For the pre-unification period a similar work had been carried out by the "Società Economiche", provincial public institutions aimed at improving agriculture, but their contribution to the southern agricultural progress had translated into a modest expansion of knowledge and a set of indicative experiments (De Rosa 1971, p. 1462).

disrepair elsewhere (Del Re 1835; Durini 1836). After the Unification, though, many scholars had actively contributed to revive the fortunes of local wines, finding in the geomorphology of the territory those characteristics that would guarantee those wines' success many decades later. One of the leading contributors to the renovation of the national wine sector, with particular reference to Abruzzo, was Francesco De Blasiis (1807–1873), born in Città Sant'Angelo.[5] He was the Minister for Agriculture in 1867, and president of the Royal Ampelographic Committee in Rome in the following years, as well as author of many essays aimed at the improvement of viticulture and winemaking techniques (De Blasiis 1857, 1869, 1870).

Starting in 1869, De Blasiis promoted a series of conferences on wine all over Italy and in 1872, together with the president of the Ancona Ampelographic Committee, he organized the *Esposizione ampelografica marchigiana-abruzzese* (Vine exhibition of Marche and Abruzzo), which took place in Ancona in September 1872, exhibiting grapes and vines from the whole territory of Marche and Abruzzo (De Bosiis 1873). In the speech given on the occasion of the exhibition, De Blasiis stated that the main fault of wines from Marche and Abruzzo was their poor adaptability to storage and consequent inadequacy to transportation. According to the scholar, this problem had not been caused by the soil unsuitability to growing grapes, or by the poor organoleptic quality of grapes, but by a faulty, incomplete fermentation process which was easily renewed and thus triggered the oxidation of sugars still contained in the wine and its consequent acescence. It was therefore necessary to pay the greatest attention to the must fermentation phase, favouring it and making sure it was complete, in order to obtain a dry wine, free of sugar components. According to the scholar, the must obtained from grapes from Abruzzo had very different organoleptic characteristics than musts from other areas of Southern or Northern Italy. In particular, the vineyards from Apulia or Campania produced musts with high level of sugars, lower percentage of water and low acidity; all these elements, combined together in the fermentation process, generated a wine with

[5]Città Sant'Angelo was then in the province of Teramo, from 1927 is in the province of Pescara.

high alcohol contents, which was fit for storage and transportation. Vineyards from Northern Italy generated low-sugar musts with high water and acid components, which favoured the production of light and dry wines, in which the fermentation process—with the consequent oxidation of wine—could hardly be triggered again during transportation (Orsi 1873).

De Blasiis's conclusions contained ideas of extraordinary relevance, as he thought it necessary to favour the process of formation of local wines—either pure or blended—which were the expression of a precise territorial context. Actually, it was desirable that the wines produced kept their own qualities and distinctive features throughout successive vintages, to be easily identifiable by consumers, as that was the only way to build a market in Italy and abroad. Moreover, the most important constraint to the development of Abruzzo's wine production was shown to be related to prevailingly local consumption of products, and to the difficulties encountered in wine exportation.

The process that would lead to the growth of Abruzzo's viticulture and winemaking had to go through the selection and implantation of new vineyards with the use of the best national and international cultivars, but also through the rediscovery of the qualities of native vines that were best suited to the characteristics of the territory. For this purpose, on the occasion of the Ancona exhibition, every Ampelographic Committee of Marche and Abruzzo were required to send samples of grapes still attached to the branches, along with a few leaves and a few samples of wines, in order to allow a reconnaissance of the vine species cultivated in those areas. The establishment of an order was attempted among the multitude of local names given to vines, in order to identify the vine species common to the two territories. Such cataloguing produced a list of 27 species of vines, 13 of which were white grapes and 14 red grapes.[6]

Limiting our analysis to the provinces of Abruzzo, the following grapes samples were sent to Ancona: white grape *verdicccchio*

[6]For a more detailed examination of the classification results, see De Bosiis (1873, pp. 158–207).

(from Penne), *trebbiano*[7] (from Teramo, Penne, Loreto Aprutino and Chieti), *malvasia* (from Teramo and Chieti), *biancame* or *biancuva* (from Chieti), *pecorino* (from Teramo and Penne), *moscatello bianco* (from all the Abruzzo provinces), *chiapparone* or *montonico* (from Teramo and Penne),[8] *empibotte* (from Teramo)[9]; red-grape *balsamina* (from Penne and Teramo), *lacrima* (from Chieti and Teramo), *aleatico* (from Teramo), *sangiovese* (from Chieti and Teramo), *moscatello nero* (from all the Abruzzo provinces), *malvasia di Candia* (from Teramo), *prungentile* or *uva d'aceto* (from Chieti). To a careful reader, the absence from this list is evident of the protagonist of Abruzzo's present and past viticulture: *montepulciano*. In fact, the vine was present in the Ancona vine exhibition, although it had been counted as *sangiovese* (De Bosiis 1873, pp. 188–189).

Although nowadays the cataloguing proposed at the 1872 Ancona vine exhibition might be considered as exceedingly simplistic and undoubtedly outdated from an ampelological point of view, it still remains a major element to understand the level of knowledge related to viticulture in Abruzzo in the post-unification years.

Post-Unification Enquiries and Giuseppe Devincenzi's Contribution

In the same years when De Blasiis started his ampelological studies in the provinces of Abruzzo and Marche, the central bodies of the unified State promoted initiatives aimed at studying the economic situation in regional contexts. It is in this perspective that *Inchiesta industriale*

[7]Abruzzo local varieties that were associated with type *trebbiano* were *uva passola, passa, spampanata, ciancialuta, scenciata, buonvino, cacciadebiti, passerina, sciarrata, camplese, campolese*, and they came from Teramo, Penne e Chieti (De Bosiis 1873, p. 168).

[8]Abruzzo local varieties that were associated with type *chiapparone* were *montonico, racciappoluta, ciapparruto, fermano, racciappolone, verdolino, verdecchio, uva chiusa, rappennolo*, and they come from Teramo e Penne (De Bosiis 1873, p. 178).

[9]Abruzzo local varieties that were associated with type *empibotte*, in the province of Teramo, were *cacciuma, canaiuola, spergola, ghiotta, mostosa* (De Bosiis 1873, p. 180).

(1870–1874) must be viewed, an industrial investigation whose activity aimed mainly at acquiring data useful to revise commercial treaties with foreign countries and which at present can be viewed as an important testimony on the main economic activities that characterized the Italian territory (Inchiesta industriale 1874, pp. 44–46).

The investigation, which was mostly carried out in the province of Chieti, pinpointed the limitations of Abruzzo's wine production, with poor quality white wines and more popular red wines. Besides the inadequacy of vines and the problems related to wine storage, *Inchiesta industriale* highlighted other economic-related issues, such as the farmers' difficulty to access credit, excessive transport freights, communication problems deriving from the inadequacy of roads and railways, high taxation on landownership and, last but not least, the high cost of vine plants for the implantation of new vineyards, which allowed farmers to set only small samples of new plantations, but not extensive crops.[10]

In the early 1870s, observers unanimously agreed that the Abruzzo wine production could improve dramatically and that the process of change had to go through the replacement of the existing vineyards, namely with the replacement of *montonico* with cultivars which guaranteed better organoleptic qualities. It was also necessary for landowners to choose more carefully the areas in which to set new plants, favouring the hills, which were sunnier and drier than the land located at the bottom of valleys.

Ten years later, on the occasion of the parliamentary investigation on agriculture and on the conditions of peasantry (better known as Jacini investigation, conducted in the years between 1877 and 1885), the situation of Abruzzo's viticulture and winemaking seemed to show the first signs of improvement, with the establishment of a wine company at Mosciano S. Angelo, in the province of Teramo (Angeloni 1884, II, pp. 93–94). The Sulmona valley was beginning to stand out for its production which, after the construction of the railroad connecting Pescara

---

[10]It was estimated that the gross weight tax on land used for vineyards, with the additional benefit of the province and city, would reach an incidence between 40 and 75% of the income from the crop (Inchiesta industriale 1874, pp. 44–46).

first and Rome later, could be easily transported to the wine industries in Northern Italy.

In those years, the process of dissemination of good practices in the wine sector had to come to terms with the excessive fragmentation of agricultural estates, which was very evident in the inner areas of the Abruzzo region, where it was favoured by the region mostly mountainous conformation.[11] With passing years, the average size of private properties grew smaller and smaller, due to natural hereditary successions, to the sale of land plots by landowners grappling with the agrarian crisis (Quaranta 1884, p. 98), but also due to the sale of land belonging to the State or to the Church. Latifundism was not totally absent from the region, although it was mainly concentrated in the hills and along the coast of the provinces of Chieti and Teramo. During the years of the parliamentary investigation, with particular reference to the latter province, it was estimated that three-fifths of the arable land belonged to large over 200-hectare estates (Angeloni 1884, pp. 46–47; Felice 2007, pp. 83–84), largely owned by members of the old aristocracy and by the emerging local middle class, for whose cultivation *admeliorandum* long lease or sharecropping contracts were used (Stefanelli 1974, p. 49). The situation was different in the Sulmona valley, where viticulture had been practised for a long time with excellent results, and where the problem of land fragmentation had been solved through the use of leases (Angeloni 1884, II, p. 44).

It was in the latifunds along the coast that, by the end of the nineteenth century, the first important experiments for the progress of Abruzzo's viticulture and winemaking were carried out, as, for example, in the winery of Giuseppe Devincenzi, a native of Notaresco, in the province of Teramo,[12] a member of Destra Storica (the Historical Right), a senator, Minister for Public Works, as well as first president of the Society of Italian winegrowers, which he had founded.[13]

---

[11] More the land is made wavy and steep, less compact were the farm units (Felice 2007, p. 59).

[12] About Giuseppe Devincenzi (1813–1903) see De Lucia (1974) and Pierucci (1997).

[13] The society of Italian wine growers had been founded in 1885 with the aim of studying the conditions governing the production, the good and bad farming practices and to protect the interests of owners and growers (Piscitelli 1974, p. 79).

Devincenzi, who had studied agriculture and enology in depth, had created a model winery at Cologna Spiaggia, close to Roseto degli Abruzzi, where he had greatly cared for all the phases of wine production, starting from vineyard implantation, for which he had chosen *malbec*, *sangiovese*, *canaiolo* and *malvasia* vines, whose musts had been blended to obtain two different wines, commercially known as "Collemarino" and "Cologna" (Di Lorenzo 1892). The Devincenzi winery was much more than a wine-producing industry: indeed, it was the actual demonstration that a quality wine could be produced in Abruzzo, able to compete with the best products of the international wine industry.

Production and Trade by the End of the Nineteenth Century

The last quarter of the nineteenth century was an eventful time for viticulture in the Southern Italy, which in those years had to face the agricultural crisis, an increased demand in wines and grapes by Northern Italy and France,[14] and later the customs tariff reform. The arrival of American and Russian cereals on the European market caused most previously wheat-cultivated land to be replaced with more valuable crops, such as grapes (Ritrovato 2010). This process of change in crop specialization, partly oriented towards viticulture, had affected the Abruzzo region as early as the first half of the nineteenth century, but it was after the Unification that it became more evident, also due to improved communication routes (Bulgarelli Lukacs 2000, p. 531). In this context, a very important role was played by railway tracks, particularly the Abruzzo sections of the Adriatic railway built between 1863 and 1864, by the completion of the Pescara-Sulmona-L'Aquila rail between 1873 and 1875, and finally by the Sulmona-Rome section,

[14]Grape production in France was indeed greatly diminished as a result of the phylloxera epidemic that from 1868 onwards had attacked the French vines (Dalmasso 1961, p. 54). On the expansion of the wine sector in the last three decades of the Nineteenth century see, among others, Gangemi and Ritrovato (2002). About the spread of phylloxera in Europe and, more specifically, in Italy, see Dandolo (2010, p. 71).

which was finished in 1888.[15] In those years, railways started to generate a production specialization process which contributed to introduce *montepulciano* and *trebbiano* cultivars, most appreciated by national and international customers and which accounted for a large share of the Abruzzo viticulture and wine production in the years afterwards.

The construction of the railroad influenced productive choices in the wine sector, subjecting production features to foreign demand which, however, by its nature could not ensure a steady balance in the long term and implied high risks for the regional agriculture. The area where this influence was more evident was the Peligna Valley, near Sulmona. An increase in the production of *montepulciano*[16] was recorded in that area during the years of the Jacini investigation, at the detriment of other grapes such as *moscato*, *malvasia*, *camplese*, *verdicchio* and *aleatico,* although they had previously been produced there (Angeloni 1884, II, p. 44). The reason of this phenomenon resides in the fact that the winemaking industry in Northern Italy and other European countries demanded a particular type of wine made from *montepulciano* grapes, which was to be used for blending less robust wines. An yearly average of 350,000 hectolitres of wine was produced in the Peligna Valley, only a fifth of which was consumed in its own production area, while the rest was meant for exportation which, starting in 1876, was directed to France, Austria and Switzerland.[17]

Due to the expansion of wine industry in the early 1880s, a large capital inflow was recorded in Sulmona, that was used in workers' and industrial companies operating in the trade of wines or, more often, of grapes (Felice 2007, p. 80). A similar situation to Sulmona's was also recorded in the Pescara valley and along the coast, in areas crossed by the railway and in which production could be more easily exported outside the Abruzzo territory. In the 1870–1880 decade, the export took

---

[15]On trade by rail in Abruzzo see Bulgarelli Lukacs (2000, pp. 508–509).

[16]About ampelographic dispute linked to the characteristics of *montepulciano* and its differences with the *sangiovese* see Giuliani (1975, p. 98).

[17]In particular, in the agrarian year 1879 were exported in France between 15 and 20 thousand hectoliters of Sulmona wine (Angeloni 1884, II, p. 44). About the export of wine in France, and on the expansion of exports to other countries of Central Europe see Einaudi (1894).

place of large quantities of grapes to the detriment of the export of must or wine (Bulgarelli Lukacs 2000, p. 535). The problem of wine storing difficulties, which had been the focus of De Blasiis's concern, had been therefore partially sidestepped through the export of raw materials, which were later processed in Northern Italy and abroad.

The golden age of Southern Italy wine production, though, was destined to give way to a deep crisis in the sector, which characterized most of the 1880s. Since 1882, the introduction to France of grapes from Spain had reappraised the demand for Italian wines, bringing about a decrease in prices and the sector crisis (Bulgarelli Lukacs 2000, p. 534; Gangemi and Ritrovato 2002). Later, the change in the 1887 commercial treaty with France brought about more negative effects that added up to the existing agricultural crisis and caused huge losses to Southern Italy viticulture and winemaking.[18] In those years, the Italian politics was torn by the debate on the possible measures to take as a safeguard of winegrowers' interests. One of the most active members of parliament at that regard was Senator Devincenzi, according to whom the crisis could be overcome only by improving the quality of the Italian wine production, which had to switch from the production of blending wines to the production of good table wines, able to conquer their own place on the market (Devincenzi 1975, p. 210).

During the last decade of the nineteenth century and the first two decades of the twentieth century, the increased use of refrigerated rail cars brought about an increase in the export of table grapes, very much in demand on the markets of Central Europe. These were mostly cultivars such as *montepulciano* and *montonico*, largely used for winemaking, which, however, were also fit for food consumption, as in the case of *montonico* from Poggio delle Rose, in the province of Teramo, which due to its late production could reach markets at the end of the season.[19]

---

[18]About the effects of the 1887 Customs Tariff on the winemaking in Southern Italy see also Ritrovato (2013, p. 340).

[19]Basing on data from the Ministero di Agricoltura, Industria e Commercio (MAIC), in the agrarian year 1911–1912 the province of Teramo was ranked second nationally for quantities exported of table grapes, equivalent to 73,500 hundredweight (MAIC 1914b, p. 20).

Production Size and Characteristics

A few statistical data, processed by the Ministry for Agriculture, Industry and Commerce are available for the last decades of the nineteenth century and the first years of the twentieth century; these data allow a broad reconstruction of the size and characteristics of grapes and wine production in the Abruzzo provinces. Starting in the 1870s, a clear reduction in the mean grape-cultivated surface in Abruzzo was observed (see Table 1), together with a less than proportional decrease in the yearly average wine production (see Table 2). Coast provinces were majorly affected by this phenomenon, that can be explained by the replacement of a mixed-crop system—in which vineyards were associated to other types of crops—with a special crop system, characterized by greater productivity per hectare.

Table 1 Mean grape-cultivated surface in the Abruzzo provinces

Province	Vineyard-cultivates average surface (hectares)	
	1870–1874 mean	1879–1883 mean
Teramo	71,250	50,535
Chieti	35,600	29,751
L'Aquila	23,904	23,904
Total Abruzzo	*130,754*	*104,190*
Total Kingdom of Italy	*1,936,832*	*3,095,293*

Source our processing on MAIC data (MAIC 1900)

Table 2 Mean wine production in the Abruzzo provinces

Province	Wine mean production (in hectolitres)				
	1870–1874 mean	1879–1883 mean	1896–1898 mean	1901–1905 mean	1909–1913 mean
Teramo	783,750	550,890	396,667	1,000,000	457,000
Chieti	534,000	621,590	350,666	675,200	473,000
L'Aquila	550,200	562,337	488,667	651,000	456,000
Total Abruzzo	*1,867,950*	*1,734,817*	*1,236,000*	*2,326,200*	*1,386,000*
Total Kingdom of Italy	*27,538,649*	*35,524,360*	*29,963,333*	*38,177,500*	*46,017,000*

Source our processing on MAIC data, years from 1870 to 1913 (MAIC 1887; MAIC 1888; MAIC 1900; MAIC 1908; MAIC 1914a)

The information on production in this period are deceitful because of the very mixture of crops, the failure of registers, the lack of agricultural training in the population, the suspicion of farmers with regards to statistical surveys which could be used also for tax purposes, and finally the scantiness of means the government could rely on for survey campaigns (MAIC 1893, p. 348). However, ministerial information is still useful to reconstruct the Abruzzo wine production size in the post-unification period. In particular, with regard to the amount of wine produced in Abruzzo, between the 1870s and the 1880s it recorded a decreasing variation in absolute terms; this was in contrast with data on national production which, from 1870–1874 to the 1879–1883 period, had recorded an increase by about 22%, in response to the increase in foreign demand for the product. Shifting the focus on the ratio between local and national wine production, it appears that in the 1870–1874 period, the three Abruzzo provinces produced on average 6.8% of the Italian wine production, while this value decreased to 4.9% in the 1879–1883 period. This phenomenon can be explained by the fact that the provinces of Abruzzo were gradually turning from wine to fresh grapes exporters and in this business attained the highest values among all the provinces in the Adriatic South, including Apulia.[20] Once harvested, grapes were loaded on trains and rapidly transported North of Bologna and abroad, where they were partly used as table grapes and partly for winemaking (Cormio 1981, p. 548).

In the following years, starting in 1889, wine national production contracted due to a drop in the exports to France, to then return to pre-crisis levels from 1891 on, due to the adoption of new trade treaties with Austria and Germany, but also thanks to the first exports to America. In the second half of the 90s, wine production in Abruzzo averaged lower levels than in the 1879–1883 period, to then grow in the 1901–1905 period and finally experience another decrease in the years before the First World War (see Table 2).

[20]About 99% of the grapes exported from the provinces of Abruzzo was marketed with the brokerage of the entrepreneur Francesco Cirio (Bulgarelli Lukacs 2000, p. 539).

Table 3 Distribution of table grapes and grapes for winemaking. Year 1910

Province	Table grapes (hundred-weights × 1000)	Grapes for wine-making (hundredweights × 1000)	Total (hundred-weights × 1000)
Teramo	32.00	313.00	345.00
Chieti	12.00	345.00	357.00
L'Aquila	4.00	159.00	163.00
Total Abruzzo	*48.00*	*817.00*	*865.00*

Source our processing on MAIC data for the year 1910 (MAIC 1911)

In the years from 1910 to 1920 data on Italian agricultural production are more regular and reliable. For the year 1910, which was characterized by a modest production, the quantities of grapes destined to table consumption can be traced back, averaging a quota of 5.55% of all harvested grapes (see Table 3).

For all the years from 1909 to 1920, the size of cultivated area can be compared with the vineyards' overall yield, also making a distinction between mixed-crop and special-crop areas. The values of cultivated areas show little difference from one year to the next; therefore, by way of example, only the data relating to 1913 are reported, when Abruzzo recorded a fairly good production (see Table 4). It is noteworthy that the province of Teramo showed the largest winegrowing land extension, with 46,600 hectares, as well as the lowest incidence of mixed crops compared with total cultivated areas, with a value hovering around 20%. The province of L'Aquila followed with 36,100 hectares, 38% of which were devoted to specialized crops, and last the province of Chieti, with 25,000 hectares, 96% of which for special crops.

Finally, when considering the 1909–1913 average production, some considerations can be made on the production characteristics of red and white wines. First of all, red wine production was higher in the province of L'Aquila compared to the remaining areas of Abruzzo, also due to the contribution of the Sulmona Valley and to the latter's vocation to the cultivation of *montepulciano*. White wine production, on the other hand, was higher along the coast with the primacy of the Teramo territory on the province of Chieti. The alcohol contents of red wines attained higher peaks on the Teramo hills than in the rest of the

Table 4 Grapes production in the Abruzzo provinces in 1913

Province	Grapes production in Abruzzo. Year 1913							
	Mixed crop			Special crop			Total grapes production (cwt × 1000)	Total wine product. (hl. × 1000)
	Cultivated sufrace (hectare × 1000)	Grapes prod. (cwt × 1000)	Yield (cwt x hectare)	Cultivated surface (hectare × 1000)	Grapes prod. (cwt × 1000)	Yield (cwt x hectar)		
Teramo	37.50	438.00	11.70	9.10	480.00	52.70	918.00	668.00
Chieti	0.80	3.00	3.70	24.20	882.00	36.40	885.00	467.00
L'Aquila	30.20	549.00	18.20	5.90	146.00	24.70	695.00	515.00
Abruzzo	*68.50*	*990.00*	*33.60*	*39.20*	*1508.00*	*113.80*	*2498.00*	*1650.00*

Source our processing on MAIC data for the year 1913 (MAIC 1914a)

Abruzzo territory, whereas the alcohol contents of white wines attained higher levels in the province of L'Aquila (see Table 5).

The Viticulture Crisis Between the Two World Wars

If the first post-unification decades and the Giolitti period had marked the expansion of viticulture and wine production and the improvement of cultivation techniques in Abruzzo, the period between the two World Wars was characterized by a deep crisis in the sector, mainly marked by the widespread of phylloxera in the Abruzzo provinces, which had been spared by the disease in previous decades.[21]

At the beginning of the 1930s, despite the phylloxera attack, the territory of Abruzzo and Molise rank tenth among Italian regions as to the quantity of wine produced, with 1,450,000 hectolitres in the agricultural year 1930–1931 (Marescalchi 1934, p. 280). Like in the rest of Southern Italy, though, local viticulture and winemaking were experiencing a serious crisis, characterized by a drop in exports and by the reduction of domestic wine consumption, and countered only partially and inefficiently by measures meant for the safeguard of viticulture and wine industry.[22]

In those years, the largest vineyards were located on the hills close to the coast, whereas they were distributed among small and medium landowners in the hinterland areas, where the phenomenon of fragmentation of landownership was prevalent and where vines were grown in promiscuity with other crops. Of course, the phylloxera attack struck equally both large and small estates, although generating different effects on the land, depending whether it was divided into large or small plots. After the contagion, while large landowners were able to

[21]At the end of December 1928 on a total of 408 municipalities in the areas of Abruzzo and Molise, 201 had been infected with phylloxera (Dandolo 2010, p. 175; Felice 2007, p. 306).

[22]In this regard we can mention the Law no. 1225 of 1932 for the economic defence of viticulture (Marescalchi 1934, p. 290).

Table 5 Production of red, white and special wines in Abruzzo (1909–1913)

Production of red, white and special wines in Abruzzo (1909–1913)									
Province	Mean prod. per year (1909–1913) in hectolitres	Red wines				White wines			
		Less than 10°		More than 10°		Less than 10°		More than 10°	
		Quantity %	Mean alcohol contents	Quantity %	Mean alcohol contents	Quantity %	Mean alcohol contents	Quantity %	Mean alcohol contents
Teramo	457,000	10	9.2°	35	12.2°	20	9.0°	35	11.5°
Chieti	47,000	10	9.0°	50	11.5°	10	9.2°	30	11.0°
L'Aquila	456,000	30	9.0°	45	11.5°	10	9.0°	15	12.0°
Abruzzo	*1,386,000*	/	/	/	/	/	/	/	/

Source MAIC 1914a

Table 6 Vineyard-cultivated land in the Abruzzo provinces (hectares × 1000)

Year	Mixed crop	Special crop
1909	69.30	38.40
1919	68.60	39.20
1929	30.11	44.84
1939	30.29	45.88

Source our processing on MAIC and ISTAT data (MAIC 1910; MAIC 1920; ISTAT 1936; ISTAT 1948)

bear the costs for the replacement of diseased vines with new American-rootstock plants, organized in a more rational and innovative way, small landowners were often obliged to replace vineyards with other crops. The huge costs for replacing infected vineyards on one hand, and the fascist regime's agricultural policy more favourable to cereal cultivation on the other, ended up causing a reduction in vine-cultivated areas also in Abruzzo, as well as and the replacement of vineyards with other, more profitable crops (see Table 6). And when small farmers, at the cost of great sacrifices, were able to restore fully or in part the destroyed vineyards, the shortage of good quality cuttings led to the use of hybrids or of plants of different crop species, which generated a progressive decrease in quality and production yield (Felice 2007, p. 309).

The effects of this process can be inferred easily from Table 6, which shows that in the 1919–1929 decade, the area devoted to the cultivation of vineyards mixed with other crops had decreased by 56%, only partially balanced by a 14% increase in the surface destined to special crops.

After the phylloxera attack, cultivars were chosen during the process of vineyard renewal, whose market demand was larger, particularly *montepulciano* and *trebbiano*, whereas native vines, which contemporary literature blamed for the late nineteenth century low quality of Abruzzo wines, gradually disappeared from the countryside. In addition, in that period of crisis for the Abruzzo wine sector, farmers increased the production of table grapes, the size of which, compared with the total Abruzzo grapes production, passed from 4.4% in 1929 to 8.4% in 1939[23] (see Table 7).

---

[23]Data taken from ISTAT (1940) and ISTAT (1948). The majority of table grapes produced in Abruzzo, in this period, was carried into the North Italy or was intended for export to Germany, Denmark, Sweden and Norway (Felice 2007, p. 319).

Table 7 Grapes production in the Abruzzo provinces (hundredweights × 1000)

Province	1919	1929	1939
L'Aquila	752.00	618.09	403.75
Chieti	601.00	617.43	612.74
Teramo	844.00	1027.36	943.70
Pescara	/	306.22	310.06
Total Abruzzo	*2197.00*	*2569.10*	*2270.25*

Source our processing on MAIC and ISTAT data (MAIC 1910; MAIC 1920; ISTAT 1936; ISTAT 1948). Note that in 1927 was established the Province of Pescara who removed surface to the other three provinces of Abruzzo

The difficulties faced by the wine sector were known even to local and national political leaders who, to the effect of countering the downward trend in production, implemented initiatives aimed at improving farming techniques and at creating agriculture-supportive infrastructure. It is in this light that the regulatory measures promoting agricultural itinerant Chairs must be viewed; such Chairs operated on the territory, training the sector workers,[24] and were coupled with newly established land reclamation Consortia aimed at the construction of a water supply net for field irrigation (Felice 2007, p. 338).

The Second Post-War Period and the Extraordinary Intervention in Southern Italy

Viticulture and winemaking in the second post-war period in Abruzzo were marked by the necessity to reconstruct vineyards and winemaking plants, which the war had destroyed. The province of Chieti had recorded the most severe damages, particularly in the Ortona neighbourhood, whose vineyards had stood out for their high levels of productivity in previous decades. In the Abruzzo provinces only, over seven million grapevines had been uprooted, while four million plants had been seriously damaged, with the largest concentration of damages

[24]For an example of the activities carried out in this period from the itinerant Chairs in Abruzzo see Conte (1934).

recorded in the territory of Chieti, where the war front had halted from the end of 1943 to the first months of 1944. Consequently, the reconstruction of vineyards and the recovery of slightly damaged ones were necessary; in order to guarantee a boost to viticulture and winemaking, though, it was essential to solve the problems that had long plagued the primary sector in Abruzzo, such as the lack of infrastructure and the excessive fragmentation of landownership. The latter phenomenon, closely related to the territory geomorphological conformation, was more evident in inland areas than on coastal hills and accounted for one of the biggest obstacles to the modernization of agriculture in Abruzzo.[25] Land parcelling brought about a consequent parcelling of farms, as well as many objective difficulties in the management of fields, which in individual farms were often located at a great distance from one another. If in the past this element had been believed to bring about positive effects, as for instance with the diversification of weather-induced risks (Franchetti 1875a, p. 11), with passing years it acquired negative aspects. First of all, land fragmentation forced labourers to long journeys which took time and energy away from the already hard toil in the fields; moreover, it was an indirect obstacle to any attempt at crop modernization and rationalization, since the capital necessary for investments was virtually inaccessible to small farms.[26] Due to the high vineyard implantation costs, viticulture-devoted farms resented most of land parcelling.

The early 1950s were characterized by the progressive depopulation of the Abruzzo hinterland, caused by an increase in migration flows, which were partly domestic, with the consequent concentration of population in the large urban centres devoted to business and industry, and partly directed abroad. The demographic decrease inevitably led also to a reduction in the number of active agricultural labourers, which was why the primary sector started specializing in higher value-added crops such as, indeed, vineyards and olive groves. The Abruzzo wine sector resumed marking a growth in cultivated areas and an improvement in

[25] On the fragmentation of landownership in Abruzzo see Medici (1956, p. 224).

[26] On this topic see Rossi Doria (1958, pp. XXIV–XXV) and Felice (2007, p. 413).

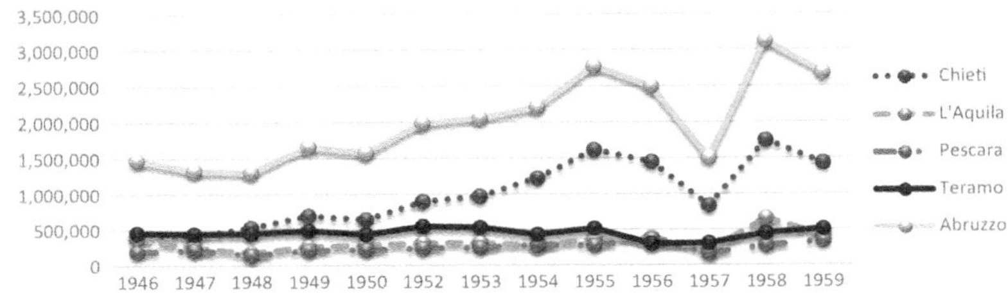

Graph 1 Grapes production in Abruzzo in hundredweights in the 1946–1959 period (*Source* our processing of ISTAT data, taken from *Annuario statistico dell'agricoltura italiana,* years 1943–1946 and 1947–1950, and on ISTAT data, *Annuario di statistica agraria*, years 1954–1959 [data for the year 1951 could not be found])

production. An important role in this agricultural modernization process was played by the *Cassa per il Mezzogiorno*,[27] whose action was initially aimed at the creation of agricultural-supportive infrastructures and to the destination of funds to crop improvement. New aqueducts were built, as well as new networks for field irrigation, roads and land reclamation works, which were paramount in the development process of local agriculture. The intervention of the *Cassa per il Mezzogiorno* was extremely important for viticulture and winemaking in Abruzzo, since it contributed to financing the first cooperative enterprises active in the wine sector. Graph 1 shows the trend of wine and table grapes production in the 1946–1959 period.

The graph shows how the province of Chieti was the one which produced the largest quantity of grapes, in contrast with the trend prior to the war, when the record was on the province of Teramo. However, it must be pointed out that the production increase in the area of Chieti depended largely on the increase in the table grapes harvest, which accounted for over half of the grapes produced in that area. The decrease in production in the years 1956 and 1957 was due to adverse weather conditions which reduced the quantity of harvested grapes by almost half, as in the case of the May 1957 frost.

[27]The *Cassa per il Mezzogiorno* was established by the Law no. 646, of 10 August 1950, and was a public body for financing and execution of extraordinary works for the economic and social progress of Southern Italy. On the role played by the *Cassa per il Mezzogiorno* in Abruzzo region, see Felice (2003).

The Emergence of Cooperation and the First Abruzzo DOC Labels

In a region characterized by a myriad of small and very small farms, cooperation was the most important tool for the revival and development of agriculture. By 31 December 1965, in the whole Abruzzo-Molise area, 315 cooperatives operating in the sector of agricultural product processing had benefited from the funds of *Cassa per il Mezzogiorno*. Among these, as many as thirteen wine cooperatives had obtained a total funding of 1 billion and 753 million liras, much more than what was provided by the *Cassa* to other forms of cooperation such as dairies, oil mills and other plants active in the processing and marketing of agricultural products (Felice 2003).

The 1960s were marked by a great ebullience in the primary sector: although valuable crops such as grapevines and olives still occupied a small share of the Abruzzo production area (Felice 2007, pp. 479–480), the progressive spreading of cooperatives had laid the foundation for the expansion of the viticulture and winemaking sector, when the constraints deriving from land fragmentation were eventually overcome. In the 1960s and the 1970s, a veritable boost took place in cooperation, that developed intensively, also due to regional laws favouring agricultural associations. The ISTAT data on the agricultural year 1969–1970 show that as many as 20 cooperative plants operating in the wine sector were located in Abruzzo: 3 winegrowers' cooperatives and 17 wine cooperatives, three of which had been founded between 1957 and 1959, and the remaining 14 between 1960 and 1970. In 1971, the overall quantity of grapes vinified in the cooperative processing plants amounted to 741,519 hundredweights, accounting for 27% of the grapes processed throughout Abruzzo in the same year (ISTAT 1972, p. 165).

In the virtuous process that led to the emergence of wine cooperatives, an important role was played by local political authorities. Actually, cooperative wine plants were sponsored partly by local representatives of *Democrazia Cristiana*—in which case they were easy to detect, as they often took the name of the patron saint of the town in which they were built—and partly by left-wing parties and organizations, in which case the name they took only included the name of the town. The rivalry between the two political parties resulted in a dramatic increase in the number of Abruzzo wineries and gave origin to an out-and-out competition, aimed at achieving primacy in the time, efficiency and control of the new plants (Felice 2007, p. 515).

Thus, initiatives and projects in the wine sector multiplied and were often successful; moreover, in time, cooperative initiatives gradually lost much of the political connotation that had led to their constitution; the rivalry between the Christian Democratic and left-wing parties faded out and this led to the constitution of consortia that included a high number of cooperative firms.

The benefits in favour of cooperative wineries' members were obvious: better and more efficient product sales channels, lower purchase price of soil fertilizers and chemicals, technical assistance to promote the technological renovation of firms, improvement of cultivation techniques. In those years, the vine Latin cultivation system was abandoned, as it hardly fit the most important mechanization techniques of agricultural work and was characterized by a poor quantitative yield. Low grapevines were replaced by canopy grapevines, whose plants were initially utilized for the production of table grapes and later gained ground in all Abruzzo also in the production of wine grapes, thanks to the possibility of mechanizing most agricultural and harvesting operations.

From a territorial point of view, in that period viticulture and winemaking developed especially along the coast and on the hills in the provinces of Chieti, Pescara and Teramo. The province of L'Aquila was only marginally affected by this phenomenon, although its areas—such as the Fucino planes and the Sulmona valley—were very well suited for grapes production. All in all, the Abruzzo agriculture showed a two-speed evolution: the territories close to the coast were the object of major infrastructure investments, farms were up-to-date and they specialized in more profitable productions and mechanized operations (Graph 2). In inner areas, the territory conformation still limited progress in the primary sector. To reduce this gap, State and EU subsidies were resorted to, but despite all efforts and the considerable resources used, the Abruzzo agricultural situation did not undergo major changes. In particular, the Community action resulted in the creation of new, agriculture-supportive public works in Abruzzo, in the financing of a

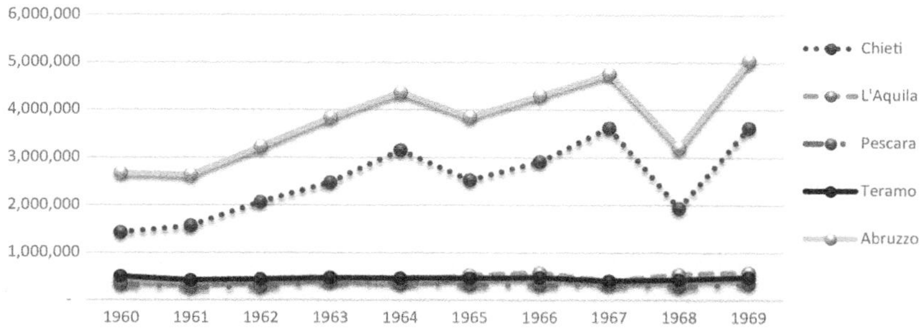

Graph 2 Grapes production in Abruzzo in hundredweights in the 1960–1969 period (*Source* our processing on ISTAT data, taken from *Annuario di statistica agraria*, years from 1960–1969)

few processing plants for agricultural products, as well as in the well-known price and market policies from which benefited especially potato and beet production. The wine sector did not draw major benefits from these intervention policies (Felice 2007, p. 507).

Much more important, though, was the approval of the rules to set the boundaries of the winegrowing areas with a designation of origin.[28] The long-anticipated recognition of Montepulciano d'Abruzzo came in the summer of 1968, followed by the acknowledgement of Trebbiano d'Abruzzo in 1972. The recognition of the designation of origin for Abruzzo wines gave a major boost to the local wine industry, generating positive effects that became more intense and appreciable starting in the 1980s.

Conclusions

After the Unification of Italy, the construction of railroads along the Adriatic coast had suddenly approached the Abruzzo viticulture and winemaking to the demand of wine industries from Northern Italy and from transalpine countries. Thus, wide hinterland areas like the

[28]It is the Law 930 of 1963. Starting in 1967 there was the first production of DOC and DOCG wines, but it was only from 1980 to 1990 decade that the production of wines with denomination of origin reached full capacity. On this topic see, among others, Fregoni 1993, pp. 3–4.

Sulmona and Pescara valleys, and areas along the coast like the hills in the provinces of Teramo and Chieti, had rediscovered their vocation to viticulture. Despite the ups and downs determined by the national economic situation, by the trend of international trade relations, by the depopulation of the hinterland and by the diseases that struck vineyards, grapes and wine production in Abruzzo grew over the years. The growth of the wine sector, though, had to grapple with the extreme parcelling of estates, which hampered production modernization and did not allow farmers from Abruzzo to obtain favourable conditions on markets. It was only in the mid-50 s that the progressive strengthening of cooperation in the primary sector led to the emergence of many wine cooperatives that, processing the products obtained by small and medium-sized farms, brought about the revival of the wine sector as well as the renewal of crop plants.

The implementation of new agricultural supportive infrastructures in the 1950s and the 1960s, together with a widening cooperation, favoured a restructuring of the wine sector, allowing farms to catch the new market opportunities that in the decades that followed were offered by the introduction of regulations safeguarding the designation of origin in wine production.

References

Angeloni, G.A. (1884). *Atti della Giunta per la Inchiesta Agraria. Relazione del commissario barone Giuseppe Andrea Angeloni, deputato al Parlamento, sulla quarta Circoscrizione (provincie di Foggia, Bari, Lecce, Aquila, Chieti, Teramo e Campobasso)* n. XII, voll. I, II. Roma: Forzani.

Bettoni, F., & Grohmann, A. (1989). *La montagna appenninica. Paesaggi ed economia* (Bevilacqua, Ed., pp. 585–641).

Bevilacqua, P. (Ed.). (1989). *Storia dell'agricoltura italiana in età contemporanea. Spazi e paesaggi*. Venezia: Marsilio.

Bulgarelli Lukacs, A. (2000). *Commercio e distribuzione (1861–1914)* (Costantini & Felice, Eds., pp. 495–553).

Calò, A., & Bertoldi Lenoci, L. (Eds.). (2010). *Storia regionale della vite e del vino in Italia. Le Puglie.* Martina Franca: Edizioni Pugliesi.

Ceccarelli, G., Grandi, A., & Magagnoli, S. (Eds.). (2013). *La typicité dans l'histoire. Tradition, innovation et terroir*. Brussels: Peter Lang.

Cercone, F. (2000). *La meravigliosa storia del Montepulciano d'Abruzzo*. Melpignano: Amaltea.

Cercone, F. (2008). *Storia della vite e del vino in Abruzzo*. Lanciano: Carabba.

Conte, G. (1934). *L'arboricoltura e la viticoltura nella vallata del Sangro*. Casalbordino: De Arcangelis.

Cormio, A. (1981). *Note sulla crisi agraria e sulla svolta del 1887 nel Mezzogiorno* (Massafra, Ed., pp. 559–567).

Corvol, A. (Ed.). (2002). *Forêt et vigne. Bois et vin*. Paris: L'Harmattan.

Costantini, M., & Felice, C. (Ed.). (2000). *Storia d'Italia. Le regioni dall'Unità ad oggi. L'Abruzzo*. Torino: Einaudi.

Cova, A. (1988). Problemi tecnici ed economici della produzione del vino in Italia tra Otto e Novecento. *Quaderni della Rivista di storia dell'agricoltura*, 1, 319–337.

d'Angiolini, P. (1969). L'Italia al termine della crisi agraria della fine del secolo XIX. *Nuova Rivista Storica*, LIII, n. 3–4, 323–365.

Dalmasso, G. (1961). La vite e il vino in Italia dagli albori del risorgimento nazionale alla fine dell'Ottocento. *Atti dell'Accademia Italiana della Vite e del Vino*, XIII, 323–406.

Dandolo, F. (2010). *Vigneti fragili, espansione e crisi della viticoltura nel Mezzogiorno in età liberale*. Napoli: Guida.

De Blasiis, F. (1857). *Istruzione teorico pratica sul modo di fare il vino e conservarlo*. Firenze: Barbera.

De Blasiis, F. (1869). *Fabbricati, recipienti ed utensili vinarj: lettura tenuta nel Comizio Agrario di Firenze nel marzo 1869*. Milano: Treves.

De Blasiis, F. (1870). *Conferenze enologiche tenute nella primavera del 1869: discorsi pronunziati da Francesco De Blasiis* [...]. Firenze: Barbera.

De Bosiis, F. (Ed.). (1873). *La esposizione ampelografica marchigiana-abruzzese tenuta in Ancona il settembre 1872 e studi sulla vite e sul vino della provincia anconitana*. Ancona: Tipografia del Commercio.

De Lucia, G. (Ed.). (1974). *Atti del 2° convegno Giuseppe Devincenzi nel Risorgimento e nella politica post-unitaria*. S. Atto: Edigrafital.

De Rosa, L. (1971). Vitivinicoltura e questione meridionale. *Rassegna economica*, XXXV, 6, 1449–1475.

Del Re, G. (1835). *Descrizione topografica fisica economica politica de' Reali Domini al di qua del Faro nel Regno delle Due Sicilie*, vol. 2. Napoli: Tip. dentro la Pietà de' Turchini.

Devincenzi, G. (1975). *Salviamo la grande industria del vino* (Villari, R., Ed., pp. 207–212).

Di Lorenzo, S. (1892). *Delle Vigne e della cantina del Senatore Devincenzi.* Roma: Forzani.

Durini, G.N. (1836). De' vini degli Abruzzi. *Annali del Regno delle Due Sicilie,* X, 24–34.

Einaudi, L. (1894). La esportazione dei principali prodotti agrari dell'Italia nel periodo 1862–92. *Giornale degli economisti,* 9, 1–22.

Felice, C. (Ed.). (1997). *Giuseppe Devincenzi: la figura e l'Opera.* S. Atto: Edigrafital.

Felice, E. (2003). *Cassa per il Mezzogiorno. Il caso dell'Abruzzo.* L'Aquila: Consiglio Regionale dell'Abruzzo.

Felice, C. (2007). *Verde a Mezzogiorno. L'agricoltura abruzzese dall'Unità a oggi.* Roma: Donzelli.

Franchetti, L. (1875a). *Abruzzi e Molise* (Franchetti, Ed., pp. 1–56).

Franchetti, L. (Ed.). (1875b). *Condizioni economiche e amministrative delle province napoletane.* Firenze: Tip. della Gazzetta.

Fregoni, M. (1993). Dalla 930 alla 164. *Bollettino del Cideao,* n. 14, 3–4.

Gangemi, M., & Ritrovato, E. (2002). *Vigne, vin et bois en Terra di Bari (1875–1914)* (Corvol, Ed., pp. 67–87).

Giuliani, G. (1975). *Il vino in Abruzzo.* L'Aquila: Japadre.

Inchiesta industriale. (1874). *Atti del Comitato di Inchiesta industriale, Deposizioni scritte,* 1. Roma: Stamperia reale.

ISTAT. (1936). *Catasto agrario, year 1929,* ff. 62–66. Rome: IPZS.

ISTAT. (1940). *Annuario statistico dell'agricoltura italiana, 1936–1938.* Roma: Failli.

ISTAT. (1948). *Annuario statistico dell'agricoltura italiana, 1939–1942.* Roma: Failli.

ISTAT. (1972). *Annuario di statistica agraria,* vol. XVIII (year 1971 with data of year 1970). Roma: Abete.

MAF (Ministero dell'Agricoltura e delle Foreste). (Ed.). (1934). *I progressi dell'agricoltura italiana in regime fascista.* Roma: Sindacato Italiano di Arti Grafiche.

MAIC (Ministero di Agricoltura, Industria e Commercio). (1887). *Annuario statistico italiano* (year 1886). Roma: Botta.

MAIC. (1888). *Annuario Statistico Italiano* (years 1887–1888). Roma: Botta.

MAIC. (1893). *Annuario statistico italiano* (year 1892). Roma: Bertero.

MAIC. (1900). *Annuario Statistico Italiano* (year 1900). Roma: Bertero.

MAIC. (1908). *Annuario Statistico Italiano* (years 1905–1907). Roma: Bertero.
MAIC. (1910). *Notizie periodiche di statistica agraria* (year 1909). Roma: Ufficio di Statistica agraria.
MAIC. (1911). *Notizie periodiche di statistica agraria* (year 1910). Roma: Bertero.
MAIC. (1914a). *Notizie periodiche di statistica agraria* (year 1913). Roma: Bertero.
MAIC. (1914b). *Il vino in Italia*. Roma: Cecchini.
MAIC. (1920). *Notizie periodiche di statistica agraria* (year 1919). Roma: Ufficio di Statistica agraria.
Marescalchi, A. (1934). *La viticoltura e l'enologia* (MAF, Ed., pp. 279–292).
Massafra, A. (Ed.). (1981). *Problemi di storia delle campagne meridionali nell'età moderna e contemporanea*. Bari: Dedalo.
Medici, G. (Ed.). (1956). *La distribuzione della proprietà fondiaria in Italia*, vol. I. Roma: INEA.
Orsi, G. (1873). *La vinificazione nell'Italia centrale* (De Bosiis, Ed., pp. 141–157).
Pierucci, P. (1997). *L'azienda agraria di Giuseppe Devincenzi* (Felice, Ed., pp. 147–156).
Piscitelli, E. (1974). *Giuseppe Devincenzi ministro e agricoltore* (De Lucia, Ed., pp. 67–85).
Quaranta, R. (1884). *Atti della Giunta per la Inchiesta Agraria. Monografia agraria della provincia dell'Aquila*, XII, III. Roma: Forzani.
Ritrovato, E. (2010). *Sviluppo dei mercati vinicoli dopo il 1860* (Calò & Bertoldi Lenoci, Eds., pp. 531–550).
Ritrovato, E. (2013). *Des vins de coupage aux étiquettes à succès. Typicité et culture oenologique dans le développement territorial des Pouilles* (Ceccarelli, Grandi, & Magagnoli, Eds., pp. 339–356).
Rossi Doria, M. (1958). *Dieci anni di politica agraria nel Mezzogiorno*. Bari: Laterza.
Stefanelli, L. (1974). *Arretratezza e patti agrari nel Mezzogiorno: la colonia miglioratoria*. Bari: De Donato.
Villari, R. (Ed.). (1975). *Il Sud nella storia d'Italia*, vol. I. Roma-Bari: Laterza.

Winegrowing in Slovenia in the Twentieth Century

Žarko Lazarević

Introduction

Slovenia is a small country in all respects. Despite its size, it boasts a rich geographical diversity, comprising the Pannonian, sub-Alpine, Alpine and Mediterranean regions. This diversity is what has determined the Slovenian viticulture and winemaking, as both the Mediterranean vines and wines as well as those specific to continental Europe are grown here. At the European level, Slovenia is a small wine production country, i.e. a niche producer.

The article is divided into four topics. The First chapter presents the general development trends of the twentieth century, while Chapter 2 covers the vine and wine varieties as well as and the structure of vineyards. Due to a very slow qualitative transformation in viticulture and winemaking processes, a special attention is paid to "self-propagated" vine and wines, and the social stigma accompanying this type

Ž. Lazarević (✉)
Institute of Contemporary History, Ljubljana, Slovenia
e-mail: zarko.lazarevic@inz.si; zarko.lazarevic@guest.arnes.si

S. A. Conca Messina et al. (eds.), *A History of Wine in Europe, 19th to 20th Centuries, Volume I*, Palgrave Studies in Economic History,
https://doi.org/10.1007/978-3-030-27772-7_11

of wine production.[1] Chapter 4 uses the example of Slovenian indigenous wine Cviček to show an intriguing correlation between wine and national identification, i.e. its socio-political connotation. Furthermore, the cultural revaluation of a brand of wine is presented as the establishment of a national wine imaginary concept which accompanied the qualitative transformation of a local wine brand that had a very bad reputation during the twentieth century. Both the wine produced from "self-propagated" vines as well as Cviček can be defined as "people's wines", as they were accessible to everyone and drank on every occasion, as opposed to quality wines that were dedicated to higher social strata. Wine was not a socially neutral product. Besides being an economic category, it also encouraged social differentiation. Namely, the production and consumption patterns had a significant impact on social status and wealth disparities, regardless of the established economic or political system, i.e. capitalist or communist.

Long-Term Characteristics

The late nineteenth century was an important turning point in the development of Slovenian viticulture. During that period, two events occurred which marked the Slovenian viticulture—the outburst of downy mildew and that of phylloxera. These two tiny organisms—a fungus and an aphid, restructured the viticulture in Slovenia. The fungus became a permanent problem which could only be neutralized by proper care of the vineyards. Problems with downy mildew in the early 1880s were soon solved by using copper vitriol. The short-term effect of downy mildew became manageable after extensive preventive spraying. Apart from the increase in production costs, downy mildew did not have any long-term consequences. However, that was not the case with phylloxera. As a result, the grape disease affected a high proportion of

[1]Please note that in Slovenia the adjective "self-propagated" designed the American vines used to graft local vines as well as the wines produced using these vines. This explains why author decided to always indicate it into brackets.

population since winemaking was very widespread in farming. A large number of farmers had small vineyards. Phylloxera spread to vineyards in the early 1880s (Seručnik 2011). After the first sporadic outbreaks, phylloxera spread across the whole Slovenian territory in the early twentieth century. In 1908, it was officially established there was no vineyard that would not be infested.

The Slovenian press closely monitored the spread of phylloxera. They reported about the first infection in France, the infection at the Klosterneuburg viticulture school, and its expansion to vineyards in Vienna surroundings and elsewhere. In the Slovenian territory, people were afraid, as they were well aware of the consequences brought by the infection. They knew that phylloxera posed a threat to the viticulture industry. Having documented the infection in Klosterneuburg, Slovenian local authorities sent the principal of the viticulture school (*Kmetijske in rokodelske novice* 1874) in order to get familiar with the appearance of the infection so that it could be identified quickly when or if it appeared in the Slovenian territory. As directed by the authorities, the population was notified not to buy vines from the infected areas. However, the Slovenian press was aware that the number of infected vineyards and areas was likely significantly greater than indicated by the already detected infections (*Kmetijske in rokodelske novice* 1875). They greatly welcomed actions by the authorities prohibiting the sale of vines with the intention to curb the epidemic, and they encouraged people to observe such measures (*Kmetijske in rokodelske novice* 1883). The press was convinced that the disease would be difficult to control. They had somehow already accepted the fact that phylloxera would not be stopped only through measures of discipline. The winegrowers were warned to prepare in advance and diversify their income (*Kmetijske in rokodelske novice* 1888). Despite the fact that phylloxera was not spreading quickly, it was still quicker than the winegrowers were able to adapt.

After the initial shock and fear, people soon received instructions on how to deal with the infection. The media regularly published instructions and decrees from the authorities. Following examples from the rest of Europe, the authorities attempted to stop phylloxera from spreading by using carbon disulphide injections (*Kmetijske in rokodelske novice* 1891a), although experts advised against this measure after it turned out to be completely ineffective during several unsuccessful attempts (*Kmetijske in rokodelske novice* 1891b). Attempts with flooding or planting the vines in sandy soils were equally unsuccessful. These two measures had a partial effect, but such natural conditions were quite rare in Slovenia, and they were also inefficient from the economical perspective (Seručnik 2005, 365–376). However, this led to a psychological turning point. There was less pessimism in the air as the vineyards were restored with new vines from an American rootstock; it gave hope for the possible recovery of viticulture, albeit at a high cost. However, the costs were not the only problem. The recognition that it was also necessary to change the methods and techniques in the recovered vineyards became apparent. Due to new work methods, vines from the American rootstock required a change in the mind-set of growers. The latter pointed to the following: "… *from the homeland of the phylloxera, America, we also received a wild vine, which is resistant to phylloxera and enables us to segregate the best indigenous vines. No one can doubt that this is the only way to save our vineyards, not even the hardest sceptics, if they look at the new plantations of the American vines, especially in Bizeljsko, where phylloxera infected every vineyard, but where most of the devastated soil is already overgrown with new vineyards of vines with juicy grapes. However, planting new vineyards is not as easy as people have been used to so far in most places. They have dug pits or trenches at most, and planted the vines. The new winemaking requires not only a lot of work but also smart actions*" (Vošnjak 1893).

Phylloxera had a strong impact on the economic and social situation; the extent of economic damage greatly exceeded the local levels. It is therefore not surprising that the government accelerated the recovery and restructuring of viticulture through mechanisms of partial coercion and by promotion with grants and rewards. The local vine nurseries were growing vines from American rootstocks in bulks and sold them at very low prices or even distributed them free of charge to farmers in order to lower the costs of vineyards recovery. The recovery of vineyards was a great financial burden for most growers. The state also offered interest-free loans with longer than usual repayment periods, i.e. from 10 to 20 years. Furthermore, the state intervened with financial incentives.

Until their recovered vineyards fully produced fruits, winemakers were exempt from property tax. But the state did not stop there. Those individuals who recovered their vineyards with special care were awarded with special premiums and presented as role models for others. Since the recovery of vineyards also presented a change in the technological paradigm, great efforts were invested in education. Several viticulture schools were established and courses were organized in winter to teach winemakers proper vine care techniques and rational winemaking (*Gorice in vino* 1976, 20–23). According to land characteristics, location and micro climate, the wine-producing regions were established and a vine sort for each wine district was recommended. The government's measures proved fruitful and the winemaking industry had recovered.

The time between both World Wars has been a major challenge for viticulture. The transition to the new country, Yugoslavia, changed the whole wine market. Due to new customs borders, the export started to decline and the domestic market was too weak because of the low purchasing power. During this period, wines were separated into two quality classes, namely the north-west class with high-quality production (Slovenian Styria) and the eastern and south-eastern class with distinctive mass production. In order to gradually improve the quality, thirteen wine districts were defined in the 1930s, where vine varieties suitable for the existing conditions were grown. Quality wines were exported mainly to Austria and the Czech Republic, while the cheaper ones, those from eastern and south-eastern parts of Slovenia, were intended for domestic consumption. During the 1930s, the wine sales further decreased due to the Great Depression, and the situation additionally deteriorated because of a big drop in prices. There was little demand for quality wines. For this reason, the stocks of Styrian winemakers increased by the year. Competitors from other parts of Yugoslavia, who have entered the market with cheaper wines, began to threaten the winegrowers in the eastern and south-eastern areas. The growing sales in table grapes could not make up for wine proceeds losses (*Spominski zbornik*… 1938, 336–338; *Krajevni leksikon*… 1938, 28–30; *Za izboljšanje*… 1939, 211–221).

However, prices and sales were not the only problems of the winemaking industry. Also worrying was the state of the vineyards in the mid-1930s, when it turned out that two-thirds of vineyards were already depleted and in need of urgent recovery. Those were mostly the vineyards that have been restored in the first wave of recovering after phylloxera. The productive lifetime of these vines was coming to an end. The state started to address this issue in 1938 as it established a fund for the recovery of vineyards, which provided the affected individuals interest-free loans for the recovery of vineyards. In a way, it was the story of phylloxera repeating itself. The costs of vineyards recovery were high and almost unaffordable for a multitude of small producers. The threatening social costs were also evaluated as high. After all, the income in one-fifth of the population was more or less dependent on revenues from wine sales. Torn between the economic and social costs, the state decided to intervene (Lazarević 1994, 85–86).

The time after World War II was different, bringing on other challenges. It was a time of great changes in viticulture and winemaking. The communist regime implemented an agrarian reform, which nationalized all large wine-producing properties and privately owned wine cellars. Under the social policy measures, the private sector became completely fragmented and was pushed aside. Its contributions remained mostly scarce up until the second half of the twentieth century. It was forced into producing merely for its own needs or had to assume the role of a supplier to the large wine cellars. The 1970s have seen changes as the capacities of private producers were included in the new agrarian policy concept. The fundamental objective of the communist government was to increase the profit from grapes and reduce wine production costs. The measures were therefore tailored to this purpose. On the one hand, the authorities were building large state-owned wine-producing complexes so that the use of the farming machinery would be as efficient as possible in the economic sense (Štern 1958, 76–146). To this end, special supporting services were established to help the development of viticulture and winemaking. The university started a study programme in vine cultivation, and the Agricultural Institute and the Viniculture Institute were established. Such organizations allowed for modern knowledge from the West, mostly from Italy and France, and later also Germany, to be transferred to the Slovenian viticulture and winemaking environment, to its daily routine (Hrček 2002, 249–280).

The first task that the communist government set to do after World War II was the much-needed restoration of vineyards. Although the regime had changed, the economic necessity remained. As many as 18.000 hectares of vineyards had to be restored, which was about 1000 per year (Štern 1958, 81). The process that had started before the war had to be realized fully. However, due to the lack of financial funds, the restoration of vineyards was a slow process. In the decade following the war, only 10% of the facilities were renovated, while the rest were mostly done in the 1960s and 1970s. The new vineyards were planted with varieties chosen in a selection process in 1935 and were set up only on the best land. It is therefore of little surprise that vineyards were persistently on the decline after World War II, so the yield had to be increased urgently. The new vineyards were planned only with the top quality grafts that were fit for the high pedological value of the soil. Analyses were conducted by the support of the state and in cooperation with institutes and university departments for viticulture and winemaking. To support the growth of plants, the new vineyards used wire supporters to make the care easier and faster. They removed or grafted the "self-propagated" varieties, filling the empty spots by new plants. Due to the good initial experience, the cultivation forms were upgraded and the distance between growing plants was increased so as to boost the yield. It was also necessary to prune the vines to allow the use of machinery on steep terrain. To this end, many vineyards were arranged in terraces wide enough to allow the use of machinery. Sufficient width in terraces was secured by adapting the distance in between rows. This resulted in a constant reduction in the number of plants per hectare of land, and later also in the wine-producing areas becoming fewer and some even abandoned due to the economic situation in the country (Pulko 2012, 27–29).

Selection of Vines, the Wine Types and Wine-Producing Land

The start of the modern territorial segmentation in winemaking dates back to the Habsburg Monarchy. From 1869 to 1871, there were three wine-producing regions in the Slovenian territory, which have, in geographical terms, remained virtually unchanged to this date. The only thing that has changed is their names. In terms of the administrative and social categorization, three wine production areas were specified at the time, i.e. the Styria, Carniola and Littoral wine-producing region. The Styria wine-producing region covered the north-eastern part of Slovenia, being linked to the winegrowing region in today's Austrian Styria.[2] The same wine-producing region in the south-western part of Austria was tied to the Carniola wine-producing areas situated at the south-east of Slovenia.[3] The wine-producing region in the central part of Slovenia was located in the western part of what was at that point called Carniola. The western wine-producing region (the Vipava valley) was connected more to the Littoral wine-producing region, which included parts of the Slovenian Istria at the rear of Trieste and also parts of the Goriško area.[4] The typology of wine-producing regions was slightly upgraded in 1905 as an inquiry was set that all plants be cultivated exclusively from the American rootstocks. Furthermore, the vine types were replaced by new ones so that the utmost level of balance between the soil and plant requirements was achieved. It was the only way to secure an optimal yield in grapes. It was recommended that (Welsh) Riesling, Silvaner, Furmin, Pinot Blanc, Chasselas, Yellow Muscat and Red Traminer be grown in the Styria wine-producing region, and in some of its terrains also the red varieties of Blaufränkisch and the two local vine types called *modra kavka* and *vranek*. Silvaner, Veltliner, Portoghese, Welsh Riesling, Chasselas, Blauer Portugieser, Žametovka and Blaufränkisch were recommended for the Carniola wine-producing region, while the Mediterranean climate in the western part of Slovenia was told to be best suited for Ribolla Gialla, Malvasia, Yellow Muscat and Garganja. In the central and eastern Slovenia, the white types of grapes were recommended to be grown,

---

[2]Today: the Podravje wine region, extending along the Drava river in north-east Slovenia, at the border with Croatia, Austria and Hungary.

[3]Today: the Posavlje wine region, extending along the Sava river in the south and south-eastern part of Slovenia, near the Croatian border.

[4]Today: the Littoral (Primorje) wine region, extending along the Italian border in western Slovenia.

while the Littoral area favoured other sorts, with the white and red varieties ratio being more balanced in this region. The white varieties included Malvasia, Sauvignon, Semillon, Yellow Muscate, and the red types comprised Refosco, Pinot Noir and Cabernet Sauvignon (Adamič 1997, 20–23). The structure established by regions was re-analysed in 1935 (*Spominski zbornik*... 1938, 336–338; *Krajevni leksikon*... 1938, 28–30; *Za izboljšanje*... 1939, 211–221). In cooperation with experts, the selection of vines and types of wine by specific regions was prescribed in details in terms of the terrain specifics in individual vineyards (*Trsni izbor*... 1935). This way, an array of wine types which was established in 1905 was preserved with slight modifications up until the end of twentieth century.

Land earmarked for wine production was scarce in Slovenia. Even during the periods when it was cultivated most intensely, in the nineteenth century, it did not take up more than 4% of all farming land. However, it would be misleading to draw any conclusions based only on this piece of information, as the economic value of vineyards was far greater than their share in the overall proportion of cultivated land. Viticulture was a highly intensive branch, providing a means of living to a larger part of population than any other plant in fertile flatlands, even in a terrain where any other plant would have barely grown or could not have grown at all.

A statistical overview shows that wine-producing areas in the early twentieth century created a dynamic category, which was subject to constant change. Over different time periods, they varied in size, gradually becoming scarcer. Through the decades, the portion of land earmarked for viticulture persistently decreased. At the same time, productivity more than amply replaced the shrinking of terrain. A historical perspective offers insight into the gradual shift from quantity to quality.

Phylloxera had a great effect on the viticulture routine as it was dramatically transformed in the two decades following its outbreak. The restoration entailed a slight decrease in vineyard surfaces. The Slovenian sum total was 5%, but the decrease varied from region to region. The land in Styria was reduced by more than 11%, in Carniola by 6.5% and in the Goriško region by 5%. In part, the decrease can be attributed to the high restoration cost, which was just too steep for small winemakers. Despite the state incentives and support, things simply did not work out for them financially and they gave up winemaking. The process of restoration sometimes included abandoning parts of vineyards that were not suitable for growing new vines due to soil erosion. And that was not yet the end of the story. In a small local area along the coast of western Slovenia, near the towns of Koper and Piran, the restoration resulted in an increase of vineyard areas. The increase amounted to a hefty 40%! Because of a healthy local market situation, the producers converted parts of meadows and even some substandard forest areas into vineyards (*Gospodarska in družbena zgodovina* 1970, 302).

A decrease in vineyard area totals was very typical for the twentieth century as shown in Table 1. A good half of all vineyards were abandoned during that time. At the same time, wine production was also on the decline, having dropped by 60% by the end of the century. The vineyard area totals reached their lowest point in 1970, when they amounted to just 38% of the area that had once been used for winegrowing (*Statistical Yearbooks* 1955–1991). Less suitable areas, which were not economically feasible in relation to the technological investment, were abandoned. Even though the cumulative vineyard surface area began to diminish in the decade preceding World War I and continued to persistently decline after the war, the biggest drop came about in the communist era, when up until the 1970s the emphasis was on quantity and state-owned wine producers. In the last couple of decades of the twentieth century, the cumulative size in vineyards slowly started to grow again. The growth coincided with two distinct processes. On the one hand, there was the gradual move from quantity towards quality, and on the other, there was the rise of private winemaking in the 1980s and 1990s. As the vineyard areas were reduced, so was the number of fruit-bearing vines. The trend line proportionally follows the reductions in area size.

An analysis in the fluctuation of vine density per hectare of vineyard surface is also interesting. The number of vines per hectare of arable land was reduced by half in the second half of the twentieth century, as a consequence of new technological methods. The new processes were all about increasing vine productivity to make up for the loss of surface area. The grape yield per vine more than tripled in the second half of the twentieth century, increasing from 0.48 to 1.5 kg. During that same period, the wine production capacity remained more or less the same, while the efficiency (measured as a ratio between grape quantity and wine yield) grew and settled at around 70% by the end of the 1960s, with some year-to-year fluctuations (*Statistical Yearbooks* 1955–1991).

Wine Bastards

Along with the restoration of noble grape vineyards, the expansion of vineyards growing self-propagated vines was recorded in the late nineteenth century (*Gospodarska in družbena zgodovina* 1970, 303). Those vines, which were of the American origin and ungrafted, such as Isabella, Othello, Noah, York and Madeira, were introduced after phylloxera began decimating the European indigenous vines. These vines were planted in the areas that were not suitable for the noble varieties. They also came in handy for individuals cultivating small vineyards and for those who saw winemaking as a peripheral endeavour and therefore could not afford to invest in noble grapevines. The area these vines of American parentage covered before World War I was quite small, which meant that the whole thing did not really attract attention from the authorities. The wine that the American vines produced was not seen as problematic, since it was still a product of nature. This meant that it was allowed to be labelled as natural wine. Such wine represented a small share of the market and did not directly compete with quality wines produced by renowned winemakers. Therefore, the authorities and the public were more concerned about counterfeit wines and mass consumption of cheap wine-like beverages.

Such conduct became widespread in the 1880s and 1890s, when peronospora and phylloxera waged their war on vineyards. The established practice of ameliorating wine with sugar to increase alcohol content was now tackled by using cheaper starch sugars. Often times, corners were cut by simply adding spirits. The public discourse was full of assumptions regarding publicans and the winemakers, who were allegedly increasing their wine stock by mixing it with water. The grape skin wine production was also on the rise. The beverage that only resembled wine from afar was made by soaking the skins in water and adding sugar or brandy. All these endeavours still resulted in natural produce. The acts might not have been morally immaculate, but they were also not detrimental to the health of the consumers. However, that was not the case when it came to chemical technology that enabled the production of knockoff wines without the use of natural substances, but often also posed a health risk.

The public was perturbed by this deceitful practice and by reports of winemaking malpractice that included the production of artificial wines and wine-like beverages, which were detrimental to health. The growing distrust was also damaging for respectable producers and retailers. The only way to set things right again was to start regulating wine production and the wine market. After the first attempt at regulating the market in 1880 failed, the Habsburg Monarchy took another swing at it in 1896, when foodstuff counterfeiting was banned by law. A big flaw in the ban was that it failed to define the notion of counterfeit wine. The flaw was remedied by a new wine act adopted in 1907. The act prescribed that wine should be made out of fresh grapes. Suitable additives[5] and circumstances in which they were permitted to be used were also prescribed. Any other production of artificial wines was forbidden. Grape skin wine production was an exception, since it was allowed for personal use in certain cases. To implement the act, the state established a special investigative force to oversee wine production and retail. By overseeing and criminalizing dubious winemaking practices, the state gradually managed to limit the amount of artificial wine on the market (Pančur 2008, 143–151).

During the interwar period, i.e. in the new country of Yugoslavia, the focus shifted from counterfeit wine to the "self-propagated" vines and the wine they produced. These vines that had been on the fringes in the last decades of the nineteenth century were now a big economic and political issue in Slovenia. During World War I and immediately

---

[5]"It was allowed to add 1% of pure alcohol, mix different varieties of wine, deacidise with lime, add tartatic acid and sodium bisulfate, and colour with fresh red wine grape skins or by adding caramel. To sweeten the wine with pure sugar, a special permission from the authorities was needed".

after it, vineyards with "self-propagated" vines expanded. Right before World War II, they amounted to more than 10% of all vineyard surface area. These vines were most widespread in Slovenian Styria, in the north-eastern part of the country, where wines of the highest quality had previously been produced. It was like a process of displacing noble grape varieties had been put in motion, a process of qualitative retardation of the entire industry. The self-propagated vines became an important part of winemaking due to their resistance to disease and economic feasibility.

The process was at odds with the plans the authorities had in gradually shifting the emphasis from quantity to quality as a measure for the standard of production. The economic effects had a lot to do with it. All the while, negative sentiment about the spread of American vines persisted. The wine they yielded, even though of inferior quality, kept snatching away portions of the market from manufacturers of superior wines. In order to protect the quality of regional wines, but also to protect the economic interest of larger winemakers with noble grapes, the state intervened. "Self-propagated" vines were to be gradually abolished. The mechanisms that regulated the growing of these vines followed two strategies, an economical one and an ideological one, both disguised under the pretence it was a health issue. The authorities realized that sheer coercion will not take them far, since the first measure from the early 1920s that forbade propagation of American vines in vineyards had not succeeded. Because the ban failed, a special act was introduced that established a system of incentives for restricting the growth of "self-propagated" vines.

The economic measures were designed in such a way that they enticed farmers to stop growing them. Monetary prizes were promised for grafted vines, while noble vines were offered in return for the removed American vines. Where the land was not suitable for winegrowing, farmers were suggested to switch to another crop, whereby the state covered the costs of such change. The "self-propagated" vines were to be substituted by fruit trees or other crops. The incentives were accompanied by legal and ideological coercion with the aim to regulate the retail of wine produced from "self-propagated" vines. The 1930 wine act excluded such wine from the ones that were allowed to be labelled as natural wines. Up until then, the label had been perfectly legal for "self-propagated" wines, since the 1907 act set forth that every wine made out of grapes was natural wine. The winemakers who produced wine from vines of North American parentage used the label to illustrate the wine's adequacy.

Paired with the looming economic crisis, the new regulation was very harsh. Wine produced from "self-propagated" vines was only allowed to be sold if the label contained information about the origin or if the product was mixed with wine made of noble grapes and sold under the name of blended wine. That way, consumers were expected to recognize inferior wine straight away. Under such conditions, the retail was allowed only during a transitional period of two years and only in places of origin. After 1932, all commercial use of wine produced from self-propagated vines was forbidden (Slabe 2007, 89–105). The wine act painstakingly defined the word wine: "*Only beverages which are produced by alcoholic fermentation of grape made out of raw grapes from domestic (noble) vines can be sold and stored as* ***wine***." Simultaneously, procedures and terms of harvest were thoroughly prescribed, as were the allowed wine additives and in part also the cellaring procedures, all this to elevate the quality of Slovenian wines in the long term. The 1907 act served as a strong foundation for the new act. Wine made from self-propagated vines was completely excluded from this thorough new definition of "real" wine. It was considered as a sort of a bastard among wines. It effectively became a wine-like beverage and was, administratively and symbolically, considered equal to spoiled, counterfeit and artificial wines, which were banned because they were considered detrimental to the health of consumers.

These health concerns were a big part of another strategy to combat wine made from vines of North American parentage. Many effects that were supposedly detrimental to health were attributed to it. Consumers of these wines were patronizingly labelled as clueless and not familiar with the consequences of consumption. They were labelled as morally weak. The methyl alcohol found in such beverages was considered to be able to lead to poisoning, degeneration, mental illness and uncontrollable violent behaviour, even suicide. Even regular consumption of small quantities could push one over the edge. All symptoms of excessive wine consumption and alcoholism were projected onto one variety of wine, i.e. that made from self-propagated vines, especially the one of the Noah variety (Slabe 2007, 85–88). Ignoring the lack of any real evidence, the ideological apparatus tried to discipline the consumers through media. At the same time, the ideological regulation had some class-based overtones since self-propagated vines were mostly grown as a supplementary crop by small and usually also very poor farmers, that one could call the unprivileged. Cheap-to-grow "self-propagated" vines were perfect for dozens of small farmers who had trouble making ends meet with their dispersed farms. These vines yielded a lot of grapes even with comparatively small monetary investments and little labour, and enabled farmers to be self-sufficient when it came to wine. But that was also all they could do with the wine since retail was frowned upon at first and then strictly forbidden in the 1930s.

The ideological construct anathematized wine made from autogenous vines and stigmatized its consumption on the basis of widespread alcoholism during the interwar period. The prevailing discourse framed alcoholism as a problem that had everything to do with production and consumption of wine made from such vines, and additionally hierarchized and deepened social differences by stigmatizing them. Such discourse was at its peak during the 1930s, as the number of socio-pathological acts increased during the economic crisis. Violations of public order, property and physical liberty tend to reverberate loudly, especially when the wrongdoers are drunk and violations are savage. Alcoholism was a common problem, but it was the most resounding in places where winemaking was widespread. The data showed that such places had comparatively higher incidence rates in gastrointestinal and cardiovascular diseases due to excessive alcohol consumption (Pirc 1939). But that was not just due to the wine made from "self-propagated" vines!

Regulating the growing of vines of North American parentage and banning this variety of wine turned out to be very inefficient. Despite the incentives, financial support and the retail ban, the expansion of "self-propagated" vineyards did not stop. The 30s were not the right time for such measures. High levels of unemployment in urban centres (around 30%) and a vastly weakened purchasing power in the rural areas meant that the official wine market shrank every year. Simultaneously, a grey market for wine began to spread. It is perfectly understandable that the demand for cheap wine rose in such circumstances. Since selling wines made from "self-propagated" vines was forbidden, the rise of an unofficial market was accompanied by an increase in the import of cheap wines from southern parts of Yugoslavia.

In the new circumstances after World War II, the vineyards of North American parentage expanded even further. At their peak in the mid-twentieth century, such vineyards represented a fifth of all vineyards as shown in Table 1. Afterwards, due to various steps taken by the authorities, the proportion began receding and at the end of the twentieth century ended up at the same point as before World War II, at around 10% of the total area. The number of fertile "self-propagated" vines declined even further. In mid-century, the grape yield in these vines amounted to a quarter of the total yield, but by the end of the century the number was only negligible (*Statistical Yearbooks* 1955–1991). The process was additionally boosted by measures from the communist state, which included a systematic removal of "self-propagated" vines from state-owned (nationalized) winemaking facilities. The private sector operated differently. Due to a lack of any economic incentives, it still swore by the vines of North American parentage, regularly pressing such grapes and turning them into wine. The appeal of simplicity in such kind of wine production was hard to resist.

It has to be said that the demand for wine made of grapes from "self-propagated" vines was still high due to the low purchasing power, which meant that such wine was sure to sell. The communist authorities tolerated both such vines and wines, even though they declared them not economical. The government also did not stigmatize or criminalize production of such wine. The reasons were partly ideological, since the consumption of wines made out "self-propagated" grapes was still associated with poverty and consequently with social stratification. However, the main argument behind the stigmatization of such wine slowly faded away after World War II. It was finally realized that the problem did not lie in the consumption of this particular wine or in the methyl alcohol, but in the quantity of wine consumed. Consequently, the authorities turned their efforts to improving the wine drinking culture. Along with the urbanization and increases in purchasing power, these social categories did more for reducing the amount of wine produced from "self-propagated" vines then all other repressive and stimulating measures of the authorities combined.

Cviček—Slovenian Indigenous Vine

When talking about the Slovenian viticulture and winemaking, we should mention the interesting story of Cviček, a local wine that has attained, in the last few decades, a mythical status of the oldest wine. Cviček is ascribed properties of a Slovenian indigenous wine and is considered part of the cultural heritage of the Dolenjska region, which is located in the central Slovenia, south from Ljubljana. The Cviček discourse comprises all the elements of an imaginarium in nationalizing a beverage, i.e. "*Cviček as the ambassador of the Slovenian nationality*". It establishes a direct link between wine as the Slovenian national identity and the narrowly defined identity of the Dolenjska region.[6] The discourse uncritically underlines that Cviček has been unfairly neglected, which means it has been attributed the moral imperative of the victim. The fact that Cviček had already been appreciated at the time of the Habsburg Monarchy in Vienna, and after the World War II by the Yugoslav president Tito, shows that Cviček remains an important element in of the historical continuity which dates back to indefinite past. Cviček is said to be the oldest wine since it also consists of Žametovka produced by the "oldest vine in the world".[7] As the

[6]For more information about the conceptual framework of correlation between food and nationalism as a definiton of common identity see Atsuko Ichijo and Ronald Ranta: *Food, National Identity and Nationalism*, Palgrave Macmillan, 2016. The concept largely relys on the "banal nationalism"—a concept which refers to everyday actions building a shared sense of national belonging and which was presented by Michael Billing in his book *Banal Nationalism*, Sage, 1995.

[7]Here it is referred to the Black Velvet (Žametna črnina or Žametovka) grapevine from Maribor, which is said to be around 400 years old. However, it is completely ignored that Cviček is not produced in the vicinity of Maribor (i.e. In eastern Slovenia).

indigenous Slovenian wine, it represents "*a piece of mosaic contributing to the Slovenia's recognition in the world*" (Kuljaj 2001, 10–12).

In the past, Cviček, which has gone through the processes of cultural revaluation and social establishment, was perceived as a low-quality sour wine suitable for farmers. It was made from different types of wine—many times, producers added wine from "self-propagated" vines. Cviček was intended for private consumption and was only sold to undemanding buyers in local areas. Throughout the entire twentieth century, Cviček was a synonym for poverty and thus social exclusion. Both producers and consumers of Cviček were somehow stigmatized. Cviček is a blend of several red (65%) and white (35%) grapevine varieties. Consumers are able to tolerate Cviček well due to a low alcohol concentration (between 8.5 and 10%), its drinkability and pleasant acidic taste (Terčelj 1974, 15). In resources, the name Cviček appeared before the phylloxera outburst in the late nineteenth century, denoting a very sour wine. The expression Cviček as a generic name for red wines originating from the Dolenjska region came to use after 1870; however, little is known about its composition at that early age. The first phylloxera outburst definitely led to a transformation of wine as winemakers had to invent a different blend of grape varieties. There were a lot of old vines that were no longer cultivated after the recovery of vineyards, which was necessary due to phylloxera outburst (Granda 2005, 299–300). Ever since being first mentioned in different sources, Cviček has been perceived as a non-quality wine. Some areas were said to produce wine so sour that they were no longer certain about its drinkability. During the pylloxera outburst, experts recommended winemakers in such areas to give up winemaking and focus on fruit farming instead. Besides the vines and grapes, the problem also lay in the absence of any proper viticultural work and cellaring, which was a consequence of scarce resources and insufficient technological know-how. Wine was often pressed from prematurely harvested grapes. Cviček's bad reputation increased even further after World War II. That was a time when quantity was everything. In the 1950s and 1960s, red wines were still particularly fashionable. Since wine of the highest quality barely sufficed for domestic consumption and was also expensive, and the communist system allowed the sales of a few imported wines, the demand in wine was high, even for the cheap varieties. There were no regulations, let alone any brand protection when it came to Cviček. Since it was so popular, a lot of wine from the state-owned and private sectors was marketed under its name. Often, Cviček was made of grapes that were imported from winegrowing areas in southern Yugoslavia. Such wines were definitely fakes. 1968 was the year of an ignominious record as the amount of Cviček sold was seven times larger than the total yield capacity in all winemakers from the area of origin (Kuljaj 2001, 48–49). The demand was also boosted by the low purchasing power of the population. Cviček was classified in the same tier as wine produced from "self-propagated" vines. The process of its cultural, technological and qualitative transformation began in the 1980s, after private farming had been reinstated within the communist economic policy.

Conclusion

The topic of this paper was a brief outline of viticulture and winemaking in Slovenia in the twentieth century. This broad topic has so far been scarcely researched. Although the number of resources is extensive on the one hand, and on the other hand, they are very fragmented. It is often impossible to access such resources since they are still being prepared by the authors, i.e. the winemakers in their wineries. The paper covers an extensive period, starting from the phylloxera outburst and extending into the 1970s and partly the 1980s. The article is concluded by identifying the legitimacy of private economic interest in agriculture within the communist economic system. The involvement of private winegrowers in the wine production process and a gradual promotion of a qualitative growth marked a new era. The then production and consumption patterns were upgraded and redirected. This period was not only long but also diverse, with distinct characteristics acting as lines dividing different eras. These dividing lines clearly highlight the period preceding World War I, when the Slovenians were part of the Habsburg Monarchy. After the phylloxera outburst, viticulture and winemaking were re-established in line with rules and methods applied in the Habsburg Monarchy. The wine districts, which were established in that period, roughly and with some amendments still exist today. During the interwar period, i.e. after Slovenia became part of Yugoslavia, the renewal of vines and the expansion of "self-propagated" American vine and wines posed a significant challenge. During the communist economic and political system following the World War II, a quantity-oriented approach was established in viticulture. The technological procedures and vine renewal depended on the goals of the communist authorities. The development trends were affected by the social and economic situation as well the biological aspect, i.e. the life cycle of vines.

Appendix

See Table 1.

Table 1 Indicators of viticulture after WW II

	1939	1955	1965	1975	1985	1995
Area of vineyards in ha	36,000	25,821	20,952	20,732	21,352	22,955
Quality vines in ha	33,500	24,343	14,746	15,5561	16,903	20,063
Self-propagated vines in ha	2500	5043	3777	3451	2502	
Number of quality vines (000)		146,533	73,087	65,455	61,750	63,021
Number of "self-propagated" vines (000)		35,282	24,643	20,796	12,312	
Yield of quality vines per ha in q	28.5	35.9	39.4	41.3	33.7	50.5
Yield of "self-propagated" vines per ha in q	22.7	40,3	46,3	40	22,1	
Yield of quality vine in kg		0.62	0.79	0.98	0.92	1.6
Yield of "self-propagated" vine in kg		0.58	0.71	0.66	44	
Ratio grape/wine		66.6	72.2	69.6	67.3	

Source *Statistical Yearbooks* (1955–1991)

References

Adamič, F. (1997). *Oris slovenskega vinogradništva in vinarstva*. Ljubljana: Biotehniška fakulteta.

Billing, M. (1995). *Banal Nationalism*. Sage.

Gorice in vino. (1976). Ptuj: Regional Museum.

Gospodarska in družbena zgodovina. (1970). Ljubljana: DZS.

Granda, S. (2005). K zgodovini cvička. In: Mihelič, D. *Otorepčev zbornik*. Ljubljana: ZRC, pp. 181–302.

Hrček, L. (2002). *Spomini slovenskega agronoma, vinogradniškega strokovnjaka in šolnika*. Ljubljana.

Ichijo, A., Ranta, R. (2016). *Food, National Identity and Nationalism*. Palgrave Macmillan.

Krajevni leksikon Dravske banovine. (1938). Ljubljana.

Kuljaj, I. (2001). *Cviček*. Ljubljana.

Lazarević, Ž. (1994). *Kmečki dolgovi na Slovenskem*. Ljubljana: ZPS.

Pančur, A. (2008). Ponarejanje vina pred prvo svetovno vojno. *Zgodovina za vse.*, 2, 143–151.

Pirc, I. (1939). Prehrana prebivalstva. *Socialni problemi slovenske vasi*, Book I. Ljubljana: Socialno ekonomski institut, pp. 73–113.

Pulko, B. (2012). Razvoj vinogradništva na Štajerskem od časa nadvojvode Janeza do danes. *Agricultura*, 9, 1, 21–30.

Seručnik, M. (2005). Spopad s trtno ušjo na Kranjskem v luči gradiva Deželnega zbora in odbora za Kranjsko. *Kronika*, 53, 3, 365–376.

Seručnik, M. (2011). *Trtna uš, ta strašno drobna pošast*. Ljubljana: ZRC.

Slabe, J. (2007). Proč s šmarnico. *Zgodovina za vse*, 2, 89–105.

Spominski zbornik Slovenije. (1938). Ljubljana: Jubilej.

Štern, V. (1958). Razvoj vinogradniške proizvodnje v naslednjih petih letih. In: *Stanje in perspektivni razvoj sadjarstva in vinogradništva v Sloveniji*. Ljubljana: Zadružna poslovna zveza Slovenije, pp. 76–146.

Terčelj, D. (1974). Značilnosti dolenjskega cvička. *Raziskave in študije 53*. Ljubljana: Kmetijski institute Slovenije, p. 15.

Trsni izbor in vinski tipi za Dravsko banovino. (1935). Ljubljana.

Vošnjak, J. (1893). Trtna uš in trtoreja. *Ljubljanski zvon*, year 13, 11. Retrieved from http://www.dlib.si (URN:NBN:SI:DOC-D3GRENCW).

Za izboljšanje življenjskih pogojev našega kmetijstva. (1939). Ljubljana.

Documents Online

Kmetijske in rokodelske novice (21 October 1874), 32, 42. Retrieved from http://www.dlib.si (URN:NBN:SI:DOC-U6RABG68).

Kmetijske in rokodelske novice (22 September 1875), 33, 38. Retrieved from http://www.dlib.si (URN:NBN:SI:DOC-R1D5SDQY).

Kmetijske in rokodelske novice (12 September 1883), 41, 37. Retrieved from http://www.dlib.si (URN:NBN:SI:DOC-OUT11LEC).

Kmetijske in rokodelske novice (15 August 1888), 46, 33. Retrieved from http://www.dlib.si (URN:NBN:SI:DOC-KO6GVXN2).

Kmetijske in rokodelske novice (4 March 1891a), 49, 9. Retrieved from http://www.dlib.si (URN:NBN:SI:DOC-37O7UEF9).

Kmetijske in rokodelske novice (1 April 1891b), 49, 13. Retrieved from http://www.dlib.si (URN:NBN:SI:DOC-QL76P8XN).

Statistical Yearbooks from 1955 to 1991. Retrieved from https://www.stat.si/StatWeb/en/yearbooks&year=2013.

Index

S. A. Conca Messina et al. (eds.), *A History of Wine in Europe, 19th to 20th Centuries, Volume I*, Palgrave Studies in Economic History,
https://doi.org/10.1007/978-3-030-27772-7

The manufacturer's authorised representative in the EU is Springer Nature Customer Service Centre GmbH, Europaplatz 3, 69115 Heidelberg, Germany. If you have any concerns regarding our products, please contact ProductSafety@springernature.com

Printed and bound by CPI Group (UK) Ltd, Croydon, CR0 4YY
30/09/2026
02225216-0010